THE ROUGH GUIDE TO

BRUGES &

GHENT

Forthcoming titles include

Chicago • Corfu • First-Time Around the World
Grand Canyon • Philippines • Skiing & Snowboarding
in North America • South America • The Gambia
Walks In and Around London

Forthcoming reference titles include

Chronicle series: China, England, France, India
Night Sky

Read Rough Guides online

www.roughguides.com

Rough Guide Credits

Text editor: Alison Murchie
Series editor: Mark Ellingham
Production: Andy Turner
Cartography: Maxine Repath

Publishing Information

This first edition published July 2002
by Rough Guides Ltd,
62–70 Shorts Gardens, London, WC2H 9AH

Distributed by the Penguin Group:

Penguin Books Ltd, 80 Strand, London WC2R ORL.
Penguin Putnam, Inc. 375 Hudson Street, New York 10014, USA
Penguin Books Australia Ltd, 487 Maroondah Highway,
PO Box 257, Ringwood, Victoria 3134, Australia
Penguin Books Canada Ltd, 10 Alcorn Avenue,
Toronto, Ontario, Canada M4V 1E4
Penguin Books (NZ) Ltd,
182–190 Wairau Road, Auckland 10, New Zealand

Typeset in Bembo and Helvetica to an original design by Henry Iles.
Printed in Spain by Graphy Cems.

ISBN 1-85828-888-6

THE ROUGH GUIDE TO

BRUGES & GHENT

by Phil Lee

**with additional accounts by
Luc Fossaert and Suzy Sumner**

ROUGH
GUIDES

We set out to do something different when the first Rough Guide was published in 1982. Mark Ellingham, just out of university, was travelling in Greece. He brought along the popular guides of the day, but found they were all lacking in some way. They were either strong on ruins and museums but went on for pages without mentioning a beach or taverna. Or they were so conscious of the need to save money that they lost sight of Greece's cultural and historical significance. Also, none of the books told him anything about Greece's contemporary life – its politics, its culture, its people, and how they lived.

So with no job in prospect, Mark decided to write his own guidebook, one which aimed to provide practical information that was second to none, detailing the best beaches and the hottest clubs and restaurants, while also giving hard-hitting accounts of every sight, both famous and obscure, and providing up-to-the-minute information on contemporary culture. It was a guide that encouraged independent travellers to find the best of Greece, and was a great success, getting shortlisted for the Thomas Cook travel guide award, and encouraging Mark, along with three friends, to expand the series.

The Rough Guide list grew rapidly and the letters flooded in, indicating a much broader readership than had been anticipated, but one which uniformly appreciated the Rough Guide mix of practical detail and humour, irreverence and enthusiasm. Things haven't changed. The same four friends who began the series are still the caretakers of the Rough Guide mission today: to provide the most reliable, up-to-date and entertaining information to independent-minded travellers of all ages, on all budgets.

We now publish more than 150 titles and have offices in London and New York. The travel guides are written and researched by a dedicated team of more than 100 authors, based in Britain, Europe, the USA and Australia. We have also created a unique series of phrasebooks to accompany the travel series, along with an acclaimed series of music guides, and a best-selling pocket guide to the Internet and World Wide Web. We also publish comprehensive travel information on our website: www.roughguides.com

Help us update

We've gone to a lot of trouble to ensure that this Rough Guide is as up-to-date and accurate as possible. However, things do change. All suggestions, comments and corrections are much appreciated, and we'll send a copy of the next edition (or any other Rough Guide if you prefer) for the best letters.

Please mark letters "**Rough Guide Bruges & Ghent Update**" and send to:

Rough Guides, 62–70 Shorts Gardens, London, WC2H 9AH, or Rough Guides, 4th Floor, 345 Hudson St, New York NY 10014.

Or send email to: mail@roughguides.co.uk
Online updates about this book can be found on Rough Guides' website (see opposite).

Acknowledgements

Phil Lee would like to thank Ailsa Uys of Tourism Flanders-Brussels for all her help and efficient assistance. Thanks also to Andy Turner for type-setting, Maxine Repath for maps, and Ken Bell for proof-reading. Finally, a word in appreciation of my excellent editor, Alison Murchie.

CONTENTS

MAP LIST

Introduction

I n 1896 the novelist and playwright Arnold Bennett complained, "The difference between **Bruges** and other cities is that in the latter you look about for the picturesque, while in Bruges, assailed on every side by the picturesque, you look curiously for the unpicturesque, and don't find it easily." Perhaps so, but there again Bennett had not had his senses battered and bruised by post-war development and today, for the modern palate, Bruges, with its seamless blend of antique architectural styles, from tiny brick cottages to gracious Georgian mansions, is a welcome relief – and retreat. It certainly brings out the **romance** in many of its visitors – stay here long enough and you can't help but be amazed by the number of couples wandering its canals hand-in-hand, cheek-to-cheek. Neither does it matter much that a fair slice of Bruges is not quite what it seems: many buildings are not the genuine article, but are carefully constructed to resemble their medieval predecessors. Bruges has spent time and money preserving its image, rendering almost everything that's new in various versions of medieval style, and the result is one of Europe's most beautiful city centres, whose charms are supplemented by a clutch of museums, which hold a fabulous collection of **early Flemish paintings**, plus lots of great restaurants and bars.

Ghent is a larger, more sprawling and less immediately picturesque city than Bruges, which is, in some ways, to its advantage. Like its neighbour, it possesses a stunning cluster of Gothic buildings and many delightful, intimate streetscapes, with antique brick houses woven around a skein of narrow canals, but, with the tourist hordes less in evidence, its restaurants and bars cater for a much more local market. Consequently, they are cheaper and more varied – indeed Ghent lays claim to an excellent nightlife. Ghent's museums come second-best to those of Bruges – though the city does have a very good contemporary art museum – but it's in Ghent you'll see arguably the world's greatest painting, Jan van Eyck's extraordinary *Adoration of the Mystic Lamb* – in itself worth crossing continents to view.

Belgium is such a small country, and the rail network so fast and efficient, that both Bruges and Ghent also make feasible bases for a whole raft of potential day-trips. We have selected – in Chapter 12 – seven prime destinations all within an hour's travelling time of one or the other. From Bruges, there are the seaside delights of **Ostend** and the charming little seaside resort of **De Haan**, the gentle pleasures of the village of **Damme**, and **Ieper** (formerly Ypres) with its poignant reminders of World War I. Ghent is, in its turn, within easy striking distance of two intriguing Flemish towns – **Veurne** and **Oudenaarde** – as well as big-city **Antwerp**, famous, in equal measure, for its fashion, nightlife and Rubens paintings.

Bruges

BRUGES was an obscure marshy village until the ninth century when the Count of Flanders decided to build a fortress here to protect the Flemish coast from Viking raids. The settlement prospered, and by the fourteenth century it shared effective control of the **cloth trade** with its two great rivals, Ghent and Ypres, turning high-quality English wool into clothing that was exported all over the known world. It was an immensely profitable business and one that made Bruges a focus of international trade. Through the city's harbours, Flemish cloth was exchanged for hogs from Denmark, spices from Venice, hides from Ireland, wax from Russia, gold and silver from Poland and furs from Bulgaria.

Despite (or perhaps because of) this lucrative state of affairs, Bruges was dogged by war. Its weavers and merchants were dependent on the goodwill of the kings of England for the proper functioning of the wool trade, but their feudal overlords, the counts of Flanders and their successors the dukes of Burgundy, were vassals of the rival king of France. Consequently, whenever France and England were at war – which was often – the counts either had to fight with the French against their own subjects or break their oath of fealty and campaign against France. The craftiest tried to be neutral, but this was – given the circumstances of the time – extraordinarily difficult. The **Habsburgs** swallowed Bruges – and Flanders – into their empire towards the end of the fifteenth century and the sour relations between the new rulers and the Bruggelingen – the citizens of Bruges – were a key reason for the city's decline. A general recession in the cloth trade also played its part, as did the silting of the **River Zwin** – the city's trading lifeline to the North Sea. Economically and politically marooned, Bruges simply withered away, its houses deserted, its canals empty and its money spirited north along with the merchants.

Some four centuries later, **Georges Rodenbach**'s novel *Bruges-la-Morte* alerted well-heeled Europeans to the town's aged, quiet charms, and Bruges attracted its first wave of tourists. Many of them – especially the British – settled here and came to play a leading role in both preserving the city's architectural heritage and ensuring that most refurbishments were in (a Victorian version of) Gothic/medieval style. In the twentieth century, Bruges escaped damage in both world wars, and is now one of the most popular weekend destinations in Europe. The city boasts several top-notch museums, most notably the **Groeninge** and **Memling**, each with a fabulous collection of early Flemish paintings, as well as the fascinating **Heilig Bloed Basiliek** (Basilica of the Holy Blood) and a postcard-perfect **Stadhuis** (Town Hall). It also has a phalanx of excellent hotels and superb restaurants, but it's special appeal is in its beautiful streetscapes. These are especially beguiling to the northeast of the main square, the Markt, with graceful mansions and intimate brick houses draped along a skein of slender canals, crisscrossed by dinky little stone bridges.

All of Bruges's key attractions are clustered in the city centre within easy walking distance of the Markt. They are described in Chapter 1 of our guide, whereas the more outlying parts of the centre – to the north and east of the Markt – are explored in Chapter 2. Note that almost all the city's sights are closed on Mondays.

Ghent

The seat of the counts of Flanders and the largest town in western Europe during the thirteenth and fourteenth centuries, **GHENT** was at the heart of the Flemish cloth trade. By 1350, the city boasted a population of fifty thousand, of whom no fewer than five thousand were directly involved in the industry, a prodigious concentration of labour in a predominantly rural Europe. Like Bruges, Ghent prospered throughout the Middle Ages, but it also suffered from endemic disputes between the count and his nobles (who supported France) and the cloth-reliant citizens (to whom friendship with England was vital).

The relative decline of the cloth trade in the early sixteenth century did little to ease the underlying tension, the people of Ghent still resentful of their ruling class, from whom they were now separated by language – French against Flemish – and religion – Catholic against Protestant. Adapting to the new economic situation, the town's merchants switched from industry to trade, exporting surplus grain from France, only to find their efforts frustrated by an interminable series of wars. The catalyst for conflict was taxation: Ghent's artisans found it hard to stomach the financial dictates of their rulers – the **Habsburgs** after 1482 – and time and again they rose in revolt and were punished. In 1540 the Holy Roman Emperor Charles V lost patience and stormed the town, abolishing its privileges, filling in the moat and building a new secure castle at the city's expense. Later, in 1584, with the Netherlands well on the way to independence from Spain, Ghent was captured by Philip II's Habsburg army. It was a crucial engagement. Subsequently, Ghent proved to be too far south to be included in the United Provinces – the Netherlands of today – and was reluctantly pressed into the Spanish Netherlands.

In the centuries that followed, Ghent slipped into a slow decline from which it only emerged during the **industrial boom** of the nineteenth century – in contrast to slumbering Bruges. Within the space of a decade or two, Ghent became choked with factories whose belching chimneys encrusted the old city with soot and grime, a disagreeable measure of the city's economic revival. Indeed, its entrepreneurial mayor, Emile Braun, even managed to get the **Great Exhibition**, showing the best in design and goods, staged here in 1913. Ghent is still an industrial city, but in the last twenty years its ancient centre has benefited from an extraordinarily ambitious programme of restoration and refurbishment. This has returned the string of fine Gothic buildings that dot the city centre to their original glory, a splendid architectural ensemble beginning with **St Baafskathedraal** – home of a remarkable painting by Jan van Eyck – and **St Niklaaskerk**. Close by are exquisite medieval guild houses, a clutch of enjoyable museums, and **Het Gravensteen**, the forbidding castle of the Counts of Flanders, not to mention lots of lively bars and first-class restaurants clustering the cobbled lanes of the **Patershol** district. Quite simply, Ghent's compact centre is one of the most fascinating in Europe, its attractions supplemented by several outlying sights, most notably **SMAK**, a prestigious Museum of Contemporary Art, and the **Museum voor Schone Kunsten** (Fine Art).

When to go

Both Bruges and Ghent are all-year destinations with most attractions and nearly all its bars and restaurants open winter and summer alike. Obviously enough, you can expect the weather to be sunnier and warmer in summer, but this advantage is offset by the excessive number of tourists visiting Bruges – but not so much Ghent - in the high season, especially July and August. If you're having a short break in either city, it's worth noting that many museums – and almost all of them in Bruges – are closed on Mondays.

Climate

Bruges and Ghent – and Belgium as a whole – enjoy a fairly standard **temperate climate**, with warm, if mild, summers and cold winters, without much snow. The warmest months are usually June, July and August, the coldest December and January, when short daylight hours and weak sunlight can make the weather seem colder (and wetter) than it actually is. Rain is always a possibility, even in summer, which actually sees a greater degree of rainfall than autumn or winter. Warm days in April and May, when the light has the clarity of springtime, are especially appealing.

	C°	RAINFALL
	AVERAGE DAILY	AVERAGE MONTHLY
		MM
Jan	1	66
Feb	4	61
March	7	53
April	11	60
May	13	55
June	18	76
July	19	95
Aug	18	80
Sept	17	63
Oct	12	83
Nov	7	75
Dec	3	88

BASICS

Bruges

ARRIVAL

Bruges is easy to reach by road and rail. The **E40 motor-way**, linking Brussels, Ghent and Ostend, runs just to the south of the city and there are fast and frequent **trains** from Brussels and Ghent, amongst several Belgian cities. Long-distance international **buses** run direct to Bruges from a number of capital cities, including London, and Bruges is well-connected by road and rail to two major North Sea **ports**: Ostend, with Hoverspeed services from Dover, and Zeebrugge, which is linked to Hull by car ferry. The nearest **airport** is Brussels (see p.4).

Bruges has only one principal **point of arrival**, the train and adjacent bus station about 2km to the southwest of the city centre. If the twenty-minute walk into the centre doesn't appeal, most of the **local buses** that leave from outside the train station head off to the Markt, with some services stopping on the square and others stopping on adjacent Wollestraat, both bang in the centre. All local buses have destination signs at the front, but if in doubt check with the driver. A **taxi** from the train station to the centre should be about €7.

> For the return journey, back from the centre to the train station, go to the bus stops outside the Biekorf centre, on Kuipersstraat, just to the northwest of the Markt. There's a more frequent service here than elsewhere.

BY AIR

Arriving in Belgium by air, you'll land at **Brussels' international airport**. From here, there are three or four trains every hour to the capital's three main stations: Bruxelles-Nord, Bruxelles-Centrale and Bruxelles-Midi. The journey-time to Bruxelles-Nord is about twenty minutes, a few minutes more to the others. You can change at any of these stations for the twice-hourly train from Brussels to Bruges, though changing at Bruxelles-Nord is a tad more convenient. The journey from Bruxelles-Nord to Bruges takes an hour. Once or twice an hour, the train from the airport goes on from the capital to Ghent, where you can also change for Bruges, but there's no saving on time. There are trains from Ghent to Bruges every twenty minutes and the journey takes twenty minutes.

BY CAR – AND PARKING

Most motorists arrive via the **E40**, which runs west from Brussels to Ostend, skirting Ghent and Bruges on the way. Bruges is clearly signed from the E40 and its oval-shaped centre is encircled by the **R30** ring road, which follows the course of the old city walls. Though it's easy to get to, **parking** in central Bruges can be a real pain with on-street parking almost impossible to find and the city centre's handful of car parks often filled to the gunnels. Easily the best option is to use the massive car park by the train station, particularly as the price – merely €2.50 per day –

ARRIVAL

includes the cost of the bus ride into (and out of) the centre. The price is deliberately kept low to attract motorists and thereby reduce city-centre congestion.

BY BOAT

Hoverspeed (in the UK contact ☎0870/240 8070, ⓕ01304/865203, ⓦwww.hoverspeed.co.uk) operates a **catamaran** service from Dover to Ostend, and P&O North Sea **Ferries** (UK contacts: ☎0870/129 6002, ⓕ01842/706438, ⓦwww.poferries.com) link Hull with Zeebrugge. The ferries operate all year, the catamarans for most of it, and both ports are within thirty minutes' drive of Bruges. In Ostend, the catamarans dock next to the train station, from where there's a twice hourly train to Bruges; the train journey takes fifteen minutes. Matters are a bit more complicated in Zeebrugge, where P&O ferries dock a couple of kilometres from Zeebrugge train station; P&O will provide onward transportation from the dock to the station, but this has to be arranged at least a couple of days beforehand. From Zeebrugge train station, trains run the fifteen-minute trip to Bruges hourly.

BY BUS

International **buses** to Bruges, including Eurolines (UK: ☎0990/143219, ⓕ01582/400694, ⓦwww.eurolines.com) services from Britain, terminate at the bus station, next to the train station, about 2km to the southwest of the city centre.

BY TRAIN – AND EUROSTAR

The only international **train** direct to Bruges is the **Thalys** service from Paris to Ostend via Brussels and Ghent. In

ARRIVAL

addition, Bruges is very well-served by the domestic network with fast and frequent services to and from a number of Belgian towns, including Brussels, Ghent, Ostend and Kortrijk. Trains from Brussels to Bruges stop at all three of the capital's mainline stations including Bruxelles-Midi, the terminus of **Eurostar** trains from London's Waterloo station. On Eurostar it takes two hours and forty minutes to get from London to Bruxelles-Midi station and another hour or so to get to Bruges. An alternative is to get off Eurostar at Lille – a two-hour journey – and then catch the train north to Kortrijk (1 hourly; 30min), where you change for the train to Bruges (2 hourly; 40min). This can save twenty minutes or so, but it depends on the times of the connections. Bruxelles-Midi station is also a stopping point for **Thalys** express trains from Amsterdam, Cologne, Aachen and Paris.

**Details of international trains to and from Belgium
can be found on the following websites:
Eurostar Ⓦ www.eurostar.com; Belgian Railways
Ⓦ www.b-rail.be; and Thalys Ⓦ www.thalys.com.**

INFORMATION AND MAPS

Bruges has two tourist offices. Inside the train station, the first **tourist office** (Mon–Sat 10am–6pm; ☎050/44 86 86) concentrates on making hotel reservations, which they will complete on your behalf at no charge, though they do require a small deposit which is deducted from the final bill. They also carry a limited range of tourist information, but this is of secondary importance here. The main **tourist office** is right in the centre of town at Burg 11 (April–Sept Mon–Fri 9.30am–6.30pm, Sat & Sun 10am–noon & 2–6.30pm; Oct–March Mon–Fri 9.30am–5pm, Sat & Sun

9.30am–1pm & 2–5.30pm; ℡050/44 86 86, Ⓕ44 86 00, Ⓔtoerisme@brugge.be, Ⓦwww.brugge.be). They also offer an accommodation-booking service and, in addition, sell all manner of brochures about the city, with one of the most useful being a general guide with suggested walking routes and museum opening times for €0.70.

Amongst a variety of free leaflets, there's a comprehensive accommodation listings brochure and a bi-monthly, multi-lingual events booklet, though the latter is not nearly as detailed as "**EXit**", a free monthly, Flemish-language newssheet available here and at many city-centre bars, cafés and bookshops. The tourist office also has currency exchange facilities and sells tickets for many events and per-formances. They also have local bus and train timetables.

If you need a large city **map**, buy the *Geocart Bruges City Map* (1:15.000), which comes complete with an index. It's available at most city-centre bookshops at around €5.50.

GETTING AROUND

The most enjoyable way to explore Bruges is to **walk**, and the centre is certainly compact – and flat – enough to make this an easy proposition. The city is also ideal for **cycling** with cycle lanes on many of the roads and cycle racks dot-ted across the centre. There are half a dozen **bike rental** places in Bruges, but Belgian Railways sets the benchmark, hiring out bikes at the railway station (℡050/30 23 29) for €8.80 per day. Two other options are Christophe's, Dweersstraat 4 (℡050/33 86 04; €8.70 per day), and the Bauhaus International Youth Hostel, Langestraat 135 (℡050/34 10 93; €8.70 per day). The tourist office issues a free and useful leaflet detailing five **cycle routes** in the countryside around Bruges – logically enough it's called "5x by bike around Bruges" – and Quasimodo Tours (see box on p.9) offers two guided cycling tours.

Bruges has an excellent network of local **bus** services, shuttling round the centre and the suburbs from the main bus station. These are operated by De Lijn, who have an information kiosk at the bus station (Mon–Fri 7.30am–6pm, Sat 9am–6pm & Sun 10am–5pm) as well as a regional information line (☏ 059/56 53 53). Most local services are routed through the city centre, calling at either the **Markt**, the main square, or the **Biekorf**, at the foot of Kuipersstraat a few metres to the northwest. The standard single fare is €1, or a booklet of ten tickets costs €7.50; pay the driver. The information kiosk also sells a 24-hour city bus pass, the Dagpas, for €2.90.

GUIDED TOURS

Guided tours are big business in Bruges and the tourist office has all the details. On offer are all sorts of ways of exploring the centre, from bus rides and walking tours to horse and carriage jaunts and boat trips, as well as excursions out into the Flemish countryside, most notably to the battlefields of World War I (see box pp.236–237). Sightseeing Line (☏ 050/35 50 24) operates fifty-minute **mini-coach tours** of the city centre for €10 per adult – pay the driver. Departures are from the Markt and passengers are issued with individual headphones in the language of their choice. Rather more sociable are the guided **walking tours** organized by the tourist office. Advance booking is required and the cost is €5 per adult. It is also possible to hire your own guide, again through the tourist office, with a two-hour tour costing €40 for a maximum of thirty people. Alternatively, **horse-drawn carriages** line up on the Markt offering a thirty-minute canter round town for €27.50. These are extremely popular, so expect to queue at the weekend.

QUASIMODO TOURS

Quasimodo Tours (℡ 050/37 04 70, ⓦ www.quasimodo.be) is the pick of the city's tour operators, offering a first-rate programme of excursions both in and around Bruges and out into Flanders. Highly recommended is their laid-back, but fully guided, Flanders Fields minibus tour of the World War I battlefields near Ypres – now Ieper. This focuses on the many visible remains, such as trenches, bunkers and craters, and includes stops at Ieper's Menin Gate War Memorial and Tyne Cot, the largest British Commonwealth war cemetery in the world. Tours run from mid-February to mid-November on Sundays, Tuesdays and Thursdays, last seven and a half hours and cost €45 (under-26 €38) including picnic lunch. Their second minibus tour, called "Triple Treat" (mid-Feb to mid-Nov Mon, Wed & Fri; 7hr 30min; €45, under-26 €38), sticks to the outskirts of Bruges. Highlights here include visits to Damme, the Gothic tithe barn at Ter Doest, the castle of Tillegem and the Chateau of Loppem, plus stops involving chocolate, waffles and beer – Belgian's gastronomic trinity. In both cases, reservations are required and hotel or railway station pick-up (in Bruges) can be arranged.

Quasimodo also runs two bike tours. Beginning at 10am, their three-hour "Bruges by Bike" excursion (daily April–Sept; €16, under-26 €14) zips round the main sights and then explores less visited parts of the city, trimming along quiet backstreets and canals. Their second bike tour, "Border by Bike", begins at 1pm and takes four hours (daily April–Sept; €16/14). This is a 25-kilometre-ride out along the poplar-lined canals to the north of Bruges, visiting Damme and Oostkerke with stops and stories along the way. Both are good fun and the price includes bottled water and mountain bike and rain-jacket hire. Reservations are required and the starting point is the Burg.

BOAT TRIPS

Half-hour **boat trips** around the city's central canals leave from a number of jetties south of the Burg (March–Nov daily 10am–6pm; €5.20). Boats depart every few minutes, but long queues still build up during high season with few visitors seemingly concerned by the clichéd commentary. In wintertime (Dec–Feb), there's a spasmodic service at weekends only. As for **trips out of town**, excursions to Damme (Easter–Sept 5 daily; 40min; one-way €5, return €6.50) start at the Noorweegse Kaai, 2km north of the town centre. Connecting bus #4 runs to the Noorweegse Kaai from the Markt, except in July and August when you need to catch the Bruges–Damme bus, #799. This is a pleasant excursion to an attractive little town – for a description of Damme, see p.214 – but it's much less expensively done by bike. Another option is the Polder Cruise to Ostend (July & Aug twice daily; €17), operated by Seastar (☎058/23 24 25). The cruise travels through some attractive countryside and the price includes the return trip back to Bruges by train (at any time you choose). Departures are from the Steenkaai, a couple of kilometres northwest of the centre; for a description of Ostend, see p.219.

Ghent

ARRIVAL

Ghent is easy to reach by road and rail. The **E40 motorway**, connecting Brussels and Ostend, runs just to the south of the city and there are fast and frequent **trains** from Brussels and Bruges, amongst several Belgian towns and cities. Long-distance **international buses** run direct to Ghent from a number of capital cities, including London, and the city is also well-connected by road and rail to two major North Sea **ports**, Ostend, with Hoverspeed services from Dover, and Zeebrugge, which is linked to Hull by car ferry. The nearest **airport** is Brussels, an hour by train from Ghent.

Ghent has only one principal **point of arrival**, St Pieters train station about 2km to the south of the city centre. The city's other two train stations – Gentbrugge and Gent-Dampoort – are used mainly by suburbanites. The city **bus station** is next to St Pieters. From beside St Pieters train station, **trams** (#1, #10, #11, #12 and #13) run up to the Korenmarkt, right in the city centre, every few minutes, mostly passing along Kortrijksesteenweg and Nederkouter. All trams have destination signs and numbers at the front, but if in doubt check with the driver. The **taxi** fare from the train station to the Korenmarkt is about €6.

BY AIR

Arriving in Belgium by air, you'll land at **Brussels' international airport**. From here, there is a once hourly train to Ghent (via Brussels) with a journey time of one hour. If you've just missed the train to Ghent, note that there are trains from the airport to Brussels every fifteen or twenty minutes and all of them stop at the capital's three main stations – Bruxelles-Nord, Bruxelles-Centrale, and Bruxelles-Midi. The journey-time to Bruxelles-Nord is about twenty minutes, a few minutes more to the others. You can change at any of these stations for the twice-hourly train from Brussels to Ghent. The journey from Bruxelles-Nord to Ghent takes forty minutes.

BY CAR – AND PARKING

Most motorists arrive via the **E40**, which runs west from Brussels to Ostend, skirting Ghent on the way. Ghent is clearly signed from the E40 and its oval-shaped centre is encircled by the **R40** ring road. Ghent is easy to get to, but **parking** in the centre can be a real headache with on-street parking difficult to find and the city centre's car parks often jam-packed. To help, the city has signed two **parking routes** (*parkeerroute*), one signed with yellow arrows, the other with green, both of which lead to – or past – the ten car parks that lie in or close to the centre. The green route is better for the central car parks and is a little less convoluted than the other. The 24-hour car park beneath the Vrijdagmarkt is one of the best placed.

BY BOAT

Hoverspeed (UK: ⓣ0870/240 8070, ⓕ01304/865203, ⓦwww.hoverspeed.co.uk) operates a **catamaran** service from Dover to Ostend, and P&O North Sea **Ferries** (UK: ℡0870/129 6002, ℻01482/706438, ⓦwww.poferries.com) link Hull with Zeebrugge. The ferries operate all year, the catamarans for most of it, and both ports are within an hour's drive of Ghent. In Ostend, the catamarans dock next to the train station, from where there's a twice-hourly train to Ghent; the train journey takes forty minutes. Matters are a bit more complicated in Zeebrugge, where P&O ferries dock a couple of kilometres from Zeebrugge train station; P&O will provide onward transportation from the dock to the station, but this has to be arranged at least a couple of days beforehand. From Zeebrugge train station there are hourly trains to Bruges, where you change for the thrice-hourly service to Ghent; Zeebrugge to Bruges takes fifteen minutes, Bruges to Ghent twenty minutes.

BY BUS

Most local and domestic **bus** services to and from Ghent pull in at the bus station, beside Ghent St Pieters train station, some 2km south of the city centre. Eurolines buses (UK: ℡0990/143219, ℻01582/400694, ⓦwww.euro-lines.com) from London to Ghent, departing once daily and taking seven hours, terminate at the bus company's offices at Koningin Elisabethlaan 73. From here, it's a couple of minutes walk southwest to St Pieters train station.

BY TRAIN – AND EUROSTAR

The only international **train** direct to Ghent is the **Thalys** service from Paris to Bruges and Ostend via Brussels. In addition, Ghent is supremely well-served by the domestic network with frequent and fast services to and from a number of Belgian towns, including Brussels, Bruges, Ostend and Kortrijk. Trains from Brussels to Ghent pause at all

ARRIVAL

three of the capital's mainline stations including Bruxelles-Midi, the terminus of **Eurostar** trains from London's Waterloo station. On Eurostar it takes two hours and forty minutes to get from London to Bruxelles-Midi station and another thirty minutes to get to Ghent. An alternative is to get off Eurostar at Lille – a two-hour journey – and then catch the train north to Ghent (1 hourly; 50min). This can save an hour or so, but it depends on the times of the connections. Bruxelles-Midi station is also a stopping point for **Thalys** express trains from Amsterdam, Cologne, Aachen and Paris.

Details of international trains to and from Belgium can be found on the following websites: Eurostar Ⓦ www.eurostar.com; Belgian Railways Ⓦ www.b-rail.be; and Thalys Ⓦ www.thalys.com.

INFORMATION AND MAPS

Ghent's **tourist office** is right in the centre of the city, in the crypt of the old cloth hall, the Lakenhalle (daily: April–Oct 9.30am–6.30pm; Nov–March 9.30am–4.30pm; Ⓣ 09/226 52 32, Ⓦ www.gent.be). They have a wide range of city information, including a booklet detailing places of interest along with opening times. Another of their booklets carries a list of selected restaurants and, more usefully, has a full list of local **accommodation**, including hotels and hostels along with prices. The tourist office will book hotel accommodation on your behalf for a small deposit, which is deducted from your final hotel bill – an especially useful service on busy summer weekends.

If you need a large city **map**, buy the *Geocart Ghent City Map* (1:10.000), which comes complete with an index. It's available at most city-centre bookshops at around €5.50.

GETTING AROUND

The best way of seeing the sights is on foot, but Ghent is a large city and you may find you have to use a **tram** or **bus** at some point. This is easy enough, especially as all services are operated by De Lijn (information line ℡09/210 93 11). A standard one-way fare costs €1 and tickets are valid for an hour; a ten-journey Rittenkaart costs €7.50. One-way tickets are bought direct from the driver, who will give change if required. Rittenkaarts are sold at selected shops and newsstands all over town and at De Lijn **kiosks**. There are De Lijn kiosks by the tram stops on the Korenmarkt (Mon–Fri 7am–7pm, Sat 10.30am–5.30pm) and at St Pieters train station (Mon–Fri 7am–7pm). These kiosks also sell a 24-hour city transport pass, the Dagpas, which represents good value at just €2.90, and issue free maps of the transport system (the Netplan). Tickets are also valid for the city's one and only **trolley bus line** (#3), which cuts across the city from east and west; this is the service you'll need to get to the Bourgoyen-Ossemeersen nature reserve (see p.115).

Ghent is very flat and thus especially good for **cycling** with cycle lanes on many of the roads and cycle racks dotted across the centre. There are a couple of **bike rental** outlets in Ghent, but Belgian Railways sets the benchmark, hiring out bikes at St Pieters railway station (℡09/241 22 24; daily 7am–8pm) for €8.80 per day.

GUIDED TOURS

Guided walking tours are particularly popular in Ghent. The standard walking tour, organized by the tourist office, is a two-hour jaunt round the city centre (April Sat & Sun at 2.30pm; May–Oct daily at 2.30pm; €6); advance booking – at least a few hours ahead of time – is strongly recom-

BOAT TRIPS

Throughout the year, **boat trips** explore Ghent's inner water-ways, departing from the Korenlei and Graslei quays, just near the Korenmarkt (March to early Nov daily 10am–6pm, mid-Nov to Feb Sat & Sun 11am–4pm). Trips last forty minutes, cost €4.50, and leave roughly once every fifteen minutes, though the wait can be longer as boats often only leave when reasonably full.

Other, longer nautical excursions leave from near the Recollettenbrug, behind the Recollettenlei (Law Courts), at the west end of Zonnestraat. They include trips along the River Leie to Sint-Martens Latem (June–Sept 1–4 times weekly 1.30–6.30pm; €9) and day-trips to Bruges (July–Aug 4 times monthly, 9am–8pm; €13) – though the latter aren't quite as good as they sound: food and drink are expensive, and long sections of the canal are too deep to see over the banks. Further details can be obtained from the tourist office or from Benelux Rederij, the boat operators, at Recollettenlei 32 (℡09/225 15 05).

mended. In addition, the Association of Guides of Ghent (℡09/233 07 72, ℱ223 08 65) run more specialist, themed walking tours – including an evening excursion to several of the city's more traditional bars – on a more ad hoc basis. A two-hour guided tour with them costs about €50. Alternatively, **horse-drawn carriages** line up outside the Lakenhalle, on St Baafsplein, offering a thirty-minute canter round town for €23 (Easter to October daily 10am–6pm and most winter weekends), and you can even fly over the city, weather permitting, by helicopter or balloon (1–1hr 30min). Balloon trips cost in the region of €120 per person, the helicopter €160. Balloon & Heli Adventure (℡09/232 46 48, ⓦwww.balloonadventure.com) do both;

Dream Ballooning (℡ & Ⓕ 09/355 59 94, Ⓦ www.fly.to /dreamballooning) just do balloons – and are a good bit cheaper.

THE GUIDE

THE GUIDE

Bruges city centre

Passing through Bruges in 1820, William Wordsworth declared that this was where he discovered "a deeper peace than in deserts found". He was neither the first nor the last Victorian to fall in love with the place and by the 1840s there was a substantial British colony here, its members captured and enraptured by the city's medieval architecture and air of lost splendour. Civil service and army pensions went much further in Bruges than back home and the expatriates were not slow to exercise their economic muscle, applying an architectural **Gothic Revival** brush to parts of the city that weren't "medieval" enough. Time and again, they intervened in municipal planning decisions, allying themselves to like-minded Flemings in a movement that changed, or at least modified, the face of the city – and ultimately paid out mega bucks with the arrival of mass tourism in the 1960s. Thus, Bruges is not the perfectly preserved medieval city of much tourist literature, but rather a clever, frequently seamless combination of medieval original and nineteenth- and sometimes twentieth-century addition. This is especially true of the **city centre**, where all the leading attractions are clustered within easy walking distance of each other.

The obvious place to start an exploration of the centre is in the two principal squares: the **Markt**, overlooked by the mighty belfry; and the **Burg**, flanked by the city's most impressive architectural ensemble. Almost within shouting distance, along the Dijver, are the city's three main museums, amongst which the **Groeninge Museum** offers a wonderful sample of early Flemish art. Another short hop brings you to **St Janshospitaal** and the important paintings of the fifteenth-century artist **Hans Memling** as well as Bruges' most satisfying churches, **Onze Lieve Vrouwekerk** and **Sint Salvatorskathedraal**. It's possible to amble round the sights in two or three hours, but really it's much, much better to dilly and dally, especially if you're visiting out of high season when the crowds are rarely bothersome.

**Be aware that almost all the city's
sights are closed on Mondays.**

THE MARKT

At the heart of Bruges is the **Markt** (Map 3, D8), an airy open space edged on three sides by rows of gabled buildings and with horse-drawn buggies clattering over the cobbles. The burghers of nineteenth-century Bruges were keen to put something suitably civic in the middle of the square and the result is the conspicuous **monument** to Pieter de Coninck, of the guild of weavers, and Jan Breydel, dean of the guild of butchers. Standing close together, they clutch the hilt of the same sword, their faces turned to the south in slightly absurd poses of heroic determination – and a far cry from the gory events which first made them local heroes. At dawn on Friday, May 18, 1302, in what was later called the Bruges Matins, their force of rebellious Flemings crept into the city and massacred the unsuspecting French

THE MARKT

garrison, putting to the sword anyone who couldn't correctly pronounce the Flemish shibboleth schild en vriend
("shield and friend"). Later the same year, the two guildsmen went on to lead the city's contingent in the Flemish
army that defeated the French at the Battle of the Golden
Spurs – no surprise, then, that the monument takes its cue
from the battle rather than the massacre. Nevertheless, the
statue was still controversial and, bizarrely enough, it was
unveiled twice. In July 1887, a local committee pulled back
the drapes to celebrate Coninck and Breydel as Flemings,
whilst the City Council organised an official opening in
August, when King Leopold II honoured them as Belgians.

The biscuit-tin buildings flanking most of the Markt are a
charming ensemble, largely mellow ruddy-brown brick,
each gable compatible with but slightly different from its
neighbour. Most are late nineteenth-or even twentieth-century re-creations – or re-inventions – of older buildings,
though the **Post Office**, which hogs the east side of the
square, is a thunderous neo-Gothic edifice that refuses to
camouflage its modern construction. The **Craenenburg
Café**, on the corner of St Amandsstraat at Markt 16, occupies a modern building too, but it marks the site of the
eponymous medieval mansion in which the guildsmen of
Bruges imprisoned the Habsburg heir, Archduke
Maximilian, for three months in 1488. The reason for their
difference of opinion was the archduke's efforts to limit the
city's privileges, but whatever the justice of their cause, the
guildsmen made a big mistake. To escape their clutches,
Maximilian made all sorts of promises, but a few weeks
after his release his dad, the Emperor Frederick III, turned
up with an army to take imperial revenge. Maximilian
became emperor in 1493 and he never forgave Bruges,
doing his considerable best to push trade north to its great
rival, Antwerp.

THE MARKT

23

Among the pavement cafés and restaurants
that edge the Markt, the **Craenenburg Café**
has the most character. Unlike its more touristy
neighbours, it has a loyal local following.

The Belfort (belfry)

Map 3, E9. Tues–Sun 9.30am–5pm; €5.

Filling out the south side of the Markt, the domineering
Belfort, with its blind arcading, turrets and towers, is a
potent symbol of civic pride and municipal independence,
its distinctive octagonal lantern visible for miles across the
surrounding polders. It was begun in the thirteenth century,
when the town was at its richest and most extravagant, but
it has had a blighted history. The original wooden version
was struck by lightning and burned to the ground in 1280
and its brick replacement received its stone octagonal
lantern – and a second wooden spire – in the 1480s. The
new spire didn't last long – it was lost to a thunderstorm a
few years later – but undeterred, the Flemings promptly
added a third. This went up in smoke in 1741 and the locals
gave up, settling for the present structure with the addition
of a stone parapet in 1822. It's a pity they didn't have
another go, if only to sabotage Longfellow's metre in his
dire but oft-quoted poem *The Belfry of Bruges*: "In the market place of Bruges, Stands the Belfry old and brown,
Thrice consumed and thrice rebuilt …" and so on. Few
would say the Belfort is good-looking – it's large and really
rather clumsy – but it does have a particular charm, though
this was lost on G.K. Chesterton who described it as "an
unnaturally long-necked animal, like a giraffe".

Entry to the belfry is via the quadrangular **Hallen** at its
base. Now used for temporary exhibitions, the Hallen is a
much-restored edifice dating from the thirteenth century,

its style and structure modelled on the Lakenhalle (cloth hall) at Ieper (see p.232). In the middle, overlooked by a long line of galleries, is a rectangular courtyard, which originally served as the town's principal market, its cobblestones once crammed with merchants and their wares. On the north side of the courtyard, up a flight of steps, is the entrance to the belfry. Inside, the **belfry staircase** begins innocuously, but gets steeper and much narrower nearer the top. On the way up, it passes several chambers, beginning with the **Treasury Room**, where the town charters and money chest were locked for safe keeping behind the fancy iron grilles that have survived in surprisingly good condition. Here also is an iron trumpet with which a watchman could warn the town of a fire outbreak – though, given the size of the trumpet, it's hard to believe this was very effective.

Further up is the **Carillon Chamber**, where you can observe the slow turning of the large spiked drum that controls the 47 bells of the municipal carillon. The base is the largest bell and it weighs no less than six tons. Like other Flemish cities, bells were first used in Bruges in the fourteenth century as a means of regulating the working day and as such reflected the development of a wage economy – employers were keen to keep tabs on their employees. Bells also served as a sort of public address system with everyone understanding the signals: pealing bells, for example, announced good news; tolling bells summoned the city to the Markt; and a rapid sequence of bells warned of danger. By the early fifteenth century, a short peal of bells marked the hour and from this developed the **carillon** (*beiaard*) with Bruges installing its present version in the middle of the eighteenth century. The city still employs a full-time bell ringer – you're likely to see him fiddling around in the Carillon Room – and he puts on **Carillon Concerts** (late June to Sept Mon, Wed & Sat 9–10pm plus Sun 2.15–3pm; Oct to mid-June Wed, Sat & Sun 2.15–3pm; free).

THE MARKT

25

Obviously enough, you can hear these concerts all over town, but if you're keen to watch him doing his thing, you'll need to head for the small and oddly intimate little **Carillon Room** right near the top of the belfry. A few stairs up from here and you emerge onto the belfry roof, which offers fabulous views over the city, especially in the late afternoon when the warm colours of the town are at their deepest.

- -

The belfry staircase does get very narrow at the top – narrow enough to upset the more nervous of visitors, especially young children.

- -

THE BURG

From the east side of the Markt, Breidelstraat leads through to the city's other main square, the Burg (Map 3, F8), named after the fortress built here by the first count of Flanders, Baldwin Iron Arm, in the ninth century. The fortress disappeared centuries ago, but the Burg long remained the centre of political and ecclesiastical power with the Stadhuis (town hall) – which has survived – on one side, and St Donatian's cathedral – which hasn't – on the other. The southern half of the Burg is fringed by the city's finest group of buildings, including the Stadhuis and, on the right, the Basilica of the Holy Blood.

Heilig Bloed Basiliek (The Basilica of the Holy Blood)

Map 3, F9. Daily: April–Sept 9.30am–noon & 2–6pm; Oct–March Mon–Tues & Thurs–Sun 10am–noon & 2–4pm, Wed 10am–noon; free. The **Heilig Bloed Basiliek** is named after the holy relic that found its way here in the Middle Ages. The church divides into two parts. Tucked away in the corner, the **lower chapel** is a shadowy, crypt-like affair, originally built at the beginning of the twelfth century to shelter another relic, that of St Basil, one of the great figures of the early Greek Church. The chapel's heavy and simple Romanesque lines are decorated with just one relief, which is carved above an interior doorway – a representation of the baptism of Basil in which a strange giant bird, depicting the Holy Spirit, plunges into a pool of water. Next door, approached up a wide, low-vaulted curving staircase, the **upper chapel** was built a few years later, but has been renovated so frequently that it's impossible to make out the original structure. In addition, the interior has been spoiled by excessively rich nineteenth-century decoration.

The building may be disappointing, but the rock-crystal phial that contains the Holy Blood is stored within a magnificent silver **tabernacle**, the gift of Albert and Isabella of Spain in 1611. One of the holiest relics in medieval Europe, the phial purports to contain a few drops of blood and water washed from the body of Christ by Joseph of Arimathea. Local legend asserts that it was the gift of Diederik d'Alsace, a Flemish knight who distinguished himself by his bravery during the Second Crusade and was given the phial by a grateful patriarch of Jerusalem in 1150. It is, however, rather more likely that the relic was acquired during the sacking of Constantinople in 1204, when the Crusaders simply ignored their collective job description and robbed and slaughtered the Byzantines instead – hence the historical invention. Whatever the truth, after several weeks in Bruges, the relic was found to be dry, but thereafter it proceeded to liquefy every Friday at 6pm until 1325, a miracle attested by all sorts of church dignitaries, including Pope Clement V.

The Holy Blood is still venerated and, despite modern scepticism, reverence for it remains strong, not least on Ascension Day when it is carried through the town in a colourful but solemn procession, the *Heilig-Bloedprocessie*.

THE BURG

The reliquary that holds the phial when it's moved from the basilica during the procession is displayed in the tiny **treasury** (same times as basilica; €1.25), next to the upper chapel. Dating to 1617, it's a superb piece of work, the gold and silver superstructure encrusted with jewels and decorated with tiny religious scenes. The treasury also has an incidental collection of vestments and lesser reliquaries plus the *Life of St Barbara*, by the Master of the St Barbara Legend – it's displayed by the window. One of the most popular saints of medieval Flanders, the story goes that St Barbara, a third-century saint from Rome or possibly Egypt, was a woman of great beauty whose father, Dioscurus, locked her up in a tower to discourage her many admirers. During her captivity, Dioscurus discovered that she was a Christian and promptly handed her over to the authorities for punishment. Barbara was tortured, but refused to abjure her faith, whereupon her father was ordered to kill her himself. This he did, but was promptly struck by lightning and reduced to a pile of ashes – events which made Barbara the patron saint of gunners and miners. The painting tells the tale and although it's not especially well executed, it is inventive for here, in a break from tradition, the tower is still under construction when Barbara arrives. Look out also, above the treasury door, for the faded strands of a locally woven seventeenth-century tapestry depicting St Augustine's funeral, the sea of helmeted heads, torches and pikes that surround the monks and abbots, very much a Catholic view of a muscular State supporting a holy Church.

A **combined ticket** for five of Bruges' central museums –
the Stadhuis, Renaissancezaal 't Brugse Vrije, Arentshuis,
Gruuthuse and Memling – is available at any of them as well
as from the tourist office. It costs €15. A sixth museum, the
Groeninge, is closed until 2003, but when it reopens the
combined ticket will no doubt be modified.

The Stadhuis (Town Hall)

Map 3, F9. Tues–Sun 9.30am–5pm; €2.50 including the
Renaissance Hall (see p.31).

Immediately to the left of the basilica, the **Stadhuis** has a
beautiful sandstone facade, a much-copied exterior that
dates from 1376 – though its statues (of the counts and
countesses of Flanders) are modern replacements of those
destroyed by the occupying French army in 1792. Inside,
the **entrance hall** is a grand, high-ceilinged affair that is
home to several nineteenth-century paintings, either
romantic reworkings of the city's history designed to reas-
sure the council of its distinguished pedigree, or didactic
canvases to keep it up to the mark. The biggest is Henri
Dobbelaere's (1829–1885) whopping *Seven Works of Mercy*,
but the most original, at the foot of the stairs, is Camille
van Camp's (1834–1891) *Death of Mary of Burgundy* – refer-
ring to a hunting accident of 1482.

Upstairs, the magnificent **Gothic Hall**, dating from
1400, was the setting for the first meeting of the States
General (parliamentary assembly) in 1464. The ceiling has
been restored in a vibrant mixture of maroon, dark brown,
black and gold, dripping pendant arches like decorated sta-
lactites. The ribs of the arches converge in twelve circular
vault-keys, picturing scenes from the New Testament.
These are hard to see without binoculars, but two of the
more distinguishable are the Flight to Egypt and the
Baptism of Christ. Down below – and much easier to view
– are the sixteen gilded **corbels**, which support them.
They represent the months and the four elements, beginning in the left-hand corner beside the chimney with
January and continuing in a clockwise direction right round
the hall: the gilded chariots of Air and Earth follow June,
Fire and Water come after September. The **frescoes** around
the walls were commissioned in 1895 to illustrate the history of the town – or rather history as the council wanted to

THE BURG

29

recall it. The largest scene, commemorating the victory over the French at the Battle of the Golden Spurs in 1302, has lots of noble knights hurrah-ing, though it's hard to take this seriously when you look at the dogs, one of which clearly has a mis-match between its body and head.

In the adjoining **historical room**, a display of miscellaneous artefacts, including navigational aids and the old, seven-lock municipal treasure chest, is largely redeemed by two fascinating **city maps**. The earlier version, from 1501, is interesting in so far as it represents a transition from the medieval map, which presented a theological, sometimes political view of the world, to the modern, geographically accurate map. Dotted with pictograms of windmills, churches and ships, the map gives the flavour of the city with some geography, but does not pretend to be precise. By contrast, the second map of 1562 – with its neatly painted fields, towns and rivers – purports to provide an accurate representation. Interestingly enough, this second map, by the artist Marcus Gerards, is not all that it seems. When the city council gave Gerards the commission, they were acutely aware that the silting up of the River Zwin, linking Bruges with the North Sea, had made access to Bruges much more difficult. Consequently, they told him to make the river and its tributaries look wider than they were; Gerards obliged – a good example of early municipal PR.

Renaissancezaal 't Brugse Vrije (Renaissance Hall of the Liberty of Bruges)

Map 3, F8. Tues–Sun 9.30am–12.30pm & 1.30–5pm; €2.50 including the Stadhuis (see p.29).

Next door to the Stadhuis, the bright and cheery **Oude Griffie** (no admission) was built to house the municipal records office in 1537, its elegant facade decorated with Renaissance columns and friezes superimposed on the

Gothic lines of the gables below. The adjacent **Paleis van het Brugse Vrije** (the Mansion of the Liberty of Bruges) is demure by comparison, but it has a distinguished history. Established in the Middle Ages, the Liberty was a territorial sub-division of Flanders that enjoyed extensive delegated powers, controlling its own finances and judiciary. Power was exercised by a council of Aldermen and it was they who demolished most of the original Gothic building in the early eighteenth century – with the occupying French army abolishing them in 1795.

Today the building is home to the municipal archives office, but the old *Schepenkamer* (Aldermen's Room) has survived and this – now known as the **Renaissancezaal 't Brugse Vrije** – boasts an enormous marble and oak **chimneypiece**. A fine example of Renaissance carving, it was completed in 1531 under the direction of Lancelot Blondeel, to celebrate the defeat of the French at Pavia in 1525 and the advantageous Treaty of Cambrai that followed. A paean of praise to the Habsburgs, the work is dominated by figures of the Emperor Charles V and his Austrian and Spanish relatives, each person identified by both the free leaflet and the audio-guide, although it's the trio of bulbous codpieces that really catch the eye. The alabaster frieze running below the carvings was a caution for the Liberty's magistrates, who held their courts here. In four panels, it relates the then familiar Biblical story of **Susanna**, in which – in the first panel – two old men surprise her bathing in her garden and threaten to accuse her of adultery if she resists their advances. Susanna does just that and the second panel shows her in court. In the third panel, Susanna is about to be put to death, but the magistrate, Daniel, interrogates the two men and uncovers their perjury. Susanna is acquitted and, in the final scene, the two men are stoned to death.

Quite deliberately, to remind them of the limits to their

authority, the magistrates sat in between the Habsburgs of the chimneypiece – representing the highest secular power – and a painting of the *Last Judgement*. The original painting was by Pieter Pourbus, but the version displayed today is a (poor) copy by Henri Dobbelaere. Also in the room are several Habsburg portraits, notably one of a singularly determined King Philip II as well as a surprisingly honest painting of Charles II. Charles, the last of the Spanish Habsburgs, was – according to the historian J. H. Elliott – "a rachitic and feeble-minded weakling, the last stunted sprig of a degenerate line" – and that's precisely what he looks like. He died without issue in 1700, precipitating the

CHARLES THE GOOD AND GALBERT OF BRUGES

In 1127, St Donaaskathedraal witnessed an event that shocked the whole of Bruges, when the Count of Flanders, **Charles the Good**, was murdered while he was at prayer in the choir. A gifted and far-sighted ruler, Charles eschewed foreign entanglements in favour of domestic matters – unlike most of his predecessors – and improved the lot of the poor, trying to ensure a regular supply of food and controlling prices in times of shortage. It was this – along with his piety – that earned Charles his sobriquet, but the count's attempts to curb his leading vassals, who had frequently ignored his predecessors, brought him into conflict with the powerful Erembald clan. The Erembalds had no intention of submitting to Charles, so they assassinated him and took control of the city. Their success was, however, short-lived. Supporters of Charles rallied and the murderers took refuge in the tower of St Donatians, from where they were winkled out and promptly dispatched.

Shocked by the murder, one of his clerks, a certain **Galbert of Bruges**, decided to write a detailed journal of the events

long-winded War of the Spanish Succession. Finally, the lay-out of the Aldermen's Room as of 1659 is portrayed in a canvas by Gillis van Tilborgh.

The Gerechtshof (Law Courts) and the site of St Donaaskathedraal

Adjoining the Bruges Vrije, the plodding courtyard complex of the **Gerechtshof** (Map 3, F8), dating from 1722, is now home to the main tourist office (see p.6). Beyond, in the northeast corner of the Burg, the modern Crowne Plaza Hotel marks the site of **St Donaaskathedraal** (St Donatian's Cathedral), which was razed by the French in

that led up to the assassination and the bloody chaos that ensued. Unlike other contemporary source materials, the journal had no sponsor – and indeed it appears that Galbert kept his scribblings entirely secret – which makes it a uniquely honest account of events, admittedly from the perspective of the count's entourage. Galbert does not flinch from criticising many of the city's leading figures, clergy and nobles alike, and – as a clear indication of his independence – he has an ambivalent attitude to Thierry of Alsace, who ultimately won the struggle to succeed Charles. Galbert's journal provides a fascinating insight into twelfth-century Bruges and it's well-written too (in a wordy sort of way) – as in the account of Charles' death: "when the count, according to custom, was praying, reading aloud obligingly, then at last, after so many plans and oaths and pacts among themselves, those wretched traitors ... slew the count, who was struck down with swords and run through again and again". The full text is in print in a University of Toronto Press edition, entitled *The Murder of Charles the Good*.

THE BURG

1799. By all accounts, the church was a splendid structure, in which – emulating Charlemagne's Palatine Chapel in Aachen – the octagonal main building was flanked by a sixteen-sided ambulatory and an imposing tower. The foundations were uncovered in 1955, but they were promptly reinterred and although there have been vague plans to carry out another archeological dig, nothing has happened yet.

ALONG THE DIJVER

From the arch beside the Oude Griffie, **Blinde Ezelstraat** ("Blind Donkey Street") leads south across the canal to the plain and sombre eighteenth-century Doric colonnades of the fish market – the **Vismarkt**. There's not much marine action here today and neither are there any tanners in the huddle of picturesque houses that crimp the **Huidenvettersplein**, the old tanners' quarter immediately to the west. Tourists converge on this pint-sized square in their droves, holing up in its bars and restaurants and snapping away at the postcard-perfect views of the belfry from the adjacent **Rozenhoedkaai**. From here, it's a short hop west to the Wollestraat bridge, which is overlooked by a statue of the patron saint of bridges, **St John Nepomuk**. A fourteenth-century Bohemian priest, Nepomuk was purportedly thrown bound and gagged into the River Vltava for refusing to reveal the confessional secrets of the queen to her husband, King Wenceslas IV. The bridge marks the start of the **Dijver**, which tracks along the canal as far as Nieuwstraat, passing the path to the first of the city's main museums, the Groeninge.

On Saturdays and Sundays, from mid-March to mid-November, the Dijver and the Vismarkt host an antique, souvenir and craft **market**. For more on markets, see p.187.

THE GROENINGE MUSEUM

Map 3, F11. Tues–Sun 9.30am–5pm.

Jan van Eyck

Arguably the greatest of the early Flemish masters, **Jan van Eyck** lived and worked in Bruges from 1430 until his death eleven years later. He was a key figure in the development of oil painting, modulating its tones to create paintings of extraordinary clarity and realism. The Groeninge has two gorgeous examples of his work in its permanent collection, beginning with the miniature portrait of his wife, *Margareta van Eyck*, painted in 1439 and bearing his motto, "als ich can" (the best I can do). The painting is very much a private picture and one that had no commercial value, marking a small step away from the sponsored art – and religious preoccupations – of previous Flemish artists.

The second Eyck painting is the remarkable *Madonna and Child with Canon George van der Paele*, a glowing and richly

GROENINGE MUSEUM REFURBISHMENT

The Groeninge Museum is in a state of flux. In 2002, to celebrate the city's selection as a cultural capital of Europe, the museum hosted a prestigious three-month exhibition on Jan van Eyck and his Netherlandish contemporaries. Afterwards, the museum was closed for an extensive refurbishment and will not reopen until 2003. The description below details some of the major works of the permanent collection, but it is impossible to say exactly what will be displayed and how. That said, it's unthinkable that the new, improved Groeninge will not showcase its wonderful sample of early Flemish paintings, one of the world's finest and the kernel of the permanent collection

THE GROENINGE MUSEUM

analytical work with three figures surrounding the Madonna: the kneeling canon, St George (his patron saint) and St Donatian, to whom he is being presented. St George doffs his helmet to salute the infant Christ and speaks by means of the Hebrew word "Adonai" (Lord) inscribed on his chin strap, while Jesus replies through the green parrot in his left hand: folklore asserted that this type of parrot was fond of saying "Ave", the Latin for welcome. The canon's face is exquisitely executed, down to the sagging jowls and the bulging blood vessels at his temple, and, with glasses and book in hand, he has assumed a look of deep contemplation. Audaciously, Van Eyck has broken with tradition by painting the canon amongst the saints – and not as a lesser figure – in a distinct nod to the humanism that was gathering pace in contemporary Bruges. The painting also celebrates the wealth of Bruges in the luxurious clothes and furnishings: the floor tiles are of Spanish design, the geometric tapestry at the feet of the Madonna comes from Asia and St Donatian is decked out in jewel-encrusted vestments.

Jan van Eyck's most magnificent painting, the extraordinary *Adoration of the Mystic Lamb*, is displayed in St Baafskathedraal in Ghent; see p.82.

Rogier van der Weyden, Dieric Bouts and Hugo van der Goes

The Groeninge possesses two fine and roughly contemporaneous copies of paintings by **Rogier van der Weyden** (1399–1464), one-time official city painter to Brussels. The first is a tiny *Portrait of Philip the Good*, in which the pallor of the duke's aquiline features, along with the brightness of his hatpin and chain of office, are skilfully balanced by the sombre cloak and hat. The second and much larger painting is *St Luke painting the Portrait of Our Lady*, a rendering of a popular if highly improbable legend, which claimed that Luke painted Mary – thereby becoming the patron saint of painters. The painting is notable for the detail of its Flemish background and the cheeky-chappie smile of the baby Christ.

Another key fifteenth-century work is a gruesome, oak-panel triptych, *The Martyrdom of St Hippolytus*, by **Dieric Bouts** (1410–1475) and **Hugo van der Goes** (d 1482). The right panel – by Bouts – depicts the Roman Emperor Decius, a notorious persecutor of Christians, trying to persuade the priest Hippolytus to abjure his faith. He fails and in the central panel – again by Bouts – Hippolytus is pulled to pieces by four horses; the donors who paid for the painting are on the left panel, which was van der Goes' contribution. The Hippolytus story was a popular one, but almost certainly fictitious, being derived from Greek mythology: there's no historical record of a Roman priest of this name, but the son of Theseus was called Hippolytus and he was dragged to his death by the bolting horses of his chariot.

One the most gifted of the early Flemish artists, Hugo van der Goes is a shadowy figure, though it is known that he became master of the painters' guild in Ghent in 1467. Eight years later, he entered a Ghent priory as a lay-brother and this may be related to the prolonged bouts of acute depression which afflicted him. Few of his paintings have survived, but these exhibit a superb compositional balance and a keen observational eye. His last work, the luminescent *Death of Our Lady*, is here at the Groeninge, though it was originally hung in the abbey at Koksijde on the coast. Sticking to religious legend, the Apostles have been miraculously transported to Mary's deathbed, where, in a state of agitation, they surround the prostrate woman. Mary is dressed in blue, but there are no signs of luxury, reflecting both der Goes' asceticism and his polemic – the artist may

THE GROENINGE MUSEUM

well have been appalled by the church's love of glitter and gold.

Another Groeninge highlight is the two matching panels of *The Legend of St Ursula*, the work of an unknown fifteenth-century artist known as the "**Master of the Ursula Legend**". The panels, each of which has five miniature scenes, were probably inspired by the twelfth-century discovery of the supposed bones of St Ursula and the women who were massacred with her in Cologne seven centuries before – a sensational find that would certainly have been common knowledge in Bruges. Surfacing in the ninth century, the original legend describes St Ursula as a British princess, who avoids an unwanted marriage by going on a pilgrimage to Rome accompanied by eleven female companions, sometimes referred to as nuns or virgins. On their way back, a tempest blows their ship off-course and they land at Cologne, where the (pagan) Huns promptly slaughter them. Pious women who suffered for the faith always went down a storm in medieval Christendom, but somewhere along the line the eleven women became eleven thousand – possibly because the buckets of bones found in Cologne were from an old public burial ground and had nothing to do with Ursula and her chums.

Hans Memling, Gerard David and Hieronymus Bosch

Bruges' Hans Memling Museum has a superb
collection of the artist's work – see p.57.

Other early Flemish highlights include the riotous violence of the unattributed *Scenes of the Legend of St George*, and a pair of *Annunciation* panels from a triptych by **Hans Memling** (1430–1494) – gentle, romantic representations of an angel and Mary, in contrasting shades of grey, a monochrome technique known as grisaille. Here also is

Memling's *Moreel Triptych*, in which the formality of the design is off-set by the warm colours and the gentleness of the detail – St Giles strokes the fawn and the knight's hand lays on the donor's shoulder. The central panel depicts saints Giles and Maurus to either side of St Christopher with a backdrop of mountains, clouds and sea. St Christopher, the patron saint of travellers, carries Jesus on his shoulders in an abbreviated reference to the original story which has the saint, who made his living lugging travellers across a river, carrying a child who becomes impossibly heavy. In the way of such things, it turns out that the child is Jesus and the realization turns Christopher Christian. The side panels show the donors and their sixteen children along with their patron saints – the knight St William for Willem Moreel, a wealthy spice trader and financier, and St Barbara for his wife.

Look closely and you'll see that in Gerard David's *Judgement of Cambyses* painting, the judge takes his bribe outside the Poortersloge on Jan van Eyckplein (see p.69).

Born near Gouda, the Dutchman **Gerard David** (c1460–1523) moved to Bruges in his early twenties. Soon admitted into the local painters' guild, he quickly rose through the ranks, becoming the city's leading artistic light after the death of Memling. Official commissions rained in on David, mostly for religious paintings, which he approached in a formal manner but with a fine eye for detail. The Groeninge holds two excellent examples of his work, starting with the *Baptism of Christ Triptych* in which a boyish, lightly bearded Christ is depicted as part of the Holy Trinity in the central panel. To either side are the donors, the Trompes, and their patron saints – St John and St Elizabeth. There's also one of David's few secular ventures, the intriguing *Judgement of Cambyses*, painted on two

THE GROENINGE MUSEUM

oak panels. Based on a Persian legend related by Herodotus, the first panel's background shows the corrupt judge Sisamnes accepting a bribe, with the result – his arrest by grim-faced aldermen – filling out the rest of the panel. The aldermen crowd in on Sisamnes with a palpable sense of menace and as the king sentences him to be flayed alive, a sweaty look of fear sweeps over the judge's face. In the gruesome second panel the king's servants carry out the judgement, applying themselves to the task with clinical detachment. Behind, in the top right corner, the fable is completed with the judge's son dispensing justice from his father's old chair, which is now draped with the flayed skin. Completed in 1498, the painting was hung in the council chamber by the city burghers to encourage honesty amongst its magistrates and as a sort of public apology for the imprisonment of Archduke Maximilian in Bruges in 1488. Maximilian would almost certainly have appreciated the painting – even if the gesture was itself too little too late – as the king dispenses his judgement without reference to either the church or God, a sub-text of secular authority very much to his tastes.

The Groeninge also has **Hieronymus Bosch**'s (1450–1516) *Last Judgement*, a trio of oak panels crammed with mysterious beasts, microscopic mutants and scenes of awful cruelty – men boiled in a pit or cut in half by a giant knife. It looks like unbridled fantasy, but in fact the scenes were read as symbols, a sort of strip cartoon of legend, proverb and tradition. Indeed Bosch's religious orthodoxy is confirmed by the appeal his work had for that most Catholic of Spanish kings, Philip II.

Jan Provoost, Adriaen Isenbrant and Bernard van Orley

There's more grim symbolism in **Jan Provoost**'s (1465–1529) crowded and melodramatic *Last Judgement*, painted for the Stadhuis in 1525, and his striking *The Miser* *and Death*, which portrays the merchant with his money in one panel, trying desperately to pass a promissory note to the grinning skeleton in the next. Provoost's career was typical of many of the Flemish artists of the early sixteenth century. Initially he worked in the Flemish manner, his style greatly influenced by Gerard David, but from about 1521 his work was reinvigorated by contact with the German painter and engraver Albrecht Dürer, who had himself been inspired by the artists of the early Italian Renaissance. Provoost moved around too, working in Valenciennes and Antwerp, before settling in Bruges in 1494. One of his Bruges contemporaries was **Adriaen Isenbrant** (d 1551), whose speciality was small, precisely executed panels. His *Virgin and Child* triptych is a good example of his technically proficient work.

Adriaen Isenbrant's superb *Madonna of the Seven Sorrows* is displayed in the Onze Lieve Vrouwekerk (see p.51).

Bernard van Orley (1488–1541) was a long-time favourite of the Habsburg officials in Brussels until his Protestant sympathies put him in the commercial dog house. A versatile artist, Orley produced action-packed paintings of Biblical scenes, often back-dropped by classical buildings in the Renaissance style, as well as cartoon designs for tapestries, sometimes for the creation of stained glass windows. He is represented in the Groeninge collection by the strip-cartoon *Legend of St Rochus*. A fourteenth-century saint hailing from Montpellier in France, Rochus was in northern Italy on a pilgrimage to Rome when the plague struck. He abandoned his journey to tend to the sick and promptly discovered he had miraculous healing powers. This did not stop him from catching the plague, but fortunately a remarkable dog was on hand to nurse him back to health. Recovered, Rochus went back home, but his

THE GROENINGE MUSEUM

relatives failed to recognize him and he was imprisoned as an impostor, and died there – a hard luck story if ever there was one.

Pieter, Frans the Elder and Frans the Younger Pourbus; Jacob van Oost the Elder

The Groeninge's collection of late sixteenth- and seventeenth-century paintings is not especially strong, but there's easily enough to discern the period's watering down of religious themes in favour of more secular preoccupations. In particular, **Pieter Pourbus** (1523–1584) is well represented by a series of austere and often surprisingly unflattering portraits of the movers and shakers of his day. There's also his *Last Judgement*, a much larger but atypical work, crammed with muscular men and fleshy women; completed in 1551, its inspiration came from Michelangelo's Sistine Chapel. Born in Gouda, Pourbus moved to Bruges in his early twenties, becoming the leading local portraitist of his day as well as squeezing in work as a civil engineer and cartographer. Pieter was the first of an artistic dynasty with his son, **Frans the Elder** (1545–1581), jumping municipal ship to move to Antwerp as Bruges slipped into the doldrums. Frans was a noted portraitist too, but his success was trifling in comparison with that of his son, **Frans the Younger** (1569–1622), who became one of Europe's most celebrated portraitists, working for the Habsburgs and the Medicis amongst a bevy of powerful families. In the permanent collection is a fine example of his work, an exquisite double portrait of the *Archdukes Albert and Isabella*.

Jacob van Oost the Elder (1603–1671) was the city's most prominent artist during the Baroque period and the Groeninge has a substantial cachet of his work. Frankly, however, his canvases are pretty meagre stuff, his *Portrait of a Theologian*, for example, being a stultifyingly formal and didactic affair only partly redeemed by its crisp draughtsmanship, while his *Portrait of a Bruges Family* drips with bourgeois sentimentality.

Jean Delville and Fernand Khnopff

Much more diverting are the Symbolists, amongst whom **Jean Delville** (1867–1953) takes pride of place with his enormous – and inordinately weird – *De Godmens*, a repulsive, yet compelling picture of writhing bodies yearning for salvation. Delville was an ardent and prolific polemicist for modern art, constantly re-defining its aesthetic as he himself changed his style and technique. This particular piece, of 1903, was arguably the high point of his Symbolist period and accorded with his assertion, in *La Mission de L'Art*, that art should have a messianic ideal and a redemptive quality. Delville distanced himself from Les XX art movement (see box p.44), but his contemporary – and fellow Symbolist – **Fernand Khnopff** (1858–1921) was a founding member. Khnopff is represented by *Secret Reflections*, not one of his better paintings perhaps, but interesting in so far as its lower panel, showing Sint Janshospitaal (see p.55) reflected in a canal, confirms one of the Symbolists' favourite conceits – "Bruges the dead city" (*Bruges la Morte*). The upper panel is a play on appearance and desire, but it's pretty feeble unlike Khnopff's later attempts, in which he painted his sister, Marguerite, again and again, using her refined, almost plastic beauty to stir a vague sense of passion – for she's desirable and utterly unobtainable in equal measure.

The twentieth century

The Groeninge's collection of **twentieth-century paintings** is really rather pedestrian, though there is a healthy sample of the work of the talented **Constant Permeke** (1886–1952). Wounded in World War I, Permeke's grim wartime experiences helped him develop a distinctive Expressionist style in which his subjects – usually agricultural

THE GROENINGE MUSEUM

LES XX

Founded in 1883, and now well-represented at the Groeninge, **Les XX** was an influential group of twenty Belgian painters, designers and sculptors, who were keen to bring together all the different strands of their respective crafts. For ten years, they staged an annual exhibition showcasing both domestic and international talent and it was here that Cézanne, Manet and Gauguin were all exhibited at the very beginning of their careers. With members as diverse as Ensor, Khnopff and the architect-designer Henri van de Velde, Les XX never professed to be united by the same artistic principles, but several of its members were inordinately impressed by the Post-Impressionism of Seurat, whose pointillist *The Big Bowl* created a sensation when it was exhibited by Les XX in 1887.

Les XX – and the other literary-artistic groupings which succeeded it – were part of a general avant-garde movement which flourished in Belgium at the end of the nineteenth century. This avant-garde was deeply disenchanted with Belgium's traditional salon culture, not only for artistic reasons but also because of its indifference to the plight of the Belgian working class. Such political views nourished close links with the fledgling Socialist movement, and Les XX even ran the slogan "art and the people have the same enemy – the reactionary Bourgeoisie". Indeed, the Belgian avant-garde came to see art (in all its forms) as a vehicle for liberating the Belgian worker, a project regularly proclaimed in *L'Art Moderne*, their most authoritative mouthpiece.

workers, fishermen and so forth – were monumental in form, but invested with sombre, sometimes threatening emotion. His charcoal drawing the *Angelus* is a typically dark and earthy representation of Belgian peasant life dated 1934. In similar vein is **Gustave van de Woestijne**'s

(1881–1947) enormous *Last Supper*, another excellent example of Belgian Expressionism with Jesus and the disciples, all elliptical eyes and restrained movement, trapped within prison-like walls.

For more on **James Ensor**, one of Belgium's most acclaimed modern artists, see Ostend, p.223.

In addition, there a couple of minor works by **James Ensor** (1860–1949), **Magritte**'s (1898–1967) characteristically unnerving *The Assault*, and the spookily stark surrealism of **Paul Delvaux**'s (1897–1994) *Serenity*. One of the most interesting of Belgium's modern artists, Delvaux started out as an Expressionist, but came to – and stayed with – Surrealism in the 1930s. Two of his pet motifs were train stations, in one guise or another, and nude or semi-nude women set against some sort of classical backdrop. The intention was to usher the viewer into the unconscious with dream-like images where every perspective was exact, and, largely because of the impeccable craftsmanship, there is indeed something very unsettling about his vision. At their best, his paintings achieve an almost palpable sense of foreboding and *Serenity* is a first-class example.

First published in 1892, **Georges Rodenbach**'s novel *Bruges la Morte* is a highly stylized muse on love and obsession that rapidly became a key text of the Symbolist movement. It's credited with starting a craze for visiting Bruges, the "dead city" where the action unfolds.

THE ARENTSPARK AND ST BONIFACIUSBRUG

From the entrance to the Groeninge, a footpath leads west to the first of two gateways on either side of a narrow cobbled lane. The second gateway leads into tiny **Arentspark** (Map 3, E11), where a pair of forlorn stone columns are all that remain of the Waterhalle, which once stood on the east side of the Markt. Demolished in 1787, the Waterhalle straddled the most central of the city's canals with boats sailing inside the building to unload their cargoes. When part of the canal – between Jan van Eyckplein and the Dijver – was covered over in the middle of the eighteenth century, the Waterhalle became redundant; its place has mostly been taken by the main Post Office. Also in the Arentspark, the tiniest of humpbacked bridges – **St Bonifaciusbrug** – is framed against a tumble of antique brick houses. Altogether one of Bruges' most picturesque (and photographed) spots, the bridge looks like the epitome of everything medieval, but in fact it was only built in 1910. Next to the bridge, an inconsequential, modern statue does few favours for **Juan Luis Vives**, a Spanish Jew and friend of Erasmus, who settled here in the early sixteenth century to avoid persecution. It was a wise decision: back in Spain, his family had converted to Christianity, but even that failed to save them. His father was burnt at the stake in 1525 and, to make matters worse, his dead mother was dug up and the bones burned.

St Bonifaciusbrug spans the canal behind and between two of the city's main museums – the Arentshuis and the Gruuthuse.

THE ARENTSHUIS

Map 3, E11. Tues–Sun 9.30am–5pm; €2.50.

The **Arentshuis**, the mansion in the north corner of the Arentspark at Dijver 16, is divided into two separate sections. The ground-floor is given over to temporary exhibitions, usually of fine art, and upstairs is the **Brangwyn Museum**, which displays the moody etchings, lithographs, studies and paintings of the much-travelled artist **Sir Frank**

Brangwyn (1867–1956). Born in Bruges, of Welsh parents, Brangwyn donated this sample of his work to his native town in 1936. Apprenticed to William Morris in the early 1880s and an official UK war artist in World War I, Brangwyn was a versatile artist who turned his hand to several different mediums, though his drawings are much more appealing than his paintings, which often slide into sentimentality. In particular, look out for the sequence of line drawings exploring industrial themes – powerful, almost melodramatic scenes of shipbuilding, docks, construction and the like. This penchant for dark and gloomy industrial scenes bore little relationship to the British artistic trends of his day and they attracted muted reviews. Better received were his murals, whose bold designs and strong colours attracted almost universal acclaim – and a 1920s commission to turn out a series for Britain's House of Lords. In the event, these murals, whose theme was the splendour of the British Empire, ended up in Swansea Guildhall, though several of the preparatory sketches are displayed here in the Arentshuis.

THE GRUUTHUSE MUSEUM

Map 3, E12. Tues–Sun 9.30am–5pm; €5.

The **Gruuthuse Museum**, just along the street from the Arentshuis at Dijver 17, occupies a rambling mansion that dates from the fifteenth century. A fine example of civil Gothic architecture, the house takes its name from the owners' historical right to tax the *gruit*, the dried herb and flower mixture once added to barley during the beer-brewing process to improve the flavour. In the fourteenth century, the city's brewers abandoned the *gruit* in favour of hops, but the name of the house stuck – and the tax was transferred to the new ingredient. The last lord of the *gruit* died in 1492 and the mansion lay empty until it was turned into a bank in the seventeenth century. The bank closed down in 1892 and, after extensive renovations, the accumulated knick-knacks of a local antiquarian society – one of whose board members was William Brangwyn, father of Frank (see p.46) – was installed here; it still forms the kernel of the collection.

THE BRUGES TAPESTRY INDUSTRY

Tapestry manufacture in Bruges began in the middle of the fourteenth century, an embryonic industry that soon came to be based on a dual system of **workshop** and **outworker**, the one with paid employees, the other with workers paid on a piecework basis. From the beginning, the town authorities took a keen interest in the business, ensuring consistency by a rigorous system of quality control. They were assisted by the Habsburgs, who issued a series of edicts stipulating the Flemish towns in which tapestries could be produced and exactly what materials – dyes and so forth – they could be made from. The other side of this interventionist policy was less palatable: wages were kept down and the workers were hardly ever able to accumulate enough capital to buy either their own looms or even raw materials.

The first great period of Bruges tapestry-making lasted until the middle of the sixteenth century, when religious conflict overwhelmed the town and many of its Protestant-inclined weavers, who had come into direct conflict with their Catholic masters, migrated north to Holland. In the early 1580s, Bruges was finally incorporated into the Spanish Netherlands, precipitating a revival of tapestry production, fostered by the king and queen of Spain, who were keen to support the industry and passed draconian laws banning the movement of weavers. Later, however, French occupation and the shrinking of the Spanish market led to diminishing production, with the industry finally fizzling out in the late eighteenth century.

The renovation work was undertaken by **Louis Delacenserie**, a leading local architect who had little time for the historical scruples of many of his colleagues: for him, restoration meant a complete revamp and if the original didn't match his requirements, he knocked it down and began again. Delacenserie didn't flatten the Gruuthuse, but

Tapestry production was a cross between embroidery and ordinary weaving. It consisted of interlacing a wool weft above and below the strings of a vertical linen "chain", a process similar to weaving. However, the weaver had to stop to change colour, requiring as many shuttles for the weft as he or she had colours, as in embroidery. The appearance of a tapestry was entirely determined by the weft, the design being taken from a painting – or cartoon of a painting – to which the weaver made constant reference. Standard-size tapestries took six months to make and were produced exclusively for the very wealthy, the most important of whom would, on occasion, insist on the use of gold and silver thread and the employment of the most famous artists of the day for the preparatory painting; Pieter Paul Rubens, Bernard van Orley and David Teniers all had tapestry commissions.

There were only two significant types of tapestry: **decorative**, principally *verdures*, showing scenes of foliage in an almost abstract way, and **pictorial** (the Bruges speciality) – usually variations on the same basic themes, particularly rural life, knights, hunting parties, classical gods and goddesses and religious scenes. Over the centuries, changes in style were strictly limited, though the early part of the seventeenth century saw an increased use of elaborate woven borders, an appreciation of perspective and the use of a far brighter, more varied range of colours.

THE GRUUTHUSE MUSEUM

he did add all sorts of bits and pieces, including the **equestrian statue** of Lodewijk van Gruuthuse, the last lord of the gruit, above the entrance and the fancily painted beamed ceiling in the entrance hall. By and large, it's impossible to distinguish between the earlier structure and Delacenserie's additions, though the grand chimneypieces are mostly original.

Distributed amongst the mansion's many rooms is a baffling hotchpotch of Flemish **fine**, **applied and decorative arts**, mostly dating from the medieval and early modern period. The collection holds something for most tastes, from paintings and sculptures through to silverware, lace, ceramics and musical instruments, while antique furniture crops up just about everywhere. The museum's strongest suite is its superb collection of **tapestries** (see box p.48), mostly woven in Brussels or Bruges and dating from the sixteenth and seventeenth centuries. Audio-guides are available at reception at no extra charge and each room carries multi-lingual cards explaining the more important exhibits, but there are still times when you begin to wonder if the museum is – or at least has been – a dumping ground for artefacts that no one knows anything much about.

That said, the collection starts well with the first room holding a charming set of four early seventeenth-century Bruges tapestries depicting scenes of rural merry-making. The central characters are a shepherd and shepherdess, **Gombaut and Macée**, well-known folkloric figures whose various adventures were used as fables, part morality tale but mainly a means of laughing at human frailty – with lashings of sauciness thrown in. Originally, there were nine tapestries in the set and each presented a scene in the life of the two protagonists from childhood to death, amplified by a running commentary in a series of (French) inscriptions. Of the four tapestries displayed here, *The Dance* and *The Wedding Parade* are the more engaging, with lots of singing and dancing and even a bagpipe player under an apple tree. Moving on, Room 2 boasts an acclaimed polychromatic terracotta **bust** of Charles V, a German carving of 1520 that reveals a young and disconcertingly thin-faced emperor. Nearby, Rooms 3 to 5 hold a medley of Gothic alabasters, furniture and wood carvings, including a highly polished post – from a weigh-house – that sports an especially delightful St John, shown with a huge bowl of a beard and long, skinny legs. Upstairs, look out for a bold and richly coloured set of **classical tapestries**, produced in Bruges in 1675 and entitled *De Zeven Vrije Kunsten* (the "Seven Free Arts"). The arts concerned were those skills considered necessary for the rounded education of a gentleman – rhetoric, astrology and so forth. Most intriguing of all, however, is the 1472 oak-panelled **oratory**, which juts out from the first floor of the museum to overlook the high altar of the cathedral next door. A curiously intimate room, its low, hooped ceiling is partly decorated with simple floral tracery, and its corbels are cut in the form of tiny angels. The oratory allowed the lords of the *gruit* to worship without leaving home – a real social coup.

ONZE LIEVE VROUWEKERK (THE CHURCH OF OUR LADY)

Map 3, D12. Tues–Sat 9.30am–12.30pm & 1.30–5pm, Sun 1.30–5pm; free.

Next door to the Gruuthuse, the **Onze Lieve Vrouwekerk** is a rambling shambles of a building, a clamour of different dates and different styles, whose brick spire is – at 122m – one of the tallest in Belgium. Entered from the south, the **nave** was three hundred years in the making, an architecturally discordant affair, whose thirteenth-century, grey-stone central aisle, with its precise blind arcading, is the oldest part of the church. The central aisle blends in with the south aisle, which was added two hundred years later, but the fourteenth-century north aisle doesn't mesh at all – even the columns aren't aligned. This was the result of changing fashions, not slapdash work: the High Gothic north aisle was intended to be the start of a complete remodelling of the church, but the money ran out and by the time the coffers were full again it looked distinctly passé.

At the east end of the south aisle is the church's most celebrated *objet d'art*, a delicate marble *Madonna and Child* by **Michelangelo**. A Bruges merchant commissioned the statue during a business trip to Florence in 1505, donating it to the church ten years later. It was the only one of Michelangelo's works to leave Italy during the artist's lifetime and it had a significant influence on the painters then working in Bruges, though its present setting – beneath cold stone walls at the centre of an ugly eighteenth-century altar – is hardly inspiring. It's actually remarkable that the statue is here at all: the French stole it during their occupation of the city at the end of the eighteenth century and the Germans did the same in 1944, but on both occasions it managed to work its way back to Bruges.

The chancel

Michelangelo apart, the most interesting of the church's accumulated treasures are situated in the **chancel** (€2.50), which is marked off from the nave by a chunky, black and white marble rood screen. Here, above the **choir stalls**, are the coats of arms of the knights of the Order of the Golden Fleece (see box, p.62), who met here in 1468. Much more impressive, however, are the **mausoleums** of Charles the Bold and his daughter Mary of Burgundy, two exquisite examples of Renaissance carving, whose side panels are decorated with coats of arms connected by the most intricate of floral designs. The royal figures are enhanced in the

CHARLES THE BOLD AND MARY OF BURGUNDY

Both **Mary and Charles** died in unfortunate circumstances, she after a riding accident in 1482, when she was only 25, and Charles during the siege of Nancy in 1477. However, there is some argument as to whether Charles was ever interred in Bruges at all. Initially, Charles' battle-battered body was buried in Nancy, but seventy years later his great grandson, the Emperor Charles V, ordered it to be exhumed and moved to Bruges for a more suitable burial. This greatly irritated the French, who may well have sent a dud skeleton, specifically one of the knights who died in the same engagement. In the 1970s, archeologists had a bash at solving the mystery when they dug up this part of the choir, but, amongst the assorted tombs, which had been buried here over several centuries, they failed to authoritatively identify either the body or the tomb of Charles. Mary proved more tractable, with her skeleton confirming the known details of her hunting accident; buried alongside her was the urn which contained the heart of her son, Philip the Fair, placed here in 1506. This movement of body parts was no imperial foible: in the sixteenth century the Habsburgs relocated to Spain, but they were keen to emphasize their connections with – and historical authority over – Flanders, one of the richest parts of their expanding empire. Nothing did this quite as well as the ceremonial burial – or reburial – of bits of royal body.

detail, from the helmet and gauntlets placed gracefully by Charles' side to the pair of watchful dogs nestled at Mary's feet, and her slender tapering fingers.

The hole the archeologists dug in the choir beneath the mausoleums (see box above) was never filled in and mirrors now give sight of Mary's coffin along with the brick **burial**

ONZE LIEVE VROUWEKERK

vaults of several unknown medieval dignitaries. In total, seventeen of these vaults were unearthed and three have been placed in the Lanchals Chapel (see below), just across the ambulatory. Plastered with lime mortar, the inside walls of all the vaults sport brightly coloured **grave frescoes**, a specific art that flourished hereabouts from the late thirteenth to the middle of the fifteenth century. The iconography is fairly consistent, with the long sides mostly bearing one, sometimes two angels apiece, with most of them shown swinging thuribles (the vessels in which incense was burnt during religious ceremonies). Typically, the short sides show the Crucifixion and a Virgin and Child and there's sometimes an image of the dead person or his/her patron saint too. The background decoration is more varied with crosses, stars and dots all making appearances as well as two main sorts of flower – roses and bluebells. The frescoes were painted freehand and executed at great speed – Flemings were then buried on the day they died – hence the vibrancy of the work.

The **Lanchals Chapel** is itself distinguished by the imposing Baroque gravestone of Pieter Lanchals, a one-time Habsburg official who was executed by the citizens of Bruges in 1488. Legend asserts that he was beheaded for his opposition to Maximilian's temporary imprisonment in the Craenenburg (see p.23) and that, to atone for its crime, Bruges was later obliged to introduce swans to its canals. Both tales are, however, fabrications, seemingly invented in the nineteenth century: Lanchals had his head lopped off for being corrupt and he was soon forgotten by his erstwhile sponsor, while the swan story seems to have originated with the swan that adorns his grave stone. The bird was the man's emblem, appropriately as his name means "long neck".

Finally, the chancel holds several first-rate **paintings**, beginning with Bernard van Orley's bold if somewhat sentimental *Passion* triptych above the high altar and, in the

Lanchals Chapel, a crisply executed *Last Supper* by Pieter Pourbus. Pick of the bunch – and exhibited on the railings directly opposite the Lanchals Chapel – is Adriaen Isenbrant's finely executed *Madonna of the Seven Sorrows*, in which the Virgin, hands clasped in prayer, is surrounded by seven cameos depicting her tribulations – the Flight into Egypt, the Carrying of the Cross, the Crucifixion and so forth.

For more on Bernard van Orley and Adriaen Isenbrant, see p.41.

While you're in the Onze Lieve Vrouwekerk chancel, keep an eye out for the ornately carved woodwork – and dinky little windows – of the Gothic bay window that pokes out into the ambulatory from the adjacent Gruuthuse (see p.47).

ST JANSHOSPITAAL AND THE HANS MEMLING MUSEUM

Map 3, D13. Tues–Sun 9.30am–5pm; €7.

Opposite the entrance to Onze Lieve Vrouwekerk, across Mariastraat, is **St Janshospitaal**, a sprawling complex that was used as an infirmary until the nineteenth century. The oldest part of the hospital is at the front behind two church-like gable ends. It dates from the twelfth century and has recently been turned into a sleek and slick **museum** with one large section – in the former ward – exploring the historical background to the hospital by means of documents, paintings and religious *objets d'art*. The other, smaller but much more alluring section, sited in the old hospital chapel, is dedicated to the paintings of Hans Memling. In both, the labelling is minimal, but the audio-guide, issued free at reception, provides copious background information, though the commentary is uninspired. A passageway on the right-hand side of the museum leads from Mariastraat to the hospital's old **Apotheek** (dispensary), also part of the museum and complete with row upon row of antique porcelain jars. The passageway then continues onto the elongated brick block that was added in the nineteenth-century. This is now a (boringly modern) exhibition-cum-shopping centre called – rather confusingly – **Oud St-Jan**.

Coffee Link, inside Oud St-Jan, has internet
and email facilities (see p.208).

St Janshospitaal

St Janshospitaal had just one ward, an expansive open area broken up by a series of heavyweight stone arches. The creators of the museum have filled this with all manner of medieval paraphernalia – from paintings through to hospital ledgers - all of which has at least some connection with either medieval hospitals in general, St John's in particular and/or the religious orders that managed them. The problem is that by themselves the artefacts give little indication as to what the hospital actually felt and looked like and, furthermore, many of the exhibits – of which there are over one hundred – are distinctly second rate or of only specialist interest. That said, there are a handful of highlights, kicking off with Jacob van Oost the Elder's *Lamentation* triptych (Exhibit no.20) in which the central panel is in true Baroque style, with a sobbing cherub appearing beside the Christ. This is not a very successful representation – the anatomy is a tad wonky for starters – but the side panels show the nun donors in fine detail, dressed in their fancy feast day habits. More to the point is Jan Beerblock's *St Janshospitaal* (no.27), a minutely detailed painting of the hospital ward in the late eighteenth century. Here at last you get some indications of what the ward actually looked like, the patients tucked away in row upon row of tiny cup-board-like beds. Two other paintings of note are an exquis-ite *Deposition* (no.36), a late fifteenth-century version of an original by Rogier van der Weyden, and a stylish, intimate-ly observed diptych by Jan Provoost (no.38). The latter has portraits of Christ and the donor on the front, a superbly drawn skull on the back.

For more on Jacob van Oost the Elder see p.42; Rogier van der Weyden see p.36; and Jan Provoost see p.40.

The Memling collection

Born near Frankfurt, **Hans Memling** (1433–1494) spent most of his working life in Bruges, where he was taught by Rogier van der Weyden. He adopted much of his tutor's style and stuck to the detailed symbolism of his contempo-raries, but his painterly manner was distinctly restrained, often pious and grave. Graceful and warmly coloured, his figures also had a velvet-like quality that greatly appealed to the city's burghers. Indeed, their enthusiasm made Memling a rich man – in 1480 he was listed among the town's major moneylenders. Of the six works on display in the hospital chapel, Memling's *Reliquary of St Ursula* of 1489 is the most unusual, a lovely piece of craftsmanship comprising a miniature wooden Gothic church painted with the story of St Ursula. Memling subscribed to the rather unpopular the-ory that the number of virgins accompanying Ursula was ten, whereas most of his contemporaries believed there were ten thousand. His six panels show Ursula and her ten companions on their way to Rome, only to be massacred by Huns as they passed through Germany. It is, however, the mass of incidental detail that makes the reliquary so enchanting – the tiny ships, figures and churches in the background effortlessly evoking the late medieval world.

ST JANSHOSPITAAL AND THE HANS MEMLING MUSEUM

In the background of Memling's *Mystical Marriage of St Catherine* you can see Bruges' much vaunted wooden crane (see p.68).

Moving on, the magnificent *Mystical Marriage of St Catherine* forms the middle panel of a large triptych painted for the altar of the hospital church between 1475 and 1479. Its symbolism was easily understood by the hospital's sisters, who were well versed in the stories of the saints: St Catherine, representing contemplation, receives a ring from the baby Jesus to seal their spiritual union, while the figure to the right is St Barbara, symbol of good deeds. Behind stand the patron saints of the hospital, St John with his customary chalice and St John the Baptist accompanied by a fragile-looking Lamb of God. The complementary side panels depict the beheading of St John the Baptist and a visionary St John writing the book of *Revelation* on the bare and rocky island of Patmos. Again it's the detail that impresses most: between the inner and outer rainbows above St John, for instance, the Prophets make music on tiny instruments – look closely and you'll spy a lute, a flute, a harp and a hurdy-gurdy.

Across the chapel are two more Memling triptychs, a *Lamentation* of 1480 and a superb *Adoration of the Magi*, completed the year before. In the central panel there's a gentle nervousness in the approach of the Magi, here shown as the kings of Spain, Arabia and Ethiopia, and the side panels depict the Nativity and the Presentation of Jesus in the Temple.

In the adjoining side chapel, Memling's skill as a portraitist is further demonstrated by his *Virgin and Martin van Nieuwenhove* diptych, in which the eponymous merchant has the flush of youth and, despite his prayerful position, a hint of arrogance. His lips pout, his hair cascades down to his shoulders and he is dressed in the most fashionable of doublets – by the middle of the 1480s, when the portrait was commissioned, no Bruges merchant wanted to appear too pious. Opposite, on the second panel, the Virgin gets the full stereotypical treatment from the oval face and the almond-shaped eyes through to full cheeks, thin nose and bunched lower lip. The apple she offers Jesus, with his preternaturally wise face, symbolizes the sins of the world and harks back to Adam and Eve.

There's more fine face-work in Memling's *Portrait of a Woman*, also in the side chapel, where the richly-dressed subject stares dreamily into the middle distance, her hands – in a wonderful optical illusion typical of Memling's oeuvre – seeming to clasp the picture frame. The lighting is subtle and sensuous with the woman set against a dark back-ground, her gauze veil dappling the side of her face. A high forehead was then considered a sign of great feminine beau-ty, so her hair is pulled right back and was probably plucked – as are her eyebrows. There's no knowing who the woman was, but in the seventeenth century her fancy headgear convinced observers that she was one of the legendary Persian sibyls who predicted Christ's birth. Indeed, they were so convinced that they added the cartouche in the top left hand corner, describing her as *Sibylla Sambetha* – and the painting is often referred to by this name.

ARCHEOLOGISCH MUSEUM (ARCHEOLOGY MUSEUM)

Map 3, D12. Mariastraat 36a. Tues–Sun 9.30am–12.30pm & 1.30–5pm; €2.

Often ignored, the city's **Archeologisch Museum** is admittedly quite modest – and most of the labelling is only in Dutch – but it does have several interesting displays, commencing with a feature on Bruges' medieval tanners, based on the rubbish they left behind. Continuing in the same vein, the museum's most distinctive exhibit is a pile of accumulated artefacts retrieved from a medieval cesspit and displayed in the form it was unearthed. Other displays deal with grave painting and the Roman fort established on the coast near Bruges in the third century AD.

ST SALVATORSKATHEDRAAL (HOLY SAVIOUR'S CATHEDRAL)

Map 3, C11. Mon 2–5.45pm, Tues–Fri 9am–noon & 2–5.45pm, Sat 9am–noon & 2–3.30pm, Sun 9–10.15am & 2–5.45pm; free.

From the Archeological Museum, it's a short walk north along Heilige-Geeststraat to **St Salvatorskathedraal**, a bulky Gothic edifice that mostly dates from the late thirteenth century, though the Flamboyant Gothic ambulatory was added some two centuries later. A parish church for most of its history, it was only made a cathedral in 1834 following the destruction of St Donatian's (see p.33) by the French some thirty years before. This change of status prompted lots of ecclesiastical rumblings – nearby Onze Lieve Vrouwekerk (see p.51) was bigger and its spire higher – and when part of St Salvators went up in smoke in 1839, the opportunity was taken to make its tower higher and grander. The work was entrusted to an English architect by the name of William Chantrell, who had cut his professional teeth building neo-Gothic churches in Yorkshire. Chantrell's design for the new tower top was a romantic rendition of the Romanesque, but its idiosyncratic appearance – especially its spiky turrets – created a real municipal stink with angry letters bombarding the local press. The rumpus subsided and now the tower is a well-regarded feature of the city skyline.

At the end of a long-term refurbishment, the cathedral's **nave** has recently emerged from centuries of accumulated grime, but it remains a cheerless, cavernous affair despite – or perhaps because of – the acres of browny-cream paint. An item of interest is the vainglorious **pulpit**, a Baroque extravagance dating to the 1770s, but the star turn – by a long stretch – is the set of eight **paintings** by Jan van Orley displayed in and around the transepts. Commissioned in the 1730s, the paintings were used for the manufacture of a matching set of **tapestries** from a Brussels workshop, and, remarkably enough, these have survived too and hang in sequence in the choir and transepts. Each of the eight scenes is a fluent, dramatic composition featuring a familiar episode from the life of Christ – from the Nativity to the Resurrection – complete with a handful of animals, including a remarkably determined Palm Sunday donkey. The tapestries are, of course, mirror images of the paintings as the weavers worked on the rear of the tapestries with the cartoon copies of the paintings down below them and their looms. Close by, off the north transept and also worth a peek, is the **Chapel of the Shoemakers**, where the emblem of the guild – a fancy riding boot – decorates either side of the Baroque altar piece.

The **choir** is more architecturally rewarding, enclosed by a sweeping series of pointed, early Gothic arches and with a dappled light filtering down from the stained glass windows up above. The tapestries are well worth close inspection – though the choir is often roped off – and so are the choir stalls, whose finely carved **misericords** are decorated with folksy scenes of everyday life. The coats-of-arms immediately above the stalls are those of members of the Order of the Golden Fleece (see box p.62), who met here in 1478 to appoint the Habsburg Maximilian their Grand Master. Encircling the choir is the dark and gloomy **ambulatory**, whose several side chapels hold a motley assortment of

THE ORDER OF THE GOLDEN FLEECE

The **Order of the Golden Fleece** was invented in 1430 by Philip the Good, the Duke of Burgundy, on the occasion of his marriage to Isabella of Portugal. Duke since 1419, Philip had spent much of his time curbing the power of the Flemish cities – including Bruges – and he thought, quite rightly, that he could add lustre to his dynasty by founding an exclusive, knightly club that harked back to the (supposed) age of chivalry. The choice of the name was a complimentary nod both to the wool weavers of Flanders, who provided him with most of his money, and to the legends of classical Greece. In the Greek story, Chrysomallus was a winged ram gifted with the power of speech and a golden fleece. He saved the life of Phrixus, presented him with his fleece and then flew off to become the constellation of Aries; it was this same fleece that Jason and the Argonauts sought to recover. A golden ram was the Order's emblem and you will see it here and there across the city, both on portraits and buildings.

Philip stipulated that membership of the Order be restricted to "noblemen in name and proven in valour ... born and raised in legitimate wedlock". He promptly picked the membership and appointed himself Grand Master. It was all something of a con trick, but it went down a treat and the 24 knights who were offered membership duly turned up at the first meeting in Lille in 1431. Thereafter, the Order met fairly regularly, with Bruges and Ghent being two favourite venues. However, when the Habsburgs swallowed up Burgundy in the late fifteenth century, the Order became effectively obsolete and the title "Grand Master" just one of the family's many dynastic trinkets.

ecclesiastical bric-a-brac. There's not much of any real interest here, though – entering the ambulatory on the right-hand side – the first chapel along, the Chapel of Our

Lady of Loretto, does hold an engaging fifteenth-century carved retable showing the family tree of St Anne, purportedly the mother of Mary.

There's yet more ecclesiastical tackle in the **cathedral museum** (same times, but currently closed for long-term refurbishment; €1.50), whose modest assortment of reliquaries, tombstones, vestments, croziers and so forth is ranged around the neo-Gothic cloisters adjoining the ambulatory.

SOUTH TO THE BEGIJNHOF AND THE MINNEWATER

Strolling south from St Janshospitaal, take the second turning on the right – Walstraat – for Walplein, where the brewery **Huisbrouwerij De Halve Mann** (Map 3, D14), at no. 26, offers guided visits for €3.70 per person, including a glass of beer (April–Sept frequent tours 11am–4pm; Oct–March at 11am & 3pm). Tours last about 45 minutes. From Walplein, it's another short hop to **Wijngaardstraat** (Map 2, E11), whose antique terrace houses are crammed with souvenir shops, bars and restaurants. The street and its immediate surroundings heave with tourists, unpleasantly so in summer, with one of the attractions being the mildly entertaining **Brugs Diamantmuseum** (Map 2, E11; Bruges Diamond Museum; daily 10.30am–5.30pm; €5), at Katelijnestraat 43, opposite the east end of Wijngaardstraat. Newly created, the museum tracks through the history of the city's diamond industry in a series of smartly presented displays. There are several examples of diamonds and their settings as well as daily demonstrations of diamond polishing.

Much more appealing – if just as over-visited – is the **Begijnhof** (Map 2, D12; daily 9am–6pm or sunset; free), immediately beyond the west end of Wijngaardstraat, where a rough circle of old and infinitely pretty whitewashed houses surrounds a central green. The best time to visit is in spring, when a carpet of daffodils pushes up between the wispy elms, creating one of the most photographed scenes in Bruges. There were once *begijnhofs* all over Belgium and this is one of the few to have survived in good nick. They date back to the twelfth century, when a Liège priest, a certain Lambert le Bègue, encouraged widows and unmarried women to live in communities, the better to do pious acts, especially caring for the sick. These communities were different from convents in so far as the inhabitants – the **beguines** (*begijns*) – did not have to take conventual vows and had the right to return to the secular world if they wished. Margaret, Countess of Flanders, founded Bruges' *begijnhof* in 1245 and, although most of the houses now standing date from the eighteenth century, the medieval lay-out has survived intact, retaining the impression of the *begijnhof* as a self-contained village with access controlled through two large gates. The houses are still in private hands, but, with the beguines long gone, they are occupied by Benedictine nuns, who you'll see flitting around in their habits. Only one is open to the public – the **Begijnenhuisje** (March–Nov daily 10am–noon & 1.45–5/6pm; €2), a pint-sized celebration of the simple life of the beguines. The prime exhibit here is the *schapraai*, a traditional beguine's cupboard, which was a frugal combination of dining table, cutlery cabinet and larder.

It's a short walk from the *begijnhof* to the **Minnewater** (Map 2, E13), billed in much publicity hype as the "Lake of Love". The tag certainly gets the canoodlers going, but in fact the lake – more a large pond – started life as a city harbour. The distinctive stone lock house at the head of the Minnewater recalls its earlier function, though it's actually a very fanciful nineteenth-century reconstruction of the medieval original. Located at the far end of the lake, on the west bank, the **Poertoren** (Map 2, D13) is more authentic, dating from 1398 and once part of the city wall. This is where the city kept its gunpowder – hence the name, "powder tower".

Bruges: north and east of the Markt

The gentle canals and maze-like cobbled streets of **eastern Bruges** are extraordinarily pretty and it's here that the city reveals its depth of character. In this uncrowded part of the city, which stretches east from **Jan van Eyckplein** to the old medieval moat, there's an almost seamless architectural homogeneity, layer upon layer, beginning with the classically picturesque terraces that date from the town's golden age. The most characteristic architectural feature is the crow-step gable, popular from the fourteenth to the eighteenth century and revived by the restorers of the 1880s and later, but there are also expansive Georgian mansions and humble, homely cottages. Almost always the buildings are of brick, reflecting the shortage of local stone and the abundance of polder peat and clay – with the peat firing the clay bricks. Above all, eastern Bruges excels in the detail, surprising the eye again and again with its sober and subtle variety, featuring everything from intimate arched doorways, bendy tiled roofs and wonky chimneys to a bevy of discrete shrines and miniature statues. Nevertheless, there are one or two obvious targets for the casual visitor, beginning with the **Lace Centre**, where you can buy locally made lace and watch its manufacture, and the city's most unusual church, the adjacent **Jeruzalemkerk**. In addition, the **Folklore Museum** holds a passably interesting collection of local bygones, while the **Museum of Our Lady of the Pottery** has an intriguing chapel and several quality Flemish paintings.

ST JAKOBSKERK

Map 3, C6. July & Aug Mon–Fri & Sun 2–5.30pm, Sat 2–4pm; free.

Strolling north from the Markt along busy St Jakobsstraat, it only takes a few minutes to reach **St Jakobskerk**, whose sombre exterior, mostly dating from the fifteenth century, clusters round a chunky tower. In medieval times, the church was popular with the foreign merchants who had congregated in Bruges, acting as a sort of prototype community centre; it also marked the western limit of the foreign merchants' quarter. These merchants covered the church walls with paintings and around eighty have survived. Taken as a whole, they are not especially distinguished, but look out for Jan Provoost's finely executed *Legend of St Cosmas and St Damian*, above the confessional, and the *Legend of St Lucy*, a panel triptych by an unknown, late fifteenth-century artist referred to as the Master of the St Lucy Legend; it's located in St Anthony's Chapel. In the background of the painting is one of the earliest surviving views of Bruges – the belfry has yet to receive its octagonal lantern. Martyred in Sicily in the fourth century, St Lucy was venerated for her chastity and charity, also becoming the saint of choice for those suffering with eye disease after her torturers plucked her eyeballs out - and God returned her vision. She is usually depicted holding a dish containing the two favoured eyeballs. In the left panel, Lucy gives away her possessions to the poor and, in the middle panel, her fiancé, furious at the loss of her dowry, condemns her as a Christian to the local Roman magistrate. Lucy is sentenced to work in a brothel, but is given supernatural strength to resist the two oxen employed by the brothel-keepers to drag her off. The church's other main item of interest is the early Renaissance **burial chapel** of Ferry de Gros (died 1547), to the right of the choir, which sports the elaborate, painted tomb of this well-to-do landowner. Unusually, the tomb has two shelves – on the top are the finely carved effigies of Ferry and his first wife, while down below, on the lower shelf, is his second. Here also, above the altar, is an enamelled terracotta medallion of the Virgin and Child imported from Florence some time in the fifteenth century. No one knows quite how it ended up here, but there's no doubt that it influenced the Flemish artists of the period – in the same way as Michelangelo's statue in the Onze Lieve Vrouwekerk (see p.51).

St Jakobskerk has a first-rate assortment of brass funeral plaques and, if you fancy having a bash at some **brass rubbing**, this is a good place to start – but bring your own equipment.

KRAANPLEIN AND JAN VAN EYCKPLEIN

Weaving your way east from St Jakobskerk, it's a short walk through to Vlamingstraat and adjoining **Kraanplein** (Map 3, E6) – Crane Square – whose name recalls one of the medieval city's main attractions, the enormous wooden **crane** that once unloaded heavy goods from the adjoining river. Before it was covered over, the River Reie ran south from Jan van Eyckplein to the Markt, and the Kraanplein dock was one of the busiest parts of this central waterway. Mounted on a revolving post in the manner of a windmill, the crane's pulleys were worked by means of two large treadmills, which in turn were operated by children – a grim existence by any measure. Installed in 1290 – and only dismantled in 1767 – the crane impressed visitors greatly and was as sure a sign of Bruges' economic success as the belfry.

The crane crops up as background in several medieval paintings, notably behind St John in Memling's *Mystical Marriage of St Catherine* (see p.58).

Take the narrow lane – Kraanrei – north from Kraanplein and you soon reach **Jan van Eyckplein**, which is one of the prettiest squares in Bruges, backdropped by the easy sweep of the Spiegelrei canal. The centrepiece of the square is an earnest **statue** of Van Eyck, erected in 1878, whilst on the north side is the **Tolhuis**, whose fancy Renaissance entrance is decorated with the coat of arms of the dukes of Luxembourg, who long levied tolls here. The Tolhuis dates from the late fifteenth century, but was extensively remod-elled in medieval style in the 1870s as was the **Poortersloge** (Merchants' Lodge), whose slender tower pokes up above the rooftops on the west side of the square. Theoretically, any city merchant was entitled to be a mem-ber of the Poortersloge, but in fact membership was restricted to the richest and the most powerful. An informal alternative to the Town Hall, it was here that key political and economic decisions were taken and it was also where local bigwigs could drink and gamble discreetly.

THE SPIEGELREI CANAL AND THE SPAANSE LOSKAAI

Stretching east from Jan van Eyckplein, the **Spiegelrei canal** (Map 3, F5) was once the heart of the foreign merchants' quarter, its frenetic quays overlooked by the trade missions of many of the city's trading partners. The medieval buildings were demolished long ago, but they have been replaced by an exquisite medley of architectural styles from expansive Georgian mansions to pirouetting crow-step gables. There's more of the same, if a little more modestly, just to the north on **Gouden-Handrei** and adjoining **Spaanse Loskaai** (Map 3, E4), which flank an especially attractive sliver of canal that was once used as a quay by Bruges' Spanish merchants. Round the corner, **Spanjaardstraat** was also part of the Spanish enclave; at no.9, in a house called De Pijnappel (The Fir Cone), the founder of the Jesuits, Ignatius Loyola (1491–1556), spent his holidays while he was a student in Paris. He befriended Juan Luis Vives (see p.46), who lodged down the street, but unfortunately his friend's liberality failed to temper Loyola's nascent fanaticism. Spanjaardstraat leads back to Jan van Eyckplein.

There are several charming **hotels** on and around the Spiegelrei canal, but perhaps the most appealing is the *Adornes*, at St Annarei 26. See p.128 for further details.

ST WALBURGAKERK AND ST ANNAKERK

From Jan van Eyckplein, follow Spinolarei along the south side of the canal and take the second turning on the right – Koningstraat – to reach **St Walburgakerk** (Map 3, G5;

Easter–Sept normally Mon–Fri 10am–noon & 2–4pm, Sat 10am–noon; free), a fluent Baroque extravagance built for the Jesuits in the first half of the seventeenth century. Decorated with podgy cherubs, the sinuous, flowing facade is matched by the booming interior, awash with acres of creamy-white paint. The grandiose **pulpit** is the work of Artus II Quellin (1625–1700), an Antwerp woodcarver and sculptor whose family ran a profitable sideline in Baroque pulpits; there are more of his huffing and puffing cherubs on the main altarpieces. The pick of the church's scattering of **paintings** is a Pieter Claeissens' triptych – on the right hand side of the nave – in which the central panel depicts a popular legend relating to Philip the Good, a fifteenth-century Count of Flanders and the founder of the Order of the Golden Fleece (see p.62). The story goes that while Philip was preparing to fight the French, he encountered the Virgin Mary in a scorched tree; not one to look a gift horse in the mouth, Philip promptly got on his knees and asked for victory, and his prayers were answered.

Walk down Hoornstraat immediately to the north of St Walburgakerk and you soon arrive at one of the city centre's widest canals. Turn right, walk over the bridge and on the far side, just off St Annarei, is the dinky little **St Annakerk** (Map 3, I5; April–Sept Mon–Fri 10am–noon & 2–4pm, Sat 10am–noon; free), which comes complete with the slenderest of brick towers. The original Gothic church was burnt to the ground in the religious wars of the sixteenth century and today's version is a notably homogeneous illustration of the Baroque with pride of interior place going to the marble and porphyry rood screen of 1628.

The **Oud Vlissinghe**, near the east end of the Spiegelrei at Blekerstraat 2, is one of Bruges' oldest and most distinctive bars; see p.164.

ST WALBURGAKERK AND ST ANNAKERK

THE KANTCENTRUM AND JERUZALEMKERK (LACE CENTRE AND JERUSALEM CHURCH)

Map 2, G6. Mon–Fri 10am–noon & 2–6pm, Sat 10am–noon & 2–5pm; €1.50.

Just to the east of St Annakerk, the complex of buildings that originally belonged to the wealthy Adornes family, who migrated here from Genoa in the thirteenth century, is located at the foot of Balstraat in the middle of an old working-class district of low, brick cottages. Inside the complex, the **Kantcentrum**, on the right-hand side of the entrance, has a couple of busy workshops and offers demonstrations of traditional lace-making in the afternoon.

The best lace shop in town – for locally-made lace – is 't Apostelientje, very close to the Kantcentrum at Balstraat 11. For more on lace shops, see "Shopping", p.185.

Across the passageway, to the left of the entrance, is one of the city's real oddities, the **Jeruzalemkerk** (same times and ticket). It was built by the Adornes family in the fifteenth century as a copy of the church of the Holy Sepulchre in Jerusalem after one of their number, Pieter, had returned from a pilgrimage to the Holy Land. The interior is on two levels: the lower level is dominated by a large and ghoulish altarpiece, decorated with skulls and ladders, in front of which is the black marble tomb of Anselm Adornes, the son of the church's founder, and his wife Margaretha. The pilgrimage didn't bring the Adornes family much luck: Anselm was murdered in gruesome circumstances in Scotland in 1483 while serving as Bruges' consul. There's more grisliness at the back of the church where the small vaulted chapel holds a replica of Christ's tomb – you can glimpse the imitation body down the tunnel behind the iron grating. To either side of the main altar, steps ascend to the choir, which is situated right below the eccentric, onion-domed lantern tower. Finally, the tiny **Lace Museum** (same times and ticket) behind the church is of passing interest for its samples of antique lace.

At some point in the next couple of years, the excellent lace collection that was formerly displayed in the Arentshuis (see p.46 is to be moved here to the Lace Museum. Currently, the lace is in long-term storage.

MUSEUM VOOR VOLKSKUNDE (FOLKLORE MUSEUM)

Map 3, I3. Tues–Sun 9.30am–5pm; €2.50.

A couple of minutes' walk from the Lace Centre, at the north end of Balstraat, the **Museum voor Volkskunde**, at Rolweg 40, occupies a long line of low-ceilinged almshouses set beside a trim courtyard. It's a varied collection, with the emphasis on the nineteenth and early twentieth centuries, but the labelling is well-nigh non-existent and even then it's only in Dutch, so to make much sense of the exhibits you'll need to pick up an English guidebook at reception (€2). Rooms 1–5 are to the right of the entrance, rooms 6–14 are dead ahead. Beside the entrance, in Room 15, *De Zwarte Kat* – the Black Cat – is a small tavern done out in traditional style and serving ales and snacks.

Amongst the various period rooms and workshops, a particular highlight is **Room 2**, the Confectioner's Shop, where in summer there are occasional demonstrations of traditional sweet making. Next door, in **Room 3**, is an intriguing assortment of biscuit and chocolate moulds as well as cake decorations – *patacons*. Made of clay, these *pata-*

cons were painted by hand in true folksy style, with the three most popular motifs being animals, military scenes and Bible stories. Here also is a charming panel painting, *Jan of the Doughnuts*, by one of the city's most talented eighteenth-century artists, Jan Garemijn (1712–1799). Moving on, **Room 6** holds a modest but enjoyable display of local costumes and textiles, including several samplers made by trainee lace makers, and **Room 7** is a re-created classroom circa 1920. **Room 11** focuses on popular religion with an interesting collection of pilgrimage banners plus wax, silver and iron ex-votos of arms, legs and other bits of body along with the occasional animal. Although the practice is gradually dying out, many Flemish churches are still dotted with ex-votos. Traditionally, the believer makes a promise to God – say to behave better – and then asks for a blessing, like the curing of a bad leg. Sometimes the ex-voto is hung up once the promise is made, but mostly it's done afterwards, in gratitude for the cure or blessing.

Rooms 13 and 14 hold a fascinating display on pipes and tobacco. There are all sorts of antique smokers' paraphernalia – tobacco cutters, lighters, tinder boxes and so forth – but it's the selection of pipes which catches the eye, especially the long, thin ones made of clay. Clay pipes were notoriously brittle, so smokers invested in pipe cases, of which several are exhibited. In the nineteenth century, pipe-smoking clubs were extremely popular and there was even a smoker's chair, which smokers straddled, facing the back of the chair to place their elbows on a specially designed rest. The rest had a drawer for the pipe and tobacco – as do the two displayed here.

THE GUIDO GEZELLE MUSEUM

Map 2, H5. Rolweg 64. Tues–Sun 9.30am–12.30pm & 1.30–5pm; €2.
Just along the street from the Museum voor Volkskunde,

the **Guido Gezelle Museum** commemorates a leading figure in nineteenth-century Bruges, the poet-priest Guido Gezelle (1830–1899). Gezelle was born in this substantial brick cottage, which now houses a museum containing a few original knick-knacks – for example his old chair and pipes – plus his death mask, but is mostly devoted to a biographical account of his life. The labelling is, however, only in Dutch and you really need to be a Gezelle enthusiast to get much out of it. Neither is Gezelle to everyone's tastes. His poetry is pretty average and the fact that he translated Longfellow's "Song of Hiawatha" into Dutch is the sort of detail that bores rather than inspires. More importantly, Gezelle played a key role in the preservation of many of the city's medieval buildings and was instrumental in the creation of the Gruuthuse Museum (see p.47). Gezelle's desire to preserve the past reflected his belief that modernity and secularism were one and the same – and, by extension, that the survival of the medieval city symbolized the continuity of the Catholic faith. This mind-set dovetailed neatly with the attitude of the city's Flemish nationalists, who resisted change – and championed medieval, or at least neo-Gothic architecture – to maintain Flemish "purity". Gezelle also got into a real lather about the theatre, writing "We are smothered by displays of adultery and incest... and the foundations of the family and of marriage are [being] undermined".

SCHUTTERSGILDE ST SEBASTIAAN (THE ARCHERS' GUILDHOUSE) AND THE ENGELS KLOOSTER (ENGLISH CONVENT)

Just beyond the Guido Gezelle Museum, at the east end of Rolweg, a long and wide earthen bank marks the path of the old town walls. Perched on top today are a quartet of relocated **windmills** – two close by and two about 600m further to the north. You'd have to be something of a windmill fanatic to want to visit them all, but the nearest two are mildly diverting – and the closest, **St Janshuismolen**, is in working order (Tues–Sun 9.30am–12.30pm & 1.30–5pm; €2). The other, more southerly of these two windmills is near the **Kruispoort**, a much modified and strongly fortified city gate dating from 1402. From the Kruispoort, Langestraat leads back to the city centre, but a better bet is to head for Carmersstraat – just to the north of Rolweg. Here, at no. 174, the **Schuttersgilde St Sebastiaan** (Map 2, H5; April–Sept Mon, Tues, Thurs & Fri 10am–noon & 2–5pm; €2) dates from the middle of the sixteenth century and has records of the guild alongside a modest collection of gold and silverwork. The city's archers ceased to be of any military importance by the end of the fifteenth century, but the guild had, by then, redefined itself as an exclusive social club where the bigwigs of the day could gather together, sometimes organizing archery tournaments. The favourite sport was to plonk a replica bird on top of a pole and shoot at it with bow and arrow.

Of the city's seven **medieval gates,** four have survived in relatively good condition, though they have all been heavily restored. Apart from the Kruispoort, these are the **Gentpoort** on the southeast edge of the centre on Gentpoortstraat; the **Smedenpoort** on the west side of the city centre at the end of Smedenstraat; and the **Ezelpoort** – Donkey Gate – to the northwest of the centre. All of them date from the early fifteenth century and consist of twin, heavily fortified, stone turrets.

During his stay in Bruges, Charles worshipped at the **Engels Klooster** (Mon–Sat 2–3.45pm & 4.15–5.15pm; free), just along the street from the Archer's Guildhouse at

CHARLES II IN BRUGES

Charles II of England, who spent three years in exile in Bruges from 1656 to 1659, was an enthusiastic member of the archers' guild and, after the Restoration, he sent them a whopping 3600 florins as a thank you for their hospitality. Charles' enforced exile had begun in 1651 after his attempt to seize the English crown – following the Civil War and the execution of his father in 1649 – had ended in defeat by the Parliamentarians at the battle of Worcester. Initially, Charles hightailed it to France, but Cromwell persuaded the French to expel him and the exiled king ended up seeking sanctuary in Spanish territory. He was allowed to settle in Bruges, then part of the Spanish Netherlands, though the Habsburgs were stingy when it came to granting Charles and his retinue an allowance. The royalists were, says a courtier's letter of 1657, "never in greater want … for Englishmen cannot live on bread alone". In addition, Cromwell's spies kept an eagle eye on Charles' activities, filing lurid reports about his conduct. A certain Mr Butler informed Cromwell that "I think I may truly say that greater abominations were never practised among people than at Charles Stewart's court. Fornication, drunkenness and adultery are considered no sins amongst them". It must have made Cromwell's hair stand on end. Cromwell died in 1658 and Charles may well have been informed of this whilst he was playing tennis in Bruges. The message was to the point – "The devil is dead" – and Charles was on the English throne two years later.

Carmersstraat 85. Founded in 1629, the convent was long a haven for English Catholic exiles, though – perhaps surprisingly – this didn't stop Queen Victoria from popping in during her visit to Belgium in 1843. Nowadays, the convent's nuns provide an enthusiastic, twenty-minute guided tour of their lavishly decorated Baroque church, whose finest features are the handsome cupola and the altar, an extraordinarily flashy affair made of 23 different types of marble. It was the gift of the Nithsdales, English aristocrats whose loyalty to the Catholic faith got them in no end of scrapes.

MUSEUM ONZE-LIEVE-VROUW TER POTTERIE (THE MUSEUM OF OUR LADY OF THE POTTERY)

Map 2, G2. Potterierei 79; Tues–Sun 9.30am–12.30pm & 1.30–5pm; €2.50.

From the English Convent, it's a ten-minute walk north to the canalside **Museum Onze-Lieve-Vrouw ter Potterie**. The complex was founded as a hospital in the thirteenth century on the site of an earlier pottery, though "hospital" is a tad misleading as – and this was normal – the buildings were used as much to accommodate visitors as tend the sick; only later did the emphasis fall more exclusively on medical treatment. The hospital was remodelled on several occasions and the three brick gables that front the building today span three centuries. The middle gable is the oldest, dating from 1359 and built as part of the original hospital chapel. The left-hand gable belonged to the main medieval hospital ward and the one on the right marks a second chapel, added in the 1620s. Inside, the museum occupies a handful of the old sick rooms and the second, later chapel. The rooms are sprinkled with old religious paintings of no particular distinction, though there are several spectacularly unflattering portraits of Habsburg officials and a couple of pen and ink drawings reputedly by Jan van Eyck.

The **chapel**, on the other hand, is delightful, distinguished by its splendid Baroque altarpieces and a sumptuous marble rood screen, whose two side altars recall the museum's location beside what was once one of the city's busiest quays. The altar on the left is dedicated to St Anthony, the patron saint of ship's joiners, the one on the right to St Brendan, the patron saint of seamen. There's also a finely carved thirteenth-century stone statue of the Virgin on the main altar, an *Adoration of the Magi* by Jacob van Oost the Elder behind the rood screen and an odd stained-glass window in the chapel's front wall. At first glance, the window, with its historical panorama and two kneeling and ruffed figures, looks medieval, but look closely and you'll soon see that the couple – the donors – have modern hairstyles; the window was added in the 1930s and it's hard not to think that someone was playing some sort of joke. Finally, several old tapestries are hung in the chapel from Easter to October: among them is a superb set of three depicting eighteen miracles attributed to Our Lady of the Pottery, almost all to do with being saved from the sea or a sudden change of fortune in fishing or trade.

ST GILLISKERK AND THE AUGUSTIJNENBRUG

From the Museum of Our Lady of the Pottery, it's a pleasant ten-minute stroll south along the canal back towards the Spiegelrei (see p.70) and Jan van Eyckplein (see p.69). One reasonably tempting detour is to **St Gilliskerk** (Map 3, F2; April–Sept Mon–Sat 10am–noon & 2–4pm, Sun 11–noon & 2–4pm; free), a sulky brick pile located just off the canalside Langrei down St Gilliskoorstraat. Dating from the late thirteenth century, but greatly enlarged in the 1460s, the church is unusual in so far as it possesses a timber, barrel-vaulted roof. Among the paintings on display are several by Jacob van Oost the Elder, a polyptych by Pieter Pourbus and a series of eighteenth-century works illustrating the efforts of the Trinitarian monks to ransom Christian captives from the Turks.

For more on Jacob van Oost the Elder
and Pieter Pourbus, see p.42.

If you head southwest from the church, you can regain Spanjaardstraat – and ultimately Jan van Eyckplein – via the **Augustijnenbrug** (Map 3, E4), the city's oldest surviving bridge, a sturdy, three-arched structure dating from 1391. It was built to help the monks of a nearby (and long demolished) Augustinian monastery get into the city centre speedily and the benches set into the parapet were cut to allow itinerant tradesmen to display their goods here.

Ghent city centre

The shape and structure of today's **city centre** reflects Ghent's ancient class and linguistic divide. The streets to the south of the **Korenmarkt**, the traditional focus of the city, tend to be straight and wide, lined with elegant old mansions, the former habitations of the wealthier, French-speaking classes, while, to the north, Flemish Ghent is all narrow alleys and low brick houses. They meet at the somewhat confusing sequence of squares that spread east from the Korenmarkt to **St Baafskathedraal**, Ghent's number-one attraction and home to the fabulous Jan van Eyck altarpiece. The other special highlights of the centre are the splendid Gothic guild houses that roll along the **Graslei**, beside what was once Ghent's principal harbour, and the stern former castle of the Counts of Flanders, **Het Gravensteen**. It is, however, in the detail that central Ghent excels – rather than in its set-piece buildings – with its web of cobbled lanes and alleys overlooked by an enchanting medley of antique terraces and grand mansions, all woven round a tangle of canals. It's not as neat and pretty as Bruges, but then it's more organic – much less the product of latter-day architectural tinkering, though the city was given a good medievalist spring-clean in preparation for the Great Exhibition (of trade and goods) held here in 1913.

East from the centre, Ghent's industrial character becomes more obvious, its sprawling inner suburbs mostly the result of the boom of the nineteenth century. There is one obvious target here: the beguiling remains of St Bavo's Abbey – **St Baafsabdij** – which dates back to the tenth century.

St Baafskathedraal – and the Adoration of the Mystic Lamb – can be visited every day of the week, but most of the other sights – including the museums – are closed on Mondays.

ST BAAFSKATHEDRAAL

Map 6, H6. St Baafskathedraal (St Bavo's Cathedral); daily: April–Oct 8.30am–6pm & Nov–March 8.30am–5pm; free.

The best place to start an exploration of the city centre is the mainly Gothic **St Baafskathedraal**, squeezed into the eastern corner of St Baafsplein. The third church on this site, and two hundred and fifty years in the making, the cathedral is a tad lop-sided, but there's no gainsaying the imposing beauty of its **west tower** with long, elegant windows and perky corner turrets. Some 82m high, the tower was the last major part of the church to be completed, topped off in 1554 – just before the outbreak of the religious wars that were to wrack the country.

Inside the cathedral, the mighty **nave** was begun in the fifteenth century, its tall, slender columns giving the whole interior a cheerful sense of lightness, though the seventeenth-century marble screens spoil the effect by darkening the choir.

The Adoration of the Mystic Lamb

Daily: April–Oct Mon–Sat 9.30am–5pm, Sun 1–5pm; Nov–March Mon–Sat 10.30am–4pm, Sun 2–5pm; €2.50.

In a small side **chapel** to the left of the entrance is the cathedral's – and Ghent's – greatest treasure, a winged altarpiece known as **De Aanbidding van het Lam Gods** (*The Adoration of the Mystic Lamb*), a seminal work of the early fifteenth century, though of dubious provenance. Since the discovery of a Latin verse on its frame in the nineteenth century, academics have been arguing about who actually painted the masterpiece. The inscription reads that Hubert van Eyck "than whom none was greater" began, and Jan van Eyck "second in art" completed the work, but as almost nothing is known of Hubert, some art historians doubt his existence. They argue that the citizens of Ghent invented "Hubert" to counter Jan's fame in the rival city of Bruges. No one knows for sure, but what is certain is that in their manipulation of the technique of oil painting the artist – or artists – was able to capture a needle-sharp, luminous realism that must have stunned his contemporaries.

The altarpiece is displayed with its panels open, but originally they were kept closed and the painting only revealed on high days and holidays. Consequently, it's actually best to begin round the back with the **cover screens**, which hold a beautiful Annunciation scene with the archangel Gabriel's wings reaching up to the timbered ceiling of a Flemish house, the streets of a town visible through the windows. In a brilliant coup of lighting, the darkened recesses around the shadows of the angel dapple the room, emphasizing the reality of the apparition – a technique repeated on the opposite cover panel around the figure of Mary. Below, the donor and his wife, a certain Joos Vydt and Isabella Borlout, kneel piously alongside statues of the saints.

By design, the restrained exterior was but a foretaste of what lay (and lies) within – a striking, visionary **painting** whose sheer brilliance still takes the breath away. On the **upper level** sit God the Father (some say Christ Triumphant), the Virgin and John the Baptist in gleaming

ST BAAFSKATHEDRAAL

clarity; to the right are musician-angels and a nude, pregnant Eve; and on the left is Adam plus a group of singing angels, who strain to read their music. The celebrated, sixteenth-century Flemish art critic Karel van Mander argued that the singers were so artfully painted that he could discern the different pitches of their voices – and true or not, it is the detail that impresses, especially the richly embroidered trimmings on the cloaks. In the **lower central panel** the Lamb, the symbol of Christ's sacrifice, is depicted in a heavenly paradise – "the first evolved landscape in European painting", suggested Kenneth Clark – seen as a sort of idealized Low Countries with the cathedrals of Bruges, Utrecht and Maastricht in the background. The Lamb stands on an altar whose rim is minutely inscribed with a quotation from the Gospel of St John, "Behold the Lamb of God, which taketh away the sins of the world". The apostles kneel on the right hand side of the altar, the prophets to the left and in addition four groups converge on the altar from the corners of the central panel. In the bottom left are the patriarchs of the Old Testament and above them are an assortment of bishops, dressed in blue vestments and carrying palm branches. The bottom right has a group of male saints and in the top right are their female equivalents – look closely and you'll spy St Barbara holding the tower that symbolized her imprisonment and St Agnes with her lamb. Also in the foreground is the Fountain of Life, a symbol of redemption. On the **side panels**, approaching the Lamb across symbolically rough and stony ground, are more saintly figures. On the right-hand side are two groups, the first being St Anthony and his hermits, the second St Christopher, shown here as a giant with a band of pilgrims. On the left side panel come the horsemen, the inner group symbolizing the Warriors of Christ – including St George bearing a shield with a red cross – and the outer the Just Judges, each of whom is dressed in fancy Flemish attire.

A fourth-century Roman saint, **Agnes** dedicated her body to Jesus and refused all offers of marriage. Her chastity was rewarded by summary execution in this world and sainthood in the next, the lamb selected as her symbol to recall her purity. For more on the legend of **St Barbara**, see p.28.

The Just Judges panel is not, however, authentic. It was added during the German occupation of World War II to replace the original, which was stolen in 1934 and never recovered. The theft was just one of many dramatic events to befall the painting – indeed it's remarkable that the altarpiece has survived at all. The Calvinists wanted to destroy it; Philip II of Spain tried to acquire it; the Emperor Joseph II disapproved of the painting so violently that he replaced the nude Adam and Eve with a clothed version of 1784 (exhibited today on a column just inside the church entrance); and near the end of World War II the Germans stole the altarpiece and hid it in an Austrian salt mine, where it remained until American soldiers arrived in 1945.

The stolen Just Judges panel features in **Albert Camus's** novel *The Fall* – not, as you might expect from Camus, in a straightforward manner, but as a symbol. The protagonist keeps the panel in a cupboard, declining to return it for a complex of reasons, one of which is "because those judges are on their way to meet the Lamb... [and]...there is no lamb or innocence any longer".

The remainder of the cathedral

After the altarpiece, the rest of the cathedral can't help but seem something of an anticlimax. That said, there are one or two items that catch the eye, beginning with the rococo **pulpit**, a whopping, mid-eighteenth-century oak and marble affair that lies stranded in the nave. The main timber of the pulpit represents the Tree of Knowledge and at its base a young woman, Bible in hand, brings the Christian faith to humanity, in the form of an old bearded man. Up above, two angels raise the Cross of Salvation, while a third confiscates the apple lodged in the mouth of a gilded serpent. This relates to the story of the Garden of Eden in which the serpent (the devil) persuaded Eve to bite the apple (of the Knowledge of Good and Evil) against God's wishes – hence the Fall. Similarly portentous is the **high altar**, with tons of marble and, in the centre between four columns, an enthroned St Baaf ascending to heaven on an untidy heap of clouds. According to legend, St Baaf (or Bavo) was a dissolute landowner, who repented his sins after the death of his wife. He gave his possessions to the poor, became a missionary and ultimately lived as a hermit just outside Ghent.

Nearby, in the **north transept**, is a characteristically energetic painting by Rubens (1577–1640) entitled *St Baaf entering the Abbey of Ghent*, dating to 1624 and including a self-portrait – he's the bearded head. Here also is the entrance to the dank and capacious **crypt**, a survivor from the earlier Romanesque church. The crypt is stuffed with religious bric-a-brac of some mild interest, but the highlight is Justus van Gent's superb fifteenth-century triptych, *The Crucifixion of Christ*. This depicts the crucified Christ flanked, on the left, by Moses purifying the waters of Mara with wood, and to the right by Moses and the bronze serpent which cured poisoned Israelites on sight. Also of note are the faded murals, painted between 1480 and 1540 but only rediscovered in 1936.

Beyond the transepts is the **choir**, built in the thirteenth and fourteenth centuries of blue-grey stone – in contrast to the later white stone of the rest of the building. Of the twenty-odd chapels flanking the choir's **ambulatory**, none are of outstanding interest, though – working in an anticlockwise direction from the south transept – the first chapel along has a thumpingly good triptych by Frans Pourbus the Elder (1545–1581), depicting scenes from the life of Jesus. The sixth chapel contains a competent copy of the *Adoration of the Mystic Lamb*, recalling the days when the original was kept here.

Stuck to the walls of the south transept are the hatchments of the Knights of the Golden Fleece, who met here in 1445 and 1559. For more on the Order, see p.62.

THE LAKENHALLE AND THE BELFORT (CLOTH HALL AND BELFRY)

Just to the west of the cathedral, in the middle of St Baafsplein, is a **statue–cum–water fountain** in honour of Jan Frans Willems (1793–1846), an early champion of Flemish culture. His cameo likeness is carved on the side of the plinth, beneath a soppy-looking couple draped with a Flemish banner. Across the square to the north is the cheerily restored late-nineteenth-century **municipal theatre**, which is now home to the regional repertory company, the Nederlands Toneel Gent (NTG; see p.177). The neo-Renaissance facade is decorated with a mosaic representing Apollo and the Muses. On the west side of St Baafsplein lurks the **Lakenhalle** (Map 7, I11), a gloomy hunk of a building with an unhappy history. Work began on the hall in the early fifteenth century, but the cloth trade slumped before it was finished and it was only grudgingly completed in 1903. Indeed, the Lakenhalle has never quite sorted itself out, and today it's little more than an empty shell with the city's tourist office (see p.114) tucked away in the basement on the north side. The basement was long used as the town prison and its entrance was then round to the right through the **Mammelokker** (The Suckling), a small but flashy Louis XIV-style structure propped up against the northwest side of the hall. Part gateway and part warder's lodging, the Mammelokker was added in 1741. It is adorned by a bas-relief sculpture illustrating the classical legend of Cimon, who the Romans condemned to death by starvation. He was saved by his daughter, Pero, who turned up daily to feed him from her breasts – a story that gave the building its name.

The first-floor entrance on the south side of the Lakenhalle is the only way to reach the adjoining **Belfort** (Map 7, I11; mid-March to mid-Nov 10am–1pm & 2–6pm, plus free guided tours May–Sept daily at 2pm, 3pm & 4pm; €3), a much-amended medieval edifice whose soaring spire is topped by a comically corpulent, gilded copper dragon. Once a watchtower-cum-storehouse of civic documents, the interior is now a real disappointment – an empty shell displaying a few old bells and statues alongside the rusting remains of a couple of old dragons that formerly perched on top of the spire. The belfry is equipped with a glass-sided lift that climbs up to the roof, where consolation is provided in the form of excellent views over the city centre.

THE STADHUIS

Map 7, I9. City Hall, on the Botermarkt; May–Oct Mon–Thurs guided tours only, times from the tourist office; €3.

Just up from the tourist office, the **Stadhuis** is a sturdy construction, whose main facade comprises two distinct sections. Framing the central stairway is the later section, whose austere symmetries are a good example of Italian Renaissance architecture, dating from the 1580s. This part of the facade is, however, in stark contrast to the wild, curling patterns of the section to the immediate north, carved in the Flamboyant Gothic style at the turn of the sixteenth century to a design by one of the most celebrated architects of the day, Rombout Keldermans. The original plan was to have the whole of the Stadhuis built by Keldermans, but the money ran out when the wool trade collapsed and the city couldn't afford to finish it off until much later – hence the discordant facade of today. Look carefully at Keldermans' work and you'll spot all sorts of charming details, especially in the elaborate tracery, decorated with oak leaves and acorns as well as vines laden with grapes. Each of Keldermans' ornate niches was intended to hold a statuette, but these were never installed and the present carvings, representing important historical figures in characteristic poses, were inserted at the end of the twentieth century. Look out for **Keldermans**, shown rubbing his chin and holding his plans for the Stadhuis.

Tours of the Stadhuis are mildly enjoyable and, of the series of halls open to the public, the most interesting is the old Court of Justice or **Pacificatiezaal** (Pacification Hall), the site of the signing of the Pacification of Ghent in 1576. A plaque commemorates this agreement, which momentarily bound north and south Flanders together against the Habsburgs. The carrot offered by the dominant Protestants was the promise of religious freedom, but they failed to deliver and much of the south (present-day Belgium) soon returned to the imperial fold. The hall's dark blue and white tiled floor is curiously designed in the form of a maze. No one's quite certain why, but it's supposed that more privileged felons (or sinners) had to struggle round the maze on their knees as a substitute punishment for a pilgrimage to Jerusalem – a good deal if ever there was one.

EMILE BRAUNPLEIN AND ST NIKLAASKERK

Back down the slope from the Stadhuis, the cobbled square to the west of the Belfort is **Emile Braunplein** (Map 7, F–H10), named after the reforming burgomaster who cleared many of the city's slums at the beginning of the twentieth century. In the middle of the square, there's a cameo portrait of Braun on the plinth-monument that was erected in his honour. In front is the **Bron der geknielden** (Kneelers' fountain), a mournful group of figures by Georges Minne (1866–1941), a leading light of Belgian Expressionism. This is arguably the most accomplished of the city's municipal statues – there's another top-notch statue by Minne in the St Elisabethbegijnhof (see p.100). While you're here, look out also for the bizarre and conspicuous set of six copper figures that climb all over the old facade of the former **Gildehuis van de Metselaars** (Masons' Guild Hall), across from the southwest corner of the square on Cataloniestraat, a modern idea to add a touch of humour to the city's monuments.

The west edge of Emile Braunplein abuts **St Niklaaskerk** (Mon 2–5pm, Tues–Sun 10am–5pm; free), an architectural hybrid dating from the thirteenth century – and once the favourite church of the city's wealthier merchants. Here, it's the shape and structure that pleases most, especially the arching buttresses and pencil-thin turrets which, in a classic example of the early Scheldt Gothic style, elegantly attenuate the lines of the nave. Inside, most of the Baroque furnishings and fittings which once cluttered the interior have been removed, thus returning the church to its early appearance, though unfortunately this does not apply to a clumsy and clichéd set of statues of the Apostles. Much better is the giant-sized Baroque high altar with its mammoth representation of God glowering down its back, blowing the hot wind of the Last Judgement from his mouth and surrounded by a flock of cherubic angels.

There's a fabulous view of St Niklaaskerk from the St Michielsbrug bridge (see below just to the west of the church. From here, St Niklaaskerk appears impossibly slender – as if somehow it was being sucked up by a giant, invisible vacuum cleaner.

THE KORENMARKT (CORN MARKET)

St Niklaaskerk marks the southern end of the **Korenmarkt** (Map 7, E9), a long and wide cobbled area where the grain which once kept the city alive was traded after it was unloaded from the boats that anchored on the Graslei. The one noteworthy building here is the former **post office**, whose combination of Gothic Revival and neo-Renaissance styles illustrates the eclecticism popular in Belgium at the beginning of the twentieth century. The carved heads encircling the building represent the rulers who came to the city for the Great Exhibition of 1913 and among them, bizarrely, is a bust of Florence Nightingale. The interior has recently been turned into a sleek shopping mall like a thousand others.

TO THE GUILD HOUSES OF THE GRASLEI

Behind the post office, the neo-Gothic **St Michielsbrug** bridge (Map 7, B10) offers fine views back over the towers and turrets that pierce the Ghent skyline – just as it was meant to: it was built in 1913 to provide visitors to the Great Exhibition with a vantage point to oversee the medieval city centre. As such, it was one of several schemes dreamed up to enhance the medieval appearance of the city, one of the others being the demolition of the scrabbly buildings that had sprung up in the lee of the Lakenhalle. The bridge also overlooks the city's oldest harbour, the **Tussen Bruggen** (Between the Bridges), from whose quays – the Graslei and the Korenlei – **boats** leave for trips around the city's canals (see p.16).

Clamber down the steps on the east side of the bridge for the **Graslei** (Map 7, C7–10), which holds the late medieval, gabled guild houses of the town's boatmen and grainweighers. Some of these are of particularly fine design, beginning with – and working your way north from – the **Gildehuis van de Vrije Schippers** (Guild house of the Free Boatmen), at no. 14, where the badly weathered sandstone is decorated with scenes of boatmen weighing anchor. There's also a delicate carving of a caravel, the type of Mediterranean sailing ship used by Columbus, located above the door. Medieval Ghent had two boatmen guilds – the Free, who could discharge their cargoes within the city, and the Unfree, who could not. This was typical of the complex regulations governing the guilds and, in this case, the Unfree Boatmen were obliged to unload their goods into the vessels of the Free Boatmen at the edge of the city – an inefficient arrangement by any standard.

Close by, at Graslei 12–13, is the late-seventeenth-century **Coorenmetershuis** (Corn Measurers' House), where city officials weighed and graded corn behind a facade graced by cartouches and garlands of fruit. Next door, at no. 11, is the quaint **Tolhuisje**, another delightful example of Flemish Renaissance architecture and built to house the customs officers in 1698. Of contrasting appearance, the limestone **Spijker** (Staple House), at no. 10, boasts a surly Romanesque facade and a heavy crow-stepped gable dating to around 1200. It was here that the city stored its grain supply for over five hundred years until a fire gutted the interior. Moving on, the original **Coorenmetershuis**, at no. 9, with its slender facade and dainty crow-step gable, was the home of the city's Corn Measurers until the construction of their second, larger premises just along the Graslei (see opposite). Finally, the splendid **Den Enghel**, at no. 8, takes its name from the angel bearing a banner that decorates the facade; the building was originally the stone-masons' guild house, as evidenced by the effigies of the four Roman martyrs who were the guild's patron saints.

At the north end of Graslei, just beyond the **Grasbrug**, the waterway forks with the River Leie on the right and the Lieve canal to the left.

THE GROENTENMARKT (VEGETABLE MARKET)

Just beyond the north end of Graslei, on the far side of Hooiard street, is a long line of sooty stone gables. These were once the walls of the Groot Vleeshuis (Great Butchers' Hall), a covered market where the sale of meat was carefully controlled by the city council. The gables date from the fifteenth century, but they are in poor condition and the interior is only of interest for its intricate wooden roof. The gables face onto the **Groentenmarkt** (Map 7, E7), one of the city's prettiest squares and flanked by two of its most distinctive shops – Tierenteyn, the mustard special-ist (see p.194), and the Himschoot bakery (see p.194).

Leaving the Groentenmarkt, the most enjoyable
route is to stroll north to the Gravensteen castle
(see p.95), though you might consider the short
detour south along the Korenlei to St Michielskerk.

THE KORENLEI AND ST MICHIELSKERK

From beside the Groot Vleeshuis, the Grasbrug bridge leads over to the **Korenlei** (Map 7, B7–10), which trips along the western side of the old city harbour. Unlike the Graslei opposite, none of the medieval buildings have survived here and instead there's a series of expansive, high-gabled Neoclassical merchants' houses, mostly dating from the eighteenth century. It's the general ensemble that appeals rather than any particular building, but the **Gildehuis van de Onvrije Schippers** (Guild house of the Unfree Boatmen), at no. 7, does boast a fetching eighteenth-century facade. It's decorated with whimsical stucco dolphins and lions, bewigged and all bulging eyes and rows of teeth. The Unfree Boatmen were not permitted to trade within the city, unlike their rivals, the Free Boatmen, whose guild house is on the Graslei (see p.92).

At the south end of the Korenlei, beside St Michielsbrug, rises the bulky stonework of **St Michielskerk** (Map 7, B11; April–Sept Mon–Sat 2–5pm; free), a heavy-duty Gothic structure begun in the 1440s. The city's Protestants seem to have taken a particularly strong dislike to the place, ransacking it twice – once in 1566 and again in 1579 – and the repairs were never quite finished: witness the pathetic and clumsily truncated tower. The interior is largely Gothic Revival, mediocre stuff enlivened by a scattering of six-teenth- and seventeenth-century paintings, the pick of which is a splendid, impassioned *Crucifixion* by **Anthony van Dyck** (1599–1641). Trained in Antwerp, where he worked in Rubens' workshop, van Dyck made extended visits to England and Italy in the 1620s, before returning to Antwerp in 1628. He stayed there for four years – during which time he painted this *Crucifixion* – before migrating to England to become portrait painter to Charles I and his court.

Located round the corner from the church, on Onderbergen, the former Dominican friary of **Het Pand** (Map 5, D5; usually Mon–Fri 9am–5pm; free) has been immaculately restored and is now used by the university for offices and conferences. At the front, three long matching facades overlook a zigzagging privet hedge that fills up the garden. No one bothers much if you wander into the building – or at least the wing on the right-hand side, where the cloisters have several glass cabinets displaying small pieces of brightly coloured medieval stained glass. The friary has had a chequered history, including the demolition of its church in the 1860s and the destruction of its once-magnificent library by iconoclasts in 1566. The Protestants chucked the books out of the window into the canal – crude and cruel perhaps, but not nearly as savage as the reprisals – mass executions – taken by the Catholic Habsburgs when they recaptured the town a few years later.

HET GRAVENSTEEN (THE CASTLE OF THE COUNTS) AND ST VEERLEPLEIN

A couple of minutes' walk north of the Groentenmarkt, **Het Gravensteen** (Map 7, C4; daily: April–Sept 9am–6pm; Oct–March 9am–5pm; €6.20), the castle of the Counts of Flanders, looks sinister enough to have been lifted from a Bosch painting. Its cold, dark walls and unyielding turrets were first raised in 1180 as much to intimidate the town's unruly citizens as to protect them. Considering the castle has been used for all sorts of purposes since then (it was even a cotton mill in the nineteenth century), it has survived in remarkably good nick. The imposing gateway is a deep-arched, heavily fortified tunnel that leads to the courtyard, which is framed by protective battlements complete with wooden flaps, ancient arrow slits and holes for boiling oil and water. Beside the courtyard stand the castle's two main buildings, the **keep** on the right and to the left the **count's residence**, riddled with narrow, interconnected staircases set within the thickness of the walls. A self-guided tour takes you through this labyrinth, and highlights include the cavernous state rooms of the count, a gruesome collection of instruments of torture, and a particularly dank, underground dungeon. It's also possible to walk along most of the castle's encircling wall, from where there are pleasant views over the city centre.

Like most medieval rulers, the Counts of Flanders didn't mess around when it came to imposing order and at any one time there might be decomposing bodies hanging from the castle walls, prisoners dying in the dungeons and yet more ex-enemies strung up at the gatehouse. The counts' public punishments were carried out just across from the castle entrance on **St Veerleplein** (Map 7, D5), now an attractive cobbled square, but with an ersatz punishment post, plonked here in 1913 and topped off by a lion carrying the banner of Flanders. At the back of the square, beside the junction of the city's two main canals, is the grandiloquent Baroque facade of the **Oude Vismarkt**, which is dominated by a grand relief of Neptune, who stands on a chariot drawn by sea horses. To either side are allegorical figures representing the Leie (Venus) and the Scheldt (Hercules) – the two rivers that spawned the city. The market itself is in a terrible state, scheduled for restoration – or possibly demolition.

THE DESIGN MUSEUM

Map 7, B7. Jan Breydelstraat 5. Tues–Sun 10am–6pm; €2.50.
Crossing the bridge immediately to the west of St Veerleplein, turn first left for the **Design Museum**, one of the city's more enjoyable museums, focused on Belgian dec-

orative and applied arts. The wide-ranging collection divides into two distinct sections. At the front, squeezed into what was once an eighteenth-century patrician's mansion, lies an attractive sequence of period rooms, culminating in the original dining room, complete with painted ceiling, wood panelling and Chinese porcelain. Linked to the back of the house is the other section, a gleamingly modern display area used both for temporary exhibitions and to showcase the museum's eclectic collection of applied arts dating from 1880 to 1940. There are examples of the work of many leading designers, but pride of place goes to the Art Nouveau material, especially the work of the Belgian **Henry van der Velde**, whose oeuvre is well represented by a furnished room he designed and decorated in 1899.

De Tap en de Tepel, at Gewad 7, a couple of hundred metres north of the Design Museum, is one of the city's best bars (see p.169).

TO THE LIEVEKAAI

Back at the top of Jan Breydelstraat, on the other side of Burgstraat, at no. 4, is the distinctive facade of **De Gekroonde Hoofden** (The Crowned Heads), a much-restored sixteenth-century house decorated with medallion sculptures of fourteen counts of Flanders. On the building's right hand side is narrow Gewad. Follow this as far as St Widostraat, where you turn right for the youth hostel (see p.142) and the **Lievekaai** (Map 6, D2), Ghent's second-oldest harbour, on what was once the canal to Bruges. The harbour was at its busiest in the sixteenth and seventeenth centuries, but a new, wider canal linking the city to Bruges was dug in 1753, rendering the Lievekaai well-nigh redundant. This new canal was itself made obsolete by the arrival of the railways in the nineteenth century, but not before it had been used by Wellington to move his troops east towards Brussels – and Waterloo. The cobbled area that flanks the canal was originally a turning circle for docking ships, but this was filled in long ago – hence the rather forlorn look of the houses that have survived here. Nonetheless, it is a fetching ensemble, with old and petite brick houses, graced by crow-step gables, set cheek-to-cheek with the larger houses that were inserted into the terrace much later.

NORTHWEST TO THE RABOT AND ST ELISABETHBEGIJNHOF (ST ELISABETH'S BEGUINAGE)

From the Lievekaai, the obvious route is to head for the Huis van Alijn, but you can detour northwest of the Rabot and the St Elisabeth's beguinage.

Heading northwest from the Lievekaai, a mixture of tumbledown and renovated seventeenth- and eighteenth-century properties line the sides of the **Lieve canal**. Take the north side of the canal – **Augustijnenkaai** to start with – and, after five minutes or so, you'll pass a set of modern, fancily carved stone pillars beside a footbridge. These pillars recall the days when the south side of the canal was hogged by the **Prinsenhof** (Map 5, C1), the favourite residence of the Counts of Flanders from the fourteenth century. The palace-fortress was a huge affair, with over three hundred rooms, but it was demolished when the city industrialized and the only survivor is a large, two-storey, stone and brick battlemented gateway, the **Donkere Poort** (Map 5, C1; Dark Gate), near the south end of the bridge.

Pushing on from the north side of the footbridge, the **Lieve canal** ends abruptly at the **Rabot** (Map 5, B1), a fortified medieval sluice gate which was crucial to the defence of old Ghent. This area, where the Lieve cut through the city walls, was long a defensive weak spot and it was here that the Habsburg army tried to force entry under the leadership of a mightily irritated Maximilian in 1488. Maximilian was determined to teach his subjects a lesson they wouldn't forget, but he was driven off and, both to celebrate their success and to guard against their future, the city's guilds built the Rabot. With its spiky twin towers and sturdy stonework, it remains a good-looking structure, though it's now stuck at the end of the canal à propos of nothing in particular. It's hard to imagine it today, but it was an ingenious means of defence: the water level behind the sluice was kept higher than the water level outside, and in emergencies the gate could be opened and the surrounding fields flooded, keeping the enemy safely at bay.

Strolling south from the Rabot, it takes about five minutes to reach St Elisabethplein at (what amounts to) the entrance to the **St Elisabethbegijnhof** (Map 5, B2). Most Belgian cities have – and all of them had – at least one *begijnhof* and Ghent is no exception (neither is Bruges; see p.63). They date from the early medieval period, when widows and unmarried women were encouraged to live in communities dedicated to pious acts, especially caring for the sick. The women who chose this life – the **beguines** (*begijns*) – had the right to return to the secular world, though most chose not to. The St Elisabethbegijnhof was founded in the 1240s and takes its name from Elisabeth of Hungary (1207–1235), who dedicated her life to the sick after the death of her husband. Remodelled on several occasions – most drastically during the Napoleonic occupation – today's beguinage makes only tentative hints as to its medieval lay-out, though the beguines' brick **church**, in the middle of St Elisabethplein, has survived in good condition, a sterling seventeenth-century structure with an imposing central tower. Here also, look out for St Elisabeth, in a niche above the entrance door, smiling contentedly with a Bible in her hand. On the lawn beside the church is a finely worked statue in memory of **Georges Rodenbach** (1855–1898), the melancholic symbolist who penned *Bruges la Morte,* a mournful tale that first made Bruges a popular tourist destination (see p.304). The monument was the work of the talented Belgian sculptor **Georges Minne**, who was also responsible for the *Kneelers' Fountain*, on Ghent's Emile Braunplein (see p.90). The main gateway that controlled access into St Elisabethbegijnhof was moved to the Bijlokemuseum (see p.113) years ago, but you do get the flavour of the old self-contained beguinage along **Proveniersstersstraat**. This narrow sidestreet is flanked by a long line of pretty little whitewashed cottages with green doors and effigies of the saints.

From St Elisabethplein, it takes about ten minutes to walk back to Het Gravensteen (see p.95), via Burgstraat.

HUIS VAN ALIJN MUSEUM

Map 7, F4. Kraanlei 65. Tues–Sun 11am–5pm; €2.50.

From the Lievekaai, it's a short walk back to St Veerleplein, where you turn down Kraanlei to reach one of the city's more popular attractions, the **Huis van Alijn Museum**, a rambling folklore museum that occupies a series of exceptionally pretty little almshouses set around a central courtyard. Dating from the fourteenth century, the almshouses were built following a major scandal reminiscent of *Romeo and Juliet*. In 1354, two members of the Rijms family murdered three of the rival Alijns when they were at Mass in St Baafskathedraal. The immediate cause of the affray was that one of each clan were rivals for the same woman, but the dispute went deeper, reflecting the commercial animosity of two guilds, the weavers and the fullers. The murderers fled for their lives and were condemned to death *in absentia*, but eventually – eight years later – they were pardoned on con-dition that they paid for the construction of a set of almshouses, which was to be named after the victims. The result was the Huis van Alijn, which became a hospice for elderly women and then a workers' tenement until the city council snapped it up in the 1950s.

The **museum** consists of a long series of period rooms depicting local life and work in the eighteenth and nine-teenth centuries, intermingled with rooms that illustrate a particular theme or subject. Frankly, the period rooms are not especially riveting, though the reconstructed pipe-maker's, cobbler's and cooper's workshops are all of some interest, whereas the themed rooms are often intriguing. There are good displays on funerals and death, popular entertainment – from brass bands through to sports and fairs – and on religious beliefs in an age when every ailment had its own allocated saint. The more substantial exhibits are explained in free English-language leaflets that are available in the appropriate room. Be sure also to pop into the **chapel**, a pleasantly gaudy affair built in the 1540s. When they aren't out on loan, the chapel is home to a pair of wooden "goliaths." Of obscure origin, goliaths are a com-mon feature of Belgian street processions and festivals. These two are purportedly the descendants of two disre-spectful effigies made of the much-disliked Habsburg rulers, the Archdukes Albert and Isabella, in the early seventeenth century.

Pushing on along the Kraanlei from the museum, it's a few paces more to two especially fine facades. First up, at no. 79, is **De Zeven Werken van Barmhartigheid** (The Seven Works of Mercy), a building that takes its name from its miniature tableaux. On the top level, from left to right, are visiting the sick, ministering to prisoners and burying the dead, whilst below – again from left to right – are feeding the hungry, providing water for the thirsty and clothing the naked. The seventh good work – giving shelter to the stranger – was provided inside the building, which was once an inn, so, perhaps rather too subtly, there's no decorative plaque. The adjacent **Fluitspeler** (The Flautist), the corner house at no. 81, dates from 1669 and is now occupied by the *De Hel* restaurant (see p.155). The six bas-relief terracotta panels on the facade sport allegorical representations of the five senses plus a flying deer and up above, on the cornice, are the figures of Faith, Hope and Charity.

THE PATERSHOL

Behind the Kraanlei are the lanes and alleys of the **Patershol** (Map 7, E5–G1), a tight web of brick terraced houses dating from the seventeenth century. Once the heart of the Flemish working-class city, this thriving residential quarter had, by the 1970s, become a slum threatened with demolition. After much toing and froing, the area was ultimately kept from the developers and a process of gentrification begun, the result being today's gaggle of good bars and smashing restaurants. The process is still under way – one of the stragglers being the ongoing refurbishment of the grand old Carmelite Monastery on Vrouwebroersstraat – and the fringes of the Patershol remain a ragbag of decay and restoration, but few Belgian cities can boast a more agreeable drinking and eating district.

Two of the best places to eat and drink in the
Patershol are *De Blauwe Zalm* restaurant
and the *Rococo* bar (see Chapters 6 and 7 for
further restaurant and bar recommendations).

THE VRIJDAGMARKT AND BIJ ST JACOBS

At the east end of Kraanlei, just beyond the Huis van Alijn, an antiquated little bridge leads over to **Dulle Griet** (Mad Meg), a lugubrious fifteenth-century cannon that proved more dangerous to the gunners than the enemy. Supposedly the most powerful siege gun ever manufactured, the barrel cracked the first time it was fired. Nevertheless, someone must have thought they could fix it, because the cannon was shipped here at great expense – but all to no avail and it has stayed put ever since.

From the cannon, it's a few seconds along Meerseniersstraat to the **Vrijdagmarkt** (Map 6, G3–H3), a wide, open square that was long the political centre of Ghent, the site of both public meetings and executions –

JACOB VAN ARTEVELDE

One of the shrewdest of Ghent's medieval leaders, Artevelde was elected captain of all the guilds in 1337. Initially, he steered a delicate course during the interminable wars between France and England, keeping the city neutral – and the textile industry going – despite the machinations of both warring countries. Ultimately he was, however, forced to take sides, plumping for England. This proved his undoing: in a burst of Anglomania, Artevelde rashly suggested that a son of Edward III of England become the new Count of Flanders, an unpopular notion that prompted a mob to storm his house and hack him to death. Artevelde's demise fuelled further outbreaks of communal violence and, a few weeks later, the Vrijdagmarkt witnessed a riot between the fullers and the weavers that left 500 dead. This rumbling vendetta – one of several that plagued the city – was to lead to the murders precipitating the creation of the Huis van Alijn almshouses (see p.100).

THE VRIJDAGMARKT AND BIJ ST JACOBS

and sometimes both at the same time. In the middle of the square stands a nineteenth-century **statue** of the guild leader **Jacob van Artevelde** (1290–1345), portrayed addressing the people in heroic style (see box p.103).

Of the buildings flanking the Vrijdagmarkt, the most appealing is the former **Gildehuis van de Huidevetters** (Tanners' Guild House), at no. 37, a tall, Gothic structure whose pert dormer windows and stepped gables culminate in a dainty and distinctive corner turret – the **Toreken** – which is crowned by a mermaid weathervane. Also worth a second glance are the lime-green **Lakenmetershuis** (Cloth Measurers' House), at no. 25, whose long windows and double entrance stairs are a classic example of eighteenth-century architecture, and the old headquarters of the trade unions, the whopping **Ons Huis** (Our House), a sterling edifice built in eclectic style at the turn of the twentieth century.

Adjoining the Vrijdagmarkt is the busy **Bij St Jacobs** (Map 6, I3), a sprawling square surrounding a sulky medieval church and sprinkled with antique shops. The totem-pole like modern **statue** on the near (Vrijdagmarkt) side of the square is dedicated to a nineteenth-century Ghent folk singer, a certain Karel Waeri. The singer perches on top of the column and down below are illustrations of his best-known songs. From Bij St Jacobs, it's a couple of minutes' walk up Belfortstraat back to the Stadhuis (see p.88).

THE MUSEUM VOOR INDUSTRIELE ARCHEOLOGIE EN TEXTIEL (MUSEUM FOR INDUSTRIAL ARCHEOLOGY & TEXTILES, M.I.A.T.)

Map 6, J1. Minnemeers 9; Tues–Sun 10am–6pm; €2.50.

It's a bit of a detour, and probably for aficionados only, but from the Vrijdagmarkt, it's a brisk five minutes' walk north via Waaistraat to the mildly diverting **Museum voor Industriele Archeologie en Textiel**. Housed in an ambitiously refurbished old cotton mill, the museum spreads over several large floors, mostly given over to temporary exhibitions focusing on industrial and social history. The main permanent exhibition (on Floor 5) is entitled "Our Industrial Past, 1750–2000" and hones in on the role of women. The other permanent display, on Floor 3, consists of a whole floor of cotton spinning machines in full working order.

EAST ALONG THE HOOGPOORT TO GEERAARD DE DUIVELSTEEN

Facing the Stadhuis, on the corner of Botermarkt and Hoogpoort, the **St Jorishof** restaurant (Map 6, H5; see p.158) occupies one of the city's oldest buildings, its sooty, heavy-duty stonework dating from the middle of the fifteenth century and once home to the Crossbowmen's Guild. The crossbow was a dead military duck by then, but the guild was still a powerful force – and remained so until the eighteenth century – and it was here, in 1477, that Mary of Burgundy was pressured into signing the Great Privilege confirming the city's commercial freedoms. She was obviously not too offended as later that year this was where she received the matrimonial ambassadors of the Holy Roman Emperor, Frederick III. Frederick was pressing the suit of his son, Maximilian, who Mary duly married, the end result being that Flanders became a Habsburg fiefdom.

For more on Mary of Burgundy, see p.53.

Lining up along the **Hoogpoort**, beyond St Jorishof, are some of the oldest **facades** in Ghent, sturdy Gothic structures that also date from the fifteenth century. The third house along – formerly a heavily protected aristocratic mansion called the **Grote Sikkel** (Map 6, H5) – is now the home of a music school, but the blackened remains of an antique torch-snuffer remain fixed to the wall.

Hoogpoort leads into Nederpolder and a right turn at the end brings you to the forbidding **Geeraard de Duivelsteen** (Map 6, I7; no admission), a fortified palace of splendid Romanesque design built of grey limestone in the thirteenth century. The stronghold, bordered by what remains of its moat and equipped with austere corner turrets, takes its name from Geeraard Vilain, who earned the soubriquet "duivel" (devil) for his acts of cruelty or, according to some sources, because of his swarthy features and black hair. Vilain was not the only noble to wall himself up within a castle – well into the fourteenth century, Ghent was dotted with fortified houses (*stenen*), such was the fear the privileged few had of the rebellious guildsmen. The last noble moved out of the Duivelsteen in about 1350 and since then the building has been put to a bewildering range of uses, from being an arsenal and a prison through to (dreadfully unsuitable) service as a madhouse and an orphanage.

Just beyond the Duivelsteen is the first of two interlocking squares, **Lieven Bauwensplein** (Map 6, I8), named after – and with a statue of – the local entrepreneur who founded the city's machine-manufactured textile industry. Born in 1769, the son of a tanner, Bauwens was an intrepid soul, who posed as an ordinary textile worker in England to learn how its much more technologically advanced machinery worked. In the 1790s, he managed to smuggle a "spinning jenny" over to the continent and soon opened cotton mills in Ghent. It didn't, however, do Bauwens much good:

he over-borrowed and when there was a downturn in demand, his factories went bust and he died in poverty. The adjoining **François Laurentplein** occupies the site of one of the city's medieval gates, demolished in the 1880s. It takes its name – and its statue – from François Laurent (1810–1887), a liberal politician and professor who pioneered workers' education classes in Ghent – hence the grateful figures to either side of the seated academic.

From these two squares, it's about ten minutes' walk east to St Baafsabdij (see p.108) or a short stroll north up Limburgstraat to St Baafskathedraal. On the way to the cathedral, you'll pass a **monument** to the Eyck brothers, Hubert and Jan, the painter(s) of the *Adoration of the Mystic Lamb*. It's a somewhat stodgy affair, knocked up for the Great Exhibition of 1913, but it's a piece of art propaganda too, proclaiming Hubert as co-painter of the altarpiece, when this is very speculative (see p.83). Open on Hubert's knees is the *Book of Revelations*, which may or may not have given him artistic inspiration.

The **Boatel**, an old canal barge, has been turned into one of the city's most alluring hotels (see p.137), and it is moored very close to St Bavo's Abbey at Voorhuitkaai 29A.

EAST TO ST BAAFSABDIJ

Map 6, N6. St Bavo's Abbey, Gandastraat. Wed–Sun 9.30am–5pm; free.

East of the Duivelsteen, Ghent's eighteenth- and nineteenth-century industrial suburbs stretch out toward the **Dampoort train station**. A mish-mash of terrace, factory and canal, these suburbs were spawned by the sea canals that were dug to replace the narrow – and obsolete – waterways of the city centre. Right next to the station, the large (and unappetizing) water-filled hole on **Oktrooiplein** is the link between the old and the new systems. Visitors to Ghent rarely venture into this part of the city, but there is one really enjoyable diversion, the ivy-clad ruins of **St Baafsabdij**, which ramble over a narrow parcel of land on Gandastraat, ten minutes from the Duivelsteen beside the River Leie (Lys in French) – and near its confluence with the Scheldt. Of no particular significance today, this was once a strategically important location and it was here, in 630, that the French missionary St Amand founded an abbey. St Amand was poorly received by the locals, who ultimately drowned him in the Scheldt, but his abbey survived to become a famous place of pilgrimage on account of its guardianship of the remains of the seventh-century **St Bavo**. A wealthy and dissolute Flemish landowner, Bavo – so the story goes – repented of his ways after the sudden death of his wife, giving his possessions to the poor and ending his days as a hermit outside Ghent. In the ninth century, the abbey suffered a major disaster when the Vikings decided this was the ideal spot to camp while they raided the surrounding region, but order was eventually restored, another colony of monks moved in and the abbey was rebuilt in 950. The abbey's heyday was during the fourteenth century, when, as a major landowner, its coffers were filled to overflowing with the proceeds of the wool industry. It also witnessed several important events, most notably, in 1369, the marriage of Philip the Bold, Duke of Burgundy, to Margaretha de Male, the daughter of the Count of Flanders, a union which marked the end of the independence of Flanders. Here also Edward III's wife gave birth to John of "Gaunt" (an English corruption of Ghent) at the start of the Hundred Years War.

The monks were loyal to their various rulers, but this did not save them from the ire of the Emperor Charles V when he stomped all over Ghent after an uprising in 1539.

Charles had most of the abbey demolished to make room for a new castle and the monks were obliged to decamp to St Baafskathedraal. The emperor's fortress was demolished in the 1820s, but these substantial **abbey ruins** somehow managed to survive and today, after extensive repairs, they comprise a fascinating jumble of old stone buildings. First up beyond the entrance are the remnants of the Gothic **cloister**, with its long vaulted corridors and distinctive octagonal tower, which consisted of a toilet on the bottom floor and the storage room – the sanctuarium – for the St Bavo relic up above. On the far side of the cloister, the lower level was used for workshops and as storage space. It now contains – both on its outside wall and within – an intriguing **lapidary museum**, displaying all sorts of architectural bits and pieces retrieved from the city during renovations and demolitions. There are gargoyles and finely carved Gothic heads, terracotta panels, broken off chunks of columns and capitals, and several delightful mini-tableaux. There's precious little labelling, but it's the skill of the carving that impresses and, if you've already explored the city, one or two pieces are identifiable, principally the original lion from the original punishment post outside Het Gravensteen (see p.95). A flight of steps leads up from beside the museum to the Romanesque **refectory**, a splendid chamber whose magnificent, hooped timber roof dates – remarkably enough – from the twelfth century. The refectory has a collection of old tombstones, which are stored here for safe-keeping, and on its west wall are the remaining bits of a huge seventeenth-century wooden Crucifixion. Finally, the **grounds** of the abbey may be small, but they are left partly wild on account of several rare plants that flourish here; if your Flemish is up to it, the warden may help to point them out or you can just settle down and relax.

South of Ghent city centre

Most of Ghent's attractions are within easy walking distance of the Korenmarkt, but two of the city's principal museums are located some two kilometres south of the centre, out towards St Pieters train station. These are the **Museum voor Schone Kunsten** (Fine Art Museum) and the adjacent Museum of Contemporary Art, **S.M.A.K.** Many visitors just hop on a Korenmarkt tram for the quick trip down to the two, but with more time – and energy – a circular walk of around three hours can take in several less well-known attractions too. The route suggested below begins by heading south from the city centre along **Veldstraat**, the main shopping street, and then drops by the historical collections of the **Bijlokemuseum** before proceeding onto the Museum voor Schone Kunsten and S.M.A.K. From here, the return to the city centre is via **Overpoortstraat** and **Sint Pietersnieuwstraat**, Ghent's student enclave and the location of the minor museums contained in the former **St Pietersabdij** (St Peter's Abbey).

SOUTH ALONG VELDSTRAAT

Ghent's main shopping street, **Veldstraat** (Map 6, F6–E8), leads south from the Korenmarkt, running parallel to the River Leie. By and large, it's a very ordinary shopping strip, but the eighteenth-century mansion at no. 82 does hold the **Museum Arnold Vander Haeghen** (Map 6, E7; Mon–Fri 10am–noon & 2–4.30pm; free), with small and temporary exhibitions of art and displays devoted to a trio of local worthies. Amongst the three, the poet and essayist Maurice Maeterlinck (1864–1949) is the most noteworthy as the winner of the Nobel prize for literature in 1911. The museum also has a Chinese Salon, where the original Chinese silk wall paper has survived intact. The Duke of Wellington stayed here in 1815 after the Battle of Waterloo, popping across the street to the **Hôtel d'Hane-Steenhuyse**, at no. 55 (Map 6, E7), to bolster the morale of the refugee King of France, Louis XVIII (see box, below). The grand facade of Louis's hideaway, dating from 1768, has survived in good condition, its elaborate pedi-

LOUIS XVIII IN GHENT

Abandoning his throne, Louis had hot-footed it to Ghent soon after Napoleon landed in France after escaping from Elba. While others did his fighting for him, Louis waited around in Ghent gorging himself – his daily dinner lasted all of seven hours and the bloated exile was known to polish off 100 oysters at a sitting. His fellow exile, François Chateaubriand, the writer and politician, ignored the gluttony and cowardice, writing meekly, "The French alone know how to dine with method". Thanks to Wellington's ministrations, Louis was persuaded to return to his kingdom and his entourage left for Paris on June 26, 1815, one week after Waterloo.

ment sporting allegorical representations of Time and History, but at present there's no access to the expansive salons beyond. Incidentally, the C&A store, close by at Veldstraat 45, carries a modest **memorial plaque** relating to the Treaty of Ghent. This treaty, which (almost) put an end to the Anglo-American War of 1812–14, was signed here in the city and the five-man American delegation, led by John Quincy Adams, later US president, stayed in the mansion that then occupied this site. The twist in the tale was the time it took for the news to reach the warring armies: the treaty was signed on December 24, 1814, but the British generals did not hear of it until after they had been humiliated at the Battle of New Orleans on January 8, 1815, in which the Brits lost 2000 men, the Americans 8.

Pushing on down Veldstraat, it's a couple of minutes more to a matching pair of grand, Neoclassical nineteenth-century buildings. On the left-hand side is the **Justitiepaleis** (Map 6, E9; Palace of Justice), whose pediment sports a large frieze with the figure of Justice in the middle, the accused to one side and the condemned on the other. Opposite stands the recently restored **opera house** – home of the Vlaamse Opera (see p.176) – whose facade is awash with carved stone panels.

The **walk** from the opera house to the Bijlokemuseum via the Nederkouter is dull and it's better – and no further – to get there along the banks of the River Leie. Turn off Nederkouter at Verlorenkost and then – with the Coupure canal and its dinky swing bridge dead ahead – take the first on the left along the river.

THE BIJLOKEMUSEUM

Map 5, C10. Godshuizenlaan 2. Thurs 10am–6pm, Sun 2–6pm; €2.50.

Continuing south along Nederkouter, it's an easy ten-minute stroll from the opera house to the **Bijlokemuseum**, whose rambling collection of Ghent-produced applied and decorative art has been shoehorned into the old Cistercian abbey on Godshuizenlaan. Founded in the thirteenth century, the abbey was savaged by Calvinists on several occasions, but much of the medieval complex has survived, tidy brown-brick buildings that now provide a charming setting for all sorts of (poorly labelled) bygones, from collections of guild pennants and processional banners to Masonic tackle, porcelain, pottery, keys and costumes. Parts of the complex are also used for temporary exhibitions.

At the entrance, the distinctive main **gateway** is actually a bit of a fraud – it was moved here from the St Elisabethbegijnhof (see p.99) – but it's still a handsome structure, a flowing Baroque portal decorated by a statue of St Elisabeth – for more on whom, see p.99 – with a beggar kneeling gratefully at her feet. Beyond, across the lawn, is the **cloister**, whose lower level is given over to a string of period rooms, among which the Louis XV drawing room is the most distinguished. On the upper level – though this may change – is a long set of cameo collections, notably an assortment of military hardware featuring the halberds and pikes favoured by the weaver-armies of Flanders. Amongst them there's a rare example of a *goedenday*, literally "good-day": this primitive fourteenth-century weapon, no more than a long pole with a short spike at the end, was designed to stab the Adam's apple, a part of the body poorly protected by armour. In response, the French bobbed their heads down to protect their necks, a nodding motion which the Flemish wryly referred to as a greeting, hence the weapon's name. Adjoining the cloister, the upper-level **refectory** is a massive affair with a high, vaulted ceiling and a striking, early fourteenth-century fresco of the Last Supper. Above this is the former **dormitory**, home – though again this may change – to a motley collection of guild mementoes including, in the centre of the room, a splendid model galleon that was carried in processions by the city's boatmen.

In front of the cloister, and reached by a connecting corridor, is the **house of the abbess**, where a further sequence of rooms accommodates a miscellany of antique furniture, portrait paintings and several magnificent carved and tiled fireplaces.

CITADELPARK

From the Bijlokemuseum, it's a five-minute walk along the busy boulevard to the northwest corner of **Citadelpark** (Map 5, D12–14), whose network of leafy footpaths circumnavigates a sprawling brick complex that dates from the 1910s. No one is quite sure what to do with the complex today, but parts have been hived off for various uses – there's a concert hall in one section and the Museum of Contemporary Art, S.M.A.K., in another. Citadelpark itself takes its name from the star-shaped fortress built here by the Dutch in the 1820s during the short-lived Kingdom of the Netherlands, which temporarily united both modern-day Belgium and the Netherlands. The fortress was demolished and the grounds prettified during the 1870s, hence today's grottoes and ponds, statues and fountains, waterfall and bandstand. The only part of the fort to have survived is the old main **gate**, a staunchly Neoclassical structure, whose pediment is decorated with weapons of war and Belgium's coat of arms.

THE BOURGOYEN-OSSEMEERSEN STEDELIJK NATUURRESERVAAT

Citadelpark is the nearest thing you'll get to countryside in Ghent itself, but there is a nature reserve – the **Bourgoyen-Ossemeersen Stedelijk Natuurreservaat** – comprising a mixed area of wetland, woodland and farmland beside the River Leie about 5km to the west of the city. The reserve has three colour-coded walking trails – though more are planned – with one being 5km long, the others 2km – and a rich birdlife. It's also easy to get to: take tram #3 from the Korenmarkt and get off – or ask to be put off – at the Driepikkelstraat entrance.

The park makes for a pleasant wander – there's even a hill here, quite an event for Ghent – but if you're heading straight for the art museums, you'll spot the pick of its wayside attractions – including the gate and the bandstand – as you cut across its northern edge along two signed footpaths, Jozef Mengaldreef and then Gustaaf den Duitsdreef. The latter brings you out between the Fine Art Museum and S.M.A.K., but the 1902 **statue** at the end of the path – *The Flagpole Planters*, featuring two muscular men, one black and one white, raising the Belgian flag in the Congo – is, considering Belgium's colonial history, shameless.

MUSEUM VOOR SCHONE KUNSTEN (FINE ART MUSEUM)

Map 5, E13. Fine Art Museum, Nicolaas de Liemaeckereplein 3. Tues–Sun 10am–6pm; €2.50.

The **Museum voor Schone Kunsten** occupies an imposing Neoclassical edifice on the edge of Citadelpark. Inside, the central atrium and connecting rotunda are flanked by a sequence of rooms, with the older paintings exhibited to the right in Rooms 1–13, the nineteenth-century works mostly on the left in Rooms A–L. There's not enough space to display all the permanent collection at any one time, so there's some rotation, but you can expect to see the paintings mentioned below even if they are not in the specified room. The layout of the collection does not seem to follow much of a scheme, but it's small enough to be easily manageable and free museum plans are issued at reception.

The atrium starts in style with a fine head by **Rodin** (1840–1917) and a series of grandiose eighteenth-century tapestries, flowing classical scenes depicting the *Exaltation of the Gods* to a design by Jan van Orley. To the right, in Room 1, the museum's small but eclectic collection of **early Flemish paintings** makes a promising beginning with **Rogier van der Weyden**'s (1399–1464) *Madonna with Carnation*, a charming work where the proffered flower, in all its exquisite detail, serves as a symbol of Christ's passion.

Moving on, Room 2 displays two superb works by **Hieronymus Bosch** (1450–1516), with his *Bearing of the Cross* showing Christ mocked by some of the most grotesque and deformed characters Bosch ever painted. Look carefully and you'll see that Christ's head is at the centre of two diagonals, one representing evil, the other good – the latter linking the repentant thief with St Veronica, whose cloak carries the imprint of Christ's face. This same struggle between good and evil is also the subject of Bosch's *St Jerome at Prayer*, in the foreground of which the saint prays, surrounded by a menacing landscape, while in the background a peaceful rural scene offers relief. Also in Room 2 are two other paintings of note, beginning with **Adriaen Isenbrandt**'s (d. 1551) *Mary and Child*, a gentle painting showing Mary suckling Jesus on the flight to Egypt, with the artist choosing a rural Flemish landscape as the backdrop rather than the Holy Land. In violent contrast, *The Conquest of Jerusalem by the Emperor Titus*, the work of an unknown fifteenth-century Ghent artist, depicts the terrible conclusion of the Roman siege of that city in 70AD – look closely and you'll spot a woman roasting her child on a spit for food. There's a sub-text here too: it is believed that the painter had the Habsburg Maximilian's hard-fought 1488 siege of Ghent on his mind.

Amongst the **seventeenth-century Flemish and Dutch paintings**, Room 5 weighs in with a powerful *St Francis* by **Rubens** (1577–1640), in which the sick-looking saint bears the marks of the stigmata. The robust romanticism of **Jacob Jordaens** (1593–1678) owed much to his friend Rubens, and his *Judgement of Midas*, in Room 7, is a case in point. Jordaens was, however, capable of much greater subtlety and his *Studies of the Head of Abraham Grapheus*, also in Room 7, is an example of the high-quality preparatory paintings he completed. These were destined to be recycled within larger compositions. In Room 7 too is **Anthony van Dyck**'s (1599–1641) *Jupiter and Antiope*, which wins the bad taste award for its portrayal of the lecherous god, with his tongue hanging out in anticipation of sex with Antiope.

Next door, Room 8 holds two precise works by **Pieter Bruegel the Younger** (1564–1638), who inherited his father's interest in the landscape and those who worked and lived on it, as evidenced by his *Wedding Breakfast* and *Village Lawyer*. Here also is **Roelandt Savery**'s (1576–1639) *Landscape with Animals*. Trained in Amsterdam, Savery worked for the Habsburgs in Prague and Vienna before returning to the Netherlands. Landscapes were his speciality and, to suit the tastes of his German patrons, he infused many of them with the romantic classicism that they preferred – the Garden of Eden and Orpheus were two

MUSEUM VOOR SCHONE KUNSTEN

favourite subjects. Nevertheless, the finely observed detail of his paintings was always in the true Flemish tradition – as is the case in this particular work.

There are more late-sixteenth- and seventeenth-century Dutch and Flemish paintings in Rooms 9–12, but here they are divided up thematically – by genre. They are a pretty modest bunch of paintings, but you might look out for the striking canvases of **Joachim Beuckelaer** (1533–1573), who specialized in allegorical market and kitchen scenes.

Rooms 16–19 kick off the museum's late-eighteenth- and nineteenth-century collection with a handful of romantic historical canvases, plus – and this is a real surprise – a superbly executed portrait by the Scot **Henry Raeburn** (1756–1823), in Room 17. These four rooms are to the far right of the rotunda, but the bulk of the nineteenth- and early-twentieth-century stuff is to the left of the atrium and rotunda in Rooms A–L with M–S given over to temporary displays. Frankly, the assorted canvases of Rooms A–L are a rather skimpy runaround of Belgian peasant scenes, landscapes and seascapes in a variety of styles, but there are several noteworthy paintings, beginning in Room A with a characteristically unsettling work by **René Magritte** (1898–1967). Room B features two striking Fauvist canvases by **Rik Wouters** (1882–1916), whilst the Pointillists are concentrated in Room D with **Théo van Rysselberghe** (1862–1926), a versatile Brussels artist and founder member of Les XX (see p.44), head and shoulders above the rest. The strongest paintings in Room E are the dark and broody works of the Expressionist **Constant Permeke** (1886–1952) and then it's on to Room F, where **James Ensor** (1860–1949), one of Belgium's most original modern artists, contributes two macabre paintings – *Old Woman and Masks* and the more accomplished *Skeleton looking at Chinoiserie*. A small selection of Ensor sketches is exhibited close by in Room J.

For more on Rogier van der Weyden, see p.36;
Hieronymus Bosch, see p.40; Adriaen Isenbrandt,
see p.41; and James Ensor, see p.223. There's also a
brief summary of Belgian art on pp.281–290.

S.M.A.K.

Map 5, D13. Stedelijk Museum voor Actuele Kunst (Municipal
Museum for Contemporary Art), Citadelpark, ⓦwww.smak.be.
Tues–Sun 10am–6pm; €5.

Directly opposite the Fine Art Museum, **S.M.A.K.** is one
of Belgium's more prestigious – and certainly one of its
most adventurous – contemporary art galleries, housed in a
cleverly remodelled 1910s building that previously served as
the city's casino. The ground floor is given over to temporary displays of international standing and the museum
prides itself on the depth and range of its exhibition programme – the works of Rob Birza, Miroslaw Balka and
Dirk Braeckman have all been showcased recently. Upstairs,
distilled from the museum's wide-ranging permanent collection, is a regularly rotated selection of sculptures, paintings and installations. S.M.A.K possesses examples of all the
major artistic movements since World War II – everything
from surrealism, the Dutch CoBrA group and pop art
through to minimalism, hyper realism and conceptual art –
as well as their forerunners, most notably René Magritte
and Paul Delvaux. Perennial favourites include the installations of the influential German **Joseph Beuys** (1921–86),
who played a leading role in the European avant-garde art
movement of the 1970s, and a characteristically unnerving
painting by **Francis Bacon** (1909–1992) entitled *A Figure
Sitting*. Usually on display also is a healthy selection of the
work of the Belgian **Marcel Broodthaers** (1924–76),

whose tongue-in-cheek pieces include *Tray of Broken Eggs* and his trademark *Red Mussels Casserole*.

TO ST PIETERSABDIJ

Map 5, F11. St Peter's Abbey, St Pietersplein

From behind the Fine Art Museum, **Overpoortstraat** cuts north through the heart of the city's student quarter, a gritty and grimy but very vivacious district, jampacked with late-night bars and inexpensive cafés (see p.166).

Decadance, Overpoortstraat 76, is one of Ghent's best student bars, offering the best and latest sounds. Like most other student bars, it's not open at the weekend.

Overpoortstraat finally emerges on **St Pietersplein**, a very wide and very long square that is flanked by the sprawling mass of **St Pietersabdij**. The abbey dates back to the earliest days of the city and was probably founded by St Amand (see p.262) in about 640. The Vikings razed the original buildings three centuries later, but it was rebuilt on a grand scale and became rich and powerful in equal measure. As a symbol of much that they hated, the Protestant iconoclasts destroyed the abbey in 1578 and the present complex – a real Baroque whopper – was erected in the seventeenth and eighteenth centuries. The last monks were ejected during the French occupation in 1796 and since then – as with many other ecclesiastical buildings in Belgium – it's been hard to figure out any suitable use. Today, much of the complex serves as municipal offices, but visitors can pop into the domed **church**, which was modelled on St Peter's in Rome, though the interior is no more than a plodding Baroque. To the left of the church, part of the old monastic complex has been turned into an arts exhibition centre, the **Kunsthal St Pietersabdij** (April to mid-Nov Tues–Sun

9am–5pm; free, though some exhibitions do attract an entrance fee), while the **Schoolmuseum Michel Thiery** (Mon–Thurs & Sat 9am–12.15pm & 1.30–5.15pm, Fri 9am–12.15pm; €1.50), with its tiresome educational displays, occupies a small part of the courtyard complex to the right.

Much more appealing is **Vooruit** (Map 5, F8), a brief stroll north of St Pietersplein at St Pietersnieuwstraat 23. To all intents and purposes, this café-cum-performing arts centre is the cultural heart of the city (at least for the under-40s), offering a varied programme of rock and pop through to dance (see p.178). It also occupies a splendid building, a twin-towered and turreted former Festival Hall that was built for Ghent's socialists in an eclectic rendition of Art Nouveau in 1914. The **café**, if that's what you're after, is open from mid-morning till late except on Sunday (Mon–Thurs 11.30am–2am, Fri & Sat 11.30am–3am & Sun 4pm–2am).

TO ST PIETERSABDIJ

●

121

LISTINGS

LISTINGS

Accommodation

I n both Ghent and Bruges, the tourist office will make **hotel and B&B reservations** on your behalf at no charge, though they do require a small deposit, which is deducted from the final bill. In **Bruges**, there are two tourist offices to go to. These are the **tourist office**, inside the train station (Mon–Sat 10am–6pm; ☎050/44 86 86), and the main **tourist office** at Burg 11 (April–Sept Mon–Fri 9.30am–6.30pm, Sat & Sun 10am–noon & 2–6.30pm; Oct–March Mon–Fri 9.30am–5pm, Sat & Sun 9.30am–1pm & 2–5.30pm; ☎050/44 86 86, 🖷44 86 00, 📧toerisme@brugge.be, 🌐www.brugge.be). In **Ghent**, the **tourist office** is in the crypt of the old cloth hall, the Lakenhalle (daily: April–Oct 9.30am–6.30pm; Nov–March 9.30am–4.30pm; ☎09/226 52 32, 🌐www.gent.be). Both city tourist offices also publish a free and comprehensive brochure detailing local **accommodation**, including hotels and hostels along with prices. One difference between these publications is that Bruges lists its B&Bs, but Ghent does not – Ghent tourist office prefers to hold the details itself. Hotel bookings can also be made **online**, but only in Bruges does this facility currently extend to B&Bs.

All Belgian licensed hotels carry a blue permit shield which indicates the number of **stars** allocated (up to a maximum of five). This classification system is, by necessity,

ACCOMMODATION PRICE CODES

All the **hotels and hostels** detailed in this chapter have been
graded according to the following price categories. These categories are based on the rate for the least expensive double
room during high season and do not take into account special
or weekend discounts.

❶ €25 and under   ❹ €60–80   ❼ €120–150
❷ €25–40   ❺ €80–100   ❽ €150–180
❸ €40–60   ❻ €100–120   ❾ €180 and over

measured against easily identifiable criteria – lifts, toilets,
room service, and so on – rather than aesthetics or specific
location, and consequently can only provide a general guide
to both quality and prices. In general terms, **prices** range
from an absolute minimum of around €40 for a double
room in the least expensive, one-star establishment, through
€80–120 for a double in a middle-range, three-star hotel,
and on up to around €200 for the luxury, four- and five-
star hotels. Ghent tends to be a bit cheaper than Bruges. In
addition, watch out for summer discounts and weekend
specials that can reduce costs by up to 35 percent.

BRUGES

BRUGES has over one hundred hotels, dozens of bed-
and-breakfasts and several unofficial youth hostels, but still
can't accommodate all its visitors at the height of the season. If you're arriving in July or August, be sure to **book
ahead** or, at a pinch, make sure you get here in the morning before all the rooms have gone. Given the crush, many
visitors use the hotel and B&B **accommodation service**
provided by the tourist office (see p.125) – it's efficient and
can save you endless hassle. At other times of the year,

things are usually much less pressing, though it's still a good idea to reserve ahead, especially if you are picky. Almost everyone in the accommodation business speaks (at least some) English. Thirty-odd Bruges establishments are described below, but in addition the city's tourist office issues a free accommodation booklet providing comprehensive **listings** including hotel photographs and a city map.

Fortunately, there's no need to stay on the peripheries of Bruges as the centre is liberally sprinkled with **hotels**, many of which occupy quaint and/or elegant old buildings. There's a cluster immediately to the south of the Burg, though these tend to be the most expensive places, and another – of more affordable hotels – in the vicinity of the Spiegelrei canal, one of the prettiest and quieter parts of the centre. Most of the city's hotels are small – twenty rooms, often less – and few are owned by a chain. Standards are generally high, even though the rooms tend to be on the small side, but note that hoteliers are wont to deck out their foyers rather grandly, often in contrast to the spartan rooms beyond, while many places offer rooms of widely divergent size and comfort. If you don't like your allocated room, be sure to object firmly and, lo and behold, another, better room will often materialize. Almost all hotels offer **breakfast** at no extra charge, ranging from a roll and coffee at the less expensive places through to full-scale banquets at the top end of the range.

B&Bs are generously distributed across the city centre too, and many offer an excellent standard of en-suite accommodation. A reasonable average price is €40–60 per double, but some of the more luxurious establishments charge in the region of €80. In addition, Bruges has a handful of unofficial **youth hostels**, offering dormitory beds at around €13 per person per night. Most of these places, as well as the official **HI youth hostel**, which is hidden away in the suburbs, also have a limited supply of smaller rooms with doubles at about €30–40 per night.

HOTELS (OVER €80)

- - - - - - - - - - - - - - - - - - -

Adornes

Map 3, G4. St Annarei 26
ⓣ 050/34 13 36, Ⓕ 34 20 85,
Ⓦ www.proximedia.be.
This tastefully converted old Flemish town house, with its plain, high-gabled facade, has none of the fussiness of many of its competitors – both the public areas and the comfortable bedrooms are decorated in bright whites and creams, which emphasize the antique charm of the place. Great location, too, at the junction of two canals near the east end of Spiegelrei. Three star. ❺

Castillion

Map 3, C11. Heilige-Geeststraat 1 ⓣ 050/34 30 01,
Ⓕ 33 94 75,
Ⓦ www.castillion.be.
Two old Flemish houses, with high crow-stepped gables, have been transformed into this neat hotel across from the cathedral. Just twenty small

but comfortable bedrooms with spruce and modern furnishings. The public areas are done out in a repro antique style that can be a little overpowering. Four star. ❻

Crowne Plaza Brugge

Map 3, F8. Burg 10 ⓣ 050/44 68 44, Ⓕ 44 68 68,
Ⓦ www.crowneplaza.com.
This prestigious four-star hotel, overlooking the Burg, occupies a good-looking modern building whose architectural features are designed to blend in with its historic surroundings. Every facility, but then that is hardly surprising when the top-whack for a double room is a staggering €407. The cheapest rooms weigh in at about €200. ❾

Dante

Map 2, H10. Coupure 29
ⓣ 050/34 01 94, Ⓕ 34 35 39,
Ⓦ www.hoteldante.be.
A little off the beaten track – but none the worse for that and still within ten minutes'

walk of the Markt – the *Dante* is a well turned-out, modern hotel built in traditional style with dormer windows and so forth. The twenty rooms are reasonably large with crisp patterned furnishings and lots of wicker chairs. The hotel overlooks one of the city centre's wider canals, which is still used by heavy-laden barges. Three star. ⑥

Die Swaene

Map 3, G8. Steenhouwersdijk 1 ⓣ 050/34 27 98, ⓕ 33 66 74, ⓦ www.dieswaene-hotel.com. The unassuming brick exterior of this long-established, family-run hotel is deceptive as the rooms beyond are luxuriously furnished in antique style. The location is perfect too, beside a particularly pretty section of canal a short walk from the Burg – which partly accounts for its reputation as one of the city's most "romantic" hotels. Pool and sauna. Four star. ⑨

Duc de Bourgogne

Map 3, F9. Huidenvettersplein 12 ⓣ 050/33 20 38, ⓕ 34 40 37, ⓔ duc@ssi.be.

The hotel's pride and joy is its restaurant-cum-breakfast room overlooking a particularly picturesque slice of canal close to the Burg. The public rooms are in a heavy-duty neo-baronial style somewhere between kitsch and imposing. Just ten rooms – ask for one with a canal view. To be avoided in summer, though, when herds of tourists devour the surrounding streets. Three star. ⑥

Egmond

Map 2, E13. Minnewater 15 ⓣ 050/34 14 45, ⓕ 34 29 40, ⓦ www.egmond.be.

There are only eight bedrooms in this rambling old house which stands in its own gardens just metres from the Minnewater on the southern edge of the city centre. The interior has wooden beamed ceilings and fine eighteenth-century chimneypieces, harking back to the days when it was a manor house. Attractive rooms in a quiet location at surprisingly affordable prices. Three star. ⑥

BRUGES: HOTELS

Navarra

Map 3, C6. St Jakobsstraat 41
Ⓣ 050/34 05 61, Ⓕ 33 67 90,
Ⓦ www.hotelnavarra.com.
Polished four-star hotel
occupying a grand Georgian
mansion with a delightful
wrought-iron staircase of
craning swans and high-
ceilinged public rooms. Almost
ninety bedrooms decorated in
brisk, modern style. Pool,
sauna and fitness area. Set
back from the road, behind
its own courtyard, and just a
short walk from the Markt. A
Great Western hotel. ❼

Orangerie, de

Map 3, E10.
Kartuizerinnenstraat 10
Ⓣ 050/34 16 49, Ⓕ 33 30 16,
Ⓦ www.hotelorangerie.com.
Excellent four-star hotel in a
surprisingly quiet location a
couple of minutes south of
the Burg. The original
eighteenth-century mansion
has been remodelled and
extended to house nineteen
elegant bedrooms – several of
which are quite small – and
there's a charming terrace bar
at the back overlooking the
canal. ❾

Relais Oud Huis Amsterdam

Map 3, F5. Spiegelrei 3
Ⓣ 050/34 18 10, Ⓕ 33 88 91.
Smooth, tastefully turned out
hotel in a grand eighteenth-
century mansion overlooking
the Spiegelrei canal. Many of
the furnishings and fittings
are period, but more so in
the public areas than in the
(34) rooms. Four star. ❾

Hotel Ter Brughe

Map 3, E3. Oost-Gistelhof 2
Ⓣ 050/34 03 24, Ⓕ 33 88 73.
Ⓦ www.hotelterbrughe.com.
In an old and dignified
merchant's house overlooking
one of the prettiest canals in
the city – and metres from
the Augustijnenbrug bridge –
this smart, four-star hotel has
opted for a minimalist,
modern refurbishment, with
bare wood floors and pastel-
painted walls. The (24) rooms
are comfortable and well-
appointed, though quite what
the old English prints (of
hunting, Queen Victoria etc)
are doing on the walls is hard
to fathom. A very pleasant
place to stay. ❻

Tuilerieën, de

Map 3, F10. Dijver 7 Ⓣ050/34 36 91, Ⓕ34 04 00.
Occupying an old and tastefully refurbished mansion close to the Burg, this delightful hotel is one of the best in town. Some rooms overlook the Dijver canal. Breakfast is taken in a lovely neo-Baroque salon. Four star and 45 rooms. ❾

Walburg

Map 3, H7. Boomgaardstraat 13 Ⓣ050/34 94 14, Ⓕ33 68 84.
Engaging hotel in an elegant nineteenth-century mansion – with splendidly large wooden doors – a short walk east of the Burg along Hoogstraat. The rooms are smart and comfortable, and there are also capacious suites. ❽

HOTELS (UNDER €80)

- - - - - - - - - - - - - - - - - - - -

Bauhaus Hotel

Map 2, H6. Langestraat 133 Ⓣ050/34 10 93, Ⓕ33 41 80, Ⓦwww.bauhaus.be.
Adjacent to the *Bauhaus Hostel* (see p.135), this one-star hotel offers 21 very spartan rooms, just one of which is en suite. Its popularity with backpackers is due to the prices, with singles at €26, doubles €40, triples €57 and quadruples for €70. Don't expect too much in the way of creature comforts, but the atmosphere is usually very agreeable, the clientele (usually) friendly. ❸

Cordoeanier

Map 3, E7. Cordoeaniersstraat 18 Ⓣ050/33 90 51, Ⓕ34 61 11, Ⓦwww.cordoeanier.be.
Medium-sized, family-run hotel handily located in the narrow side-streets a couple of minutes north of the Burg. Mosquitoes can be a problem here, but the small rooms are clean and pleasant. Two star. ❹

De Goezeput

Map 3, C12. Goezeputstraat 29 Ⓣ050/34 26 94, Ⓕ34 20 13.
Outstanding, two-star hotel in an immaculately refurbished, eighteenth-century convent, complete with wooden beams and oodles of antiques. Charming location, on a

BRUGES: HOTELS

quiet street near the cathedral. Fifteen en-suite rooms. Relatively new, so don't be surprised if prices go up once it's better known, but currently a snip. ❹

Europ

Map 3, D4. Augustijnenrei 18 ⓣ050/33 79 75, ⓕ34 52 66, ⓦwww.hoteleurop.com. This dignified late nineteenth-century townhouse overlooks a canal about five minutes' walk north of the Burg. The public areas are somewhat frumpy and the modern bedrooms are a little too spartan, but it's a pleasant place to stay all the same. Two star. ❺

Imperial

Map 3, B11. Dweersstraat 24 ⓣ050/33 90 14, ⓕ34 43 06. Nothing out-of-the-ordinary, but this old terrace house offers a handful of perfectly adequate en-suite rooms at a reasonable price – note that they are much more appealing than those in the annexe. A couple of doors down from the *Passage* hotel and hostel (see below). No credit cards. Two star. ❹

Jacobs

Map 3, F2. Baliestraat 1 ⓣ050/33 98 31, ⓕ33 56 94, ⓦwww.hoteljacobs.be. Pleasant hotel in a creatively modernized old brick building complete with a precipitous crowstep gable. Occupies a quiet location in one of the more attractive parts of the centre, a ten-minute walk to the northeast of the Markt via Jan van Eyckplein. Twenty-three rooms decorated in brisk modern style, though some are really rather small. Three star. ❹

Passage Hotel

Map 3, B11. Dweersstraat 28 ⓣ050/34 02 32, ⓕ34 01 40. Simple but well-maintained rooms a ten-minute stroll west of the Markt. A real steal, with en-suite doubles for just €50, shared facilities from €35, as well as three-bed (€45) and four-bed (€50) rooms. It's a very popular spot and there are only ten rooms (four en suite) so advance reservations are pretty much essential. The *Passage* also has a busy bar that's a favourite with backpackers. Next door is the *Passage Hostel* (see opposite). ❷

De Pauw

Map 3, F2. St Gilliskerkhof 8
ⓣ 050/33 71 18, ⓕ 34 51 40,
ⓦ www.hoteldepauw.be.
Not a particularly exciting hotel perhaps, but this competent two-star

establishment occupies an unassuming brick building in a pleasant, quiet part of town across from the church of St Gillis. Has eight sparse but perfectly adequate rooms, six en suite. Closed Jan. ❸

't Speelmanshuys

Map 3, A11. 't Zand 3
ⓣ 050/33 95 52, ⓕ 33 95 52.
Sparse rooms popular with budget travellers – and mosquitoes from the adjacent canal. Ten minutes' walk west of the Markt. One star. ❸

HOLIDAY APARTMENTS

Holiday apartments, available for both long- and short-term rental, are increasingly a feature of the Bruges tourist industry. The comprehensive accommodation brochure issued by the city's tourist office details about forty of them, with prices ranging from as little as €350 per week for two people (€425 for four) up to around €450 (€600). The tourist office does not, however, arrange holiday-apartment lettings – these must be arranged direct with the lessor. As ever, advance booking is strongly advised. Two B&B operators – Mr & Mrs Dieltiens and Mr & Mrs Gheeraert (see p.134) – operate good-quality holiday apartments, the first at Peerdenstraat 16 (from €350 per week for two; Map 3, G7), the second at Riddersstraat 18 (from €385 for two; Map 3, G7).

BRUGES: HOTELS

BED & BREAKFASTS

Bistro Die Maene

Map 3, D8. Markt 17 ⓣ 050/33 39 59, ⓕ 33 44 60, ⓦ huyzediemaene.be. Above a brasserie plum in the centre of town, with two well-appointed, en-suite rooms decked out in comfortable style. Open all year; credit cards accepted. ❺

Het Wit Beertje

Map 2, A10. Witte Beerstraat 4 ⓣ & ⓕ 050/45 08 88, ⓔ jp.defour@worldonline.be. Cosy little guesthouse-cum-B&B with three, en-suite rooms. Each room has a TV and a phone. No credit cards. Located just outside – and west of – the city centre, off Canadaplein, beyond the Smedenpoort. Open all year. ❸

Mrs Degraeve

Map 2, I8. Kazernevest 32 ⓣ & ⓕ 050/34 57 11, ⓦ www.stardekk.com/bedbreakfast. Two en-suite rooms pleasantly decorated in attractive modern style. On the eastern edge of town, not far from the Kruispoort, which means that you miss the tourist droves, but it's a fair old hike to the Markt. No credit cards. Open all year. ❸

Mr & Mrs Gheeraert

Map 3, G6. Riddersstraat 9 ⓣ 050/33 56 27, ⓕ 34 52 01, ⓔ paul.gheeraert@skynet.be. The three en-suite guest rooms here are immaculate, smart and precise with TVs and refrigerators. They occupy the top floor of a creatively modernized old house a short walk east from the Burg. No credit cards. Closed January. ❸

Salvators

Map 3, B12. Korte Vulderstraat 7 ⓣ 050/33 19 21, ⓕ 33 94 64, ⓦ www.hotelsalvators.be. Operated in tandem with the eponymous hotel, just round the corner on St Salvatorskerkhof, this smart guesthouse-cum-B&B offers three rooms, two en suite. Occupies an attractive, well-maintained, three-storey brick house in a handy location, metres from the cathedral. ❸–❹

Mr Van Nevel

Map 3, H3. Carmersstraat 13 ⓣ 050/34 68 60, ⓕ 34 76 16, ⓔ robert.vannevel@advalvas.be. A few euros cheaper than many of its rivals, this B&B has two unassuming guest rooms with shared bathroom. Situated in an appealing part of town near the Spiegelrei canal. No credit cards. Open all year. ❸

HOSTELS AND CAMPING

Bauhaus International Youth Hostel

Map 2, H6. Langestraat 135 ⓣ 050/34 10 93, ⓕ 33 41 80, ⓦ www.bauhaus.be. Laid-back hostel with few discernible rules, several dormitories, sleeping up to eight apiece, and a mish-mash of double and triple rooms. Not for the fastidious. There's bike hire, currency exchange and coin-operated lockers. The popular downstairs bar serves filling portions of food. The hostel is situated about fifteen minutes' walk east of the Burg, next to the bargain-basement *Bauhaus Hotel* (see p.131). From €13 per person for a dorm bed.

Camping Memling

Veltemweg 109 ⓣ & ⓕ 050/35 58 45, ⓦ www.camping -memling.be. The more agreeable of the city's two (outlying) campsites, the Memling backs onto a chunk of forest a couple of kilometres east of the Markt, out along Maalsesteenweg, the N9. Take bus #11 from the train station. It is open all year. The overnight charge per person is €2.80, plus tents €2.50–3.30, cars €3.30, caravans €3.40.

Charlie Rockets

Map 3, G7. Hoogstraat 19 ⓣ 050/33 06 60, ⓕ 34 36 30, ⓦ www.charlierockets.com. New kid on the hostel block that steals a march on its rivals by being so much closer to the Markt. Has eleven rooms on two upper floors in a variety of shapes and sizes, and with a capacity for 44. All was spick and span when it opened, but quite what the hostellers will make of – or do to – it remains to be seen. Above a busy American-style bar, so light sleepers may need to consider their options. Dormitory beds from €13, €15 with breakfast. Doubles, including breakfast, €43.

International Youth Hostel Europa

Baron Ruzettelaan 143 ⓣ 050/35 26 79, ⓕ 35 37 32, ⓦ www.vjh.be.

Big, modern HI-affiliated hostel in its own grounds, a (dreary) 2km south of the centre in the suburb of Assebroek. Over two hundred beds in a mixture of rooms from singles through to six-bed dorms. Breakfast is included in the overnight fee. Lockout 10am–1pm, till 5pm on Sunday; open all year except from Christmas to mid-January. Local, city bus #2, from the train station goes within 100 metres – ask the driver to let you off. Dorm beds €12.50.

Passage

Map 3, B11. Dweersstraat 26 ⓣ 050/34 02 32, ⓕ 34 01 40. The most agreeable hostel in Bruges. Accommodates fifty people in ten comparatively comfortable dormitories, but all with shared bathrooms. Located in an old and interesting part of town, about ten minutes' walk west of the Markt. The *Passage Hotel* next door is also a bargain – see p.132. Rates from €14 for a dorm bed.

GHENT

Compared to Bruges, **GHENT** is small beer when it comes to accommodation. The city has just twenty or so **hotels**, ranging from the delightful to the mundanely modern with several of the most stylish and enjoyable – but not necessarily the most expensive – located in the centre, which is where you want to be. There's also a cluster of less expensive hotels around the train station, but you really miss the atmosphere of the town down here. Chain hotels are more prevalent in Ghent than Bruges, but not to the exclusion of more individualistic places, and everywhere standards are usually high, though the rooms tend to be a tad cramped. Also unlike Bruges, the competition between hotels is low-key and consequently few hoteliers bother to fancify their foyers to attract visitors, but the same cautions as before apply when it comes to being allocated a room you consider sub-standard (see p.127). In all but the cheapest hotels, breakfast is included in the room rate. In addition, Ghent tourist office has the details of a modest range of **B&Bs** – reckon on €40–60 per double – and operates a hotel and B&B **accommodation service** (see p.125), which is especially useful in July and August, when vacant rooms are thin on the ground. Other bargain options in Ghent are the bright, cheerful and centrally located **youth hostel**, the several hundred **student rooms** offered to visitors by the university during the summer recess, and a large, suburban **campsite**.

HOTELS (OVER €80)

Boatel
Map 6, M6. Voorhuitkaai 29A
ⓣ 09/267 10 30, ⓕ 267 10 39,
ⓦ www.theboatel.com.
Certainly the most distinctive of the city's hotels – and in some ways the best – the *Boatel* is, as its name implies, a converted boat, an imaginatively and immaculately refurbished canal barge to be precise. The seven bedrooms are decked out in crisp, modern style – five standard at €95 and two deluxe at €119 – and breakfasts, taken on the deck, are first rate. The boat is moored in one of the city's outer canals, a ten- to fifteen-minute walk east from the centre. Two star. Recommended. ❺

GHENT: HOTELS

Golden Tulip Alfa Flanders

Map 5, A11. Koning Albertlaan 121 ⓣ 09/222 60 65, ⓕ 220 16 05, ⓦ www.goldentulip hotels.nl/gtgent.

Smart, four-star chain hotel with 49 commodious rooms. Popular with visiting business folk, but a good fifteen-minute walk from the centre. Near St Pieters station. **❺–❾**

Erasmus

Map 6, C5. Poel 25 ⓣ 09/224 21 95, ⓕ 233 42 41, ⓔ hotel .erasmus@proximedia.be.

Another contender for Ghent's most distinctive hotel, located in an old and commodious town house a few yards away from the Korenlei. A small family-run affair with each room thoughtfully decorated – though it's a touch twee in places – and furnished with antiques. The breakfast is excellent and the family friendly. Reservations strongly advised in summer. One star, but this rating does it precious little justice. Closed mid-Dec to mid-Jan. **❺**

Gravensteen

Map 6, D3. Jan Breydelstraat 35 ⓣ 09/225 11 50, ⓕ 225 18 50, ⓦ www.gravensteen.be.

Medium-sized, conducive hotel centred in an attractively restored nineteenth-century mansion adorned with Second Empire trimmings. Great location, close to the castle. The rooms in the annexe and in one wing of the original building are smart and relatively spacious with crisp and pleasing modern furnishings. Several of the older rooms are, however, poky beyond belief. Three star. **❼**

Novotel Centrum

Map 6, G5. Goudenleeuwplein 5 ⓣ 09/224 22 30, ⓕ 224 32 95, ⓦ www.novotel.com.

First-class modern, chain hotel bang in the middle of the town centre. The rooms are neat and trim, decorated in fetching if standard chain style. Has an outdoor swimming pool and offers good breakfasts. Three star. **❼**

Poortackere Monasterium

Map 6, B7. Oude Houtlei 58
ⓣ 09/269 22 10, ⓕ 269 22 30,
ⓦ www.poortackere.com.
This unusual hotel-cum-guest-house occupies a rambling and frugal former monastery, whose dusty brickwork dates from the nineteenth century. The complex includes a modest neo-Gothic chapel, but guests don't stay here. Instead they have a choice between spick and spartan, en-suite rooms in the hotel section (€120); or the more authentic monastic-cell experience in the guest house, either en suite (€95) or with shared facilities (€86). Breakfast is taken in the old chapter house. *Poortackere* is located about five minutes' walk west of Veldstraat. One star. ❺

St Jorishof-Cour St Georges

Map 6, H5. Botermarkt 2
ⓣ 09/224 24 24, ⓕ 224 26 40,
ⓦ www.courtstgeorges.com.
Facing the Stadhuis, the main building dates from the thirteenth century and is notable for its sturdy Romanesque facade, equipped with a slender crow-step gable and mullioned windows. The interior is all neo-baronial, with acres of late nineteenth-century panelling. The rooms inside the main building are decorated in broadly period style (❻), but most of the 36 rooms are in a nearby annexe and are best described as adequate to plain. One star. ❺

Sofitel Gent Belfort

Map 6, H5. Hoogpoort 63
ⓣ 09/233 33 31, ⓕ 233 11 02,
ⓦ www.sofitel.com.
One of the plushest hotels in town, daintily shoehorned behind an ancient facade across from the Stadhuis. Spacious, pastel-shaded rooms and suites as well as all mod cons, including good fitness facilities. Four star. Inquire direct for discounts. ❾

HOTELS (UNDER €80)

Adoma

St Denijslaan 19 ⓣ09/222 65 50, ⓕ245 09 37, ⓦwww.hotel-adoma.be.

Routine modern three-star with fifteen neat and trim rooms, all en suite, about 500m behind – and to the west of – the main train station. Hardly an exciting option, but perfectly adequate. ❸

Brooderie

Map 6, D4. Jan Breydelstraat 8 ⓣ09/225 06 23.

The Brooderie is an appealing café (see p.154) handily located near the Korenmarkt and its owners rent out three neat and trim little rooms above it. B&B costs €62 for the two double rooms, €37 for the single. Breakfast is excellent.

Chamade

Map 5, C14.
Blankenbergestraat 2 ⓣ09/220 15 15, ⓕ221 97 66, ⓦwww.bestwestern.be.

A chain hotel situated about five minutes' walk north of the train station. Standard three-star accommodation in bright, modern bedrooms, though the building itself – a six-storey block – is a bit of an eyesore. Prices are in the lower range of this price code and there are weekend discounts of twenty percent.

Flandria Centrum

Map 6, J6. Barrestraat 3 ⓣ09/223 06 26, ⓕ233 77 89, ⓦwww.flandria-centrum.be.

Somewhat dishevelled hotel located in the narrow sidestreets off the Reep, a five-minute walk northeast of the cathedral. Apart from the youth hostel, these are the least expensive rooms in the city centre. All sixteen (modest) rooms are en suite. One star. ❸

Ibis Centrum Kathedraal

Map 6, I7. Limburgstraat 2 ⓣ09/233 00 00, ⓕ233 10 00, ⓦwww.ibishotel.com.

Handily situated opposite the cathedral, this large hotel – one of the *Ibis* chain – offers comfortable modern rooms, though the noise from the square in front of the hotel can be irritating late at night – ask for a room at the back. Three star. ❹

Ibis Centrum Opera

Map 5, D7. Nederkouter 24–26 ⓣ 09/225 07 07, ⓕ 223 59 07, ⓦ www.ibishotel.com.
Spick and span, modern, five-storey block a five-minute walk south of the Korenmarkt. The rooms lack character, but they're perfectly functional and typical of this popular, reasonably priced chain. Three star. A few euros less than its more central rival. ❹

New Carlton Gent

Map 5, B14. Koningin Astridlaan 138 ⓣ 09/222 88 36, ⓕ 220 49 92.
Competent, mid-range, three-star, modern hotel in a six-storey block near the main train station. Nineteen rooms, all en suite. ❹

Trianon I

Sint Denijslaan 203 ⓣ 09/220 48 40, ⓕ 220 49 50,
ⓦ www.hoteltrianon.be.
Motel-style accommodation on a quiet residential street about 2km south of the centre, just beyond Ghent St Pieters train station. The nineteen rooms are comfortable and spotless, and all are en suite, but for "stylish and intimate" in their advertising, read overdone. One star. ❸

Trianon II

Voskenslaan 34 ⓣ 09/220 48 40, ⓕ 220 49 50, ⓦ www.hoteltrianon.be.
Similar to Trianon I, 50m away, though the rooms are a tad more commodious – and you're beside a much busier road. Nineteen rooms, all en suite. Two star. ❹

CAMPING, HOSTELS AND STUDENT ROOMS

- -

Camping Blaarmeersen

Zuiderlaan 12 ⓣ 09/221 53 99, ⓕ 222 41 84.
Among the woods beside the watersports centre to the west of town (bus #38 from

GHENT: HOTELS • CAMPING, HOSTELS AND STUDENT ROOMS

Korenmarkt; 10min), this large campsite is well equipped with laundry, shop, cafeteria and various sports facilities. Open March to mid-Oct. High season rate per person per night is €3 (low season €2.70), cars €1.60 (€1.50), tent or caravan €3.20 (€3).

Jeugdherberg De Draecke

Map 6, D2. St Widostraat 11 ⓣ 09/ 233 70 50, ⓕ 233 80 01, ⓔ youthhostel.gent@skynet.be. Excellent, well-equipped and smart youth hostel in the city centre, a five-minute walk north of the Korenmarkt. Over a hundred beds, in two-, three-, four-, five- and six-bed rooms. Advance reservations are advised especially in the height of the season. A single room costs €20, double €29 and a dormitory for six costs €74. A dorm bed on its own costs

€13. Breakfast is included, and the restaurant offers lunch and dinner too. There are lockers, currency exchange, bike rentals and a bar.

Universitaire Homes

Map 5, F12. Several addresses including Stalhof 4 and 6; general information and reservations on ⓣ 09/264 71 12, ⓕ 264 72 96.
Between mid-July and late September, over a thousand student rooms are let to visitors for €15 per person per night including breakfast. The rooms are dotted around the south of town in a number of complexes; ask at the tourist office for further details or enquire direct. The most central complexes are Home Vermeylen, Stalhof 6 and Home Fabiola, Stalhof 4. Stalhof is a good fifteen minutes' walk south of the centre via Overpoortstraat.

Eating

Both Bruges and Ghent boast an extraordinary number of **restaurants** and **cafés**, ranging from deluxe establishments, where you can sample exquisite Flemish and French cuisine, through to rudimentary places serving up filling meals at bargain-basement prices. The distinction between these restaurants and cafés is actually rather blurred – the only important distinction being that the former are usually more expensive and a tad more formal than the latter – but mercifully very few are owned by chains. The result is that the vast majority of places are small and cosy, with the chef – or chef-owner – hovering around to make sure everything is up to scratch.

The better Flemish chefs are eclectic, dipping into many other cuisines, especially those of the Mediterranean, and also borrowing freely from France – and, for that matter, the French-speaking regions of Belgium. This enlivens many a menu as Flemish food is characteristically plain and simple, though, in fairness, there are many interesting traditional dishes (see box overleaf). Pork, beef, game, fish and seafood, especially mussels, remain the staple items of Flemish food, often cooked with butter, cream and herbs, or sometimes beer – which is, of course, the Belgian national drink. Soup is also common, hearty stew-like affairs offered in a huge tureen from which you can help

FLEMISH SPECIALITIES

After decades in the doldrums, the regional cuisine of Flanders has experienced an extraordinary revival and in both Ghent and Bruges there are now lots of restaurants specializing in **Flemish food**. Local dishes worth seeking out include the following:

Hutsepot is a winter-warmer dish: various bits of beef and pork (including pigs' trotters and ears) are casseroled with turnips, celery, leeks and parsnips.

Karbonaden comprises cubes of beef marinated in beer and cooked with herbs and onions.

Konijn met pruimen is an old Flemish standby of rabbit with prunes.

Paling in 't groen consists of eel braised in a green – usually spinach – sauce with herbs.

Stoemp is mashed potato mixed with vegetable and/or meat purée.

Stoverij comprises stewed beef and offal – especially liver and kidneys – slowly tenderized in dark beer and served with a slice of bread covered in mustard.

Waterzooi is a delicious and filling soup-cum-stew, which is served with either chicken (*van kip*) or fish (*van riviervis*).

yourself – a satisfying and reasonably priced meal in itself. **English speakers** will find that most waiters speak at least a modicum of their language – many are fluent – and multilingual menus are commonplace. **Prices** run the gamut, but a filling main course in a café or cheaper restaurant should cost €7–12, and €15–20 in a mid-range restaurant.

The list of cafés and restaurants below gives opening times along with **holiday closures**, where these are fixed. Most places close for a week or two over the winter and many shut down for a summer break as well. **Telephone numbers** are only given where reservations are required or advised. To assist with the deciphering of menus, a Flemish glossary of food and drink terms is given on pp.311–315.

BRUGES

In **Bruges**, most of the cafés and restaurants are geared up for the tourist industry. Standards are very variable, with a whole slew of places churning out some pretty mediocre stuff to cater for the enormous number of day-trippers. There are, of course, lots of exceptions – including the places we recommend below – but the city's special strength is its top-quality restaurants, amongst which are several prestigious establishments that are generally reckoned to be among the best in the whole of Belgium – no mean feat in such a gastronomic country. The other problem is the crowds that make many city-centre establishments well-nigh unbearable in the peak season. The tourist hordes congregate in the Markt, the Burg and in the Begijnhof, leaving locals to gather in the more distinctively Flemish places tucked among the quieter streets of the rest of the centre.

Den Amand
Map 3, D8. St Amandstraat 4 ☎050/34 01 22.
Tues & Thurs–Sun noon–3pm & 6–10pm, plus Wed noon–3pm. Cosy, family-run restaurant beginning to establish a name for itself for its inventive cuisine, combining both French and Flemish traditions. Limited but well-chosen menu – swordfish, rack of lamb – with main courses averaging about €20.

Decorated in pleasant modern style and footsteps from the Markt. It's a small place, so book a few hours or so in advance.

Aneth

Map 2, A6. Maria van Bourgondiëlaan 1 ☎ 050/31 11 89.
Tues–Fri noon–7pm & Sat 4–7pm.

Gourmet restaurant with a showcase menu, featuring all sorts of imaginative dishes with pork and seafood high on the list – langoustines with a Guinness vinaigrette (at €23) is a good example. Set menus from €27, main courses from €20. Occupies a solid suburban building on the west edge of the centre, about ten minutes' walk north of 't Zand. Popular with a local clientele, so reservations are strongly advised.

Den Braamberg

Map 3, G10. Pandreitje 11 ☎ 050/33 73 70.
Mon–Wed & Fri–Sat noon–2pm & 7–9.30pm.

Polished restaurant in a good-looking eighteenth-century mansion a short walk south of the Burg. French-based cuisine served with panache and dreamed up by an award-winning chef. Set evening menus can go as high as €85, but begin at a much more affordable €45, the same price as lunch. Main courses cost around €25–35. Three house specialities are lobster, cod and veal in several different preparations.

Cafedraal

Map 3, C11. Zilverstraat 38 ☎ 050/34 08 45.
Tues–Sat 11.30am–2am, food served from 11am–2pm & 6.30–11pm.

Fashionable and tremendously popular restaurant decked out in ersatz medieval style. Big open fire in winter, outside garden terrace in summer. A lively menu runs the gamut of French and Flemish dishes, but it's hard to beat the North Sea bouillabaisse, the lobster and the veal cooked in mustard. Shares its premises with the *Cohiba* bar (see p.162). Located at the west

BRUGES: EATING

end of Zilverstraat, near the junction with Steenstraat.

Het Dagelijks Brood

Map 3, E7. Philipstockstraat 21.

Mon & Wed–Sat 7am–6pm, Sun 8am–6pm.

Excellent bread shop which doubles as a wholefood café with one long wooden table – enforced communalism, which can be good fun – and a few smaller side tables too. Mouth-watering homemade soup and bread makes a meal in itself for just €7, or you can chomp away on a range of snacks and cakes. Part of a small chain – Het Dagelijks Brood in Flemish-speaking Belgium, Pain Quotidien in the French regions. Very handy location, just off the Burg.

Le Due Venezie

Map 3, D9. Kleine Sint Amandstraat 2 ⊤ 050/33 23 26. Daily except Tues noon–2.30pm & 6–10pm.

Long-established Italian restaurant serving up all the classics at reasonable prices with main courses in the region of €12–18, though spaghetti costs as little as €7, pizzas from €6. Occupying an attractive old house close to the Markt, it prides itself on its rustic atmosphere – lit by candles and with wine bottles hanging all over the place. The same family run La Pasta, an Italian shop just along the street at no. 12 (see p.185).

Den Dyver

Map 3, F10. Dijver 5 ⊤ 050/33 60 69.

Daily noon–2pm & 6.30–9pm, but closed Wed & Thurs lunch.

Top-flight restaurant specializing in traditional Flemish dishes cooked in beer – the quail and rabbit are magnificent, though the seafood runs them close. Mains are around €25. The decor is plush and antique with tapestries on the wall beneath an ancient wood-beam ceiling. The service is attentive, but not unduly so, and the only real negative is the music/muzak which can be dire. Popular with an older clientele. Reservations advised.

BRUGES: EATING

Gran Kaffee de Passage

Map 3, B11. Dweersstraat 26
ⓣ 050/34 02 32.

Daily 6pm–midnight.

Seating seventy, this lively café is extremely popular with backpackers, many of whom have bunked down in the *Passage Hostel* (see p.136). Serves up a good and filling line in Flemish food with many dishes cooked in beer. Mussels are featured too, along with vegetarian options. Not much in the way of frills, but then main courses only cost about €10.

De Karmeliet

Map 3, I7. Langestraat 19
ⓣ 050/33 82 59.

Tues–Sat noon–2pm & 7–9.30pm, Sun noon–2pm.

Smooth and polished restaurant – one of the city's best – occupying a big, old mansion about five minutes' walk east of the Burg. A tad formal for many tastes, but there's no disputing the excellence of the service or the quality of the French cuisine, earning *De Karmeliet* three Michelin stars. As you would expect, the menu is stunningly inventive – watch out for the rabbit (*lapin royale*) and the marinated cod. Set menus from €65 and main courses average around €34. Reservations essential.

De Koetse

Map 3, D11. Oude Burg 31
ⓣ 050/33 76 80.

Daily except Thurs noon–2.30pm & 6–10pm, plus frequent extended opening hours in the summer, normally noon–10pm. Low-key, informal restaurant with a straightforward, reasonably priced menu – main courses average around €18. The seafood dishes are more interesting than the meat and, in particular, look out for their eel in spinach sauce and mussels cooked in beer.

L'Intermède

Map 3, B10. Wulfhagestraat 3
ⓣ 050/33 16 74.

Tues–Sat noon–1.30pm & 7–9.30pm.

Tastefully decorated, very chic little restaurant serving exquisite French cuisine with a Flemish twist. Reasonable prices and away from the tourist zone – which is very much to its advantage.

De Lotteburg

Map 3, C12. Goezeputstraat 43 ⓣ 050/33 75 35.

Wed–Fri & Sun noon–2pm & 7–9.30pm, plus Sat 7–9.30pm; last orders 30min before closing. Usually closed for holidays for two weeks from late Jan and again from late July. One of the best restaurants in town – and one of two outstanding fish restaurants (see *De Visscherie* p.151) – this very smart and formal little place has a superb menu. The key is its creativity, with imaginative, carefully prepared dishes like shrimps and truffle oil, sole and mushrooms. Set menus cost an arm and a leg, but main courses average €30–35 – expensive but well worth it. Lunches cost in the region of €30. Don't miss the fish soup. Reservations essential.

Jan van Eyck Restaurant-Tearoom

Map 3, E5. Jan van Eyckplein 12.

Daily except Wed 11.30am–2pm

& 6.30–10.30pm.

This brightly decorated, neat and trim little restaurant-cum-tearoom serves up a tasty line in snacks and light meals. An agreeable location beside one of the city's prettier squares, friendly service and affordable prices, plus thirteen sorts of beer. Main courses work out at about €15–18, but veggie dishes at around €10. Also has a good line in *stoemp*.

Lokkedize

Map 3, B12. Korte Vuldersstraat 33.

Tues–Fri 7pm–2am, Fri & Sat 6pm–3am.

Sympathetic café-bar, all subdued lighting, fresh flowers and jazz music, serving up a good line in Mediterranean food with main courses averaging around €9. Attracts a youthful crowd.

Patrick Devos – De Zilveren Pauw

Map 3, C10. Zilverstraat 41 ⓣ 050/33 55 66.

Mon–Fri noon–1.30pm & 7–9pm, Sat 7–9pm.

One of Bruges's premier restaurants, whose speciality is themed meals, such as Art Nouveau lunches and Belle Epoque dinners. These are the creations of Patrick Devos, a great name in Belgian cooking and the designer of such treats as jelly of seafood perfumed with garlic, and duck with rhubarb. A full meal will set you back at least €60, main courses from about €30. It's a formal – some would say staid – establishment and reservations are essential. To ogle, go to Ⓦ www .patrickdevos.be.

Rochefort

Map 3, I7. Langestraat 15.
Mon, Tues & Thurs–Sat noon–2.30pm & 6–11pm, Sun 6–11pm.
Smart little café-bistro serving up a tasty line of salads, pastas and seafood. Main courses average around €18.

De Snippe

Map 3, G13. Nieuwe Gentweg 53 Ⓣ 050/33 70 70.
Tues–Sat noon–3pm & 7–10pm, plus Mon 7–10pm.

The serious-looking, eighteenth-century facade of the *Hotel De Snippe* barely hints at the cultured extravagance that lies within, all cut flowers, heavy drapes and chandeliers. The hotel restaurant is one of the best in town, *haute cuisine* with an especially strong line in langoustines. Main courses about €30–35.

Spinola

Map 3, E5. Spinolarei 1 Ⓣ 050/34 17 85.
Mon 7–10pm, Tues–Sat noon–1.30pm & 7–10pm.
Immaculate restaurant in a beautiful old building overlooking Jan van Eyckplein, a short stroll north of the Markt. Lively modern menu, featuring unusual sauces and prime delicacies. Main courses average €22–28. The eel is particularly tasty here and so are the steaks. Everything is freshly prepared, so there's some waiting involved, but even so the service can sometimes be a little tardy.

Tanuki

Map 3, E14. Oude Gentweg 1
ⓣ 050/34 75 12.
Wed–Sun noon–2pm &
6.30–9.30pm. Closed two
weeks in Jan & July.

The best Japanese restaurant in
town and, if you've been in
Bruges long, a welcome break
from sauce-laden Belgian
cuisine. All the favourites –
noodles, sushi and sashimi –
served within a suitably Asian
decor. Prices are very
reasonable with noodles
starting at €7 and rising to
€20 for dishes like *teppan yaki*.

Taverne Curiosa

Map 3, E7. Vlamingstraat 22
ⓣ 050/34 23 34.
Tues–Fri 11am–1am, Sat
11am–2am, Sun
noon–midnight.

Occupying an old vaulted
cellar, this popular bar-
restaurant has a very
competent beer list of around
sixty different brews and
offers filling snacks and meals
– the grilled meats are best.
Reasonable prices with dishes
of the day costing about €10.
Located a couple of minutes'
walk north of the Markt.

De Verbeelding

Map 3, E10. Oude Burg 26.
Mon–Sat 11am–11pm.

Low-key, amenable café-bar
serving a reasonably satisfying
range of salads, pastas and
tapas. Few would say the
food was brilliant, but it is
inexpensive and – at its best –
very tasty. Main courses
around €10, half that for
tapas. Handy for the Markt.

De Visscherie

Map 3, F9. Vismarkt 8
ⓣ 050/33 02 12.
Daily except Tues noon–2pm &
7–10pm. Closed for holidays
from late Nov to mid-Dec.

This is the second of the
city's excellent seafood
restaurants, but unlike its rival
– *De Lotteburg*, p.149 – it
manages to be smart and
relaxed at the same time. A
well-presented and
imaginative menu features
such delights as a
spectacularly tasty fish soup
for €15, seafood *waterzooi* for
€25 and cod cooked in a
traditional Flemish style for
€30. The restaurant occupies
a spacious nineteenth-century
mansion a short walk south

of the Burg, but the decor has some intriguing modern touches – small sculptures and so on – and the chairs are supremely comfortable.

De Vlaamsche Pot

Map 3, B9. Helmstraat 3–5. Daily noon–9/10pm.
Informal and friendly, this enjoyable little restaurant, with its cosy furnishings and fittings – red check table clothes and so forth – has quickly become popular. The menu is confined to a few traditional Flemish dishes, each competently prepared and excellent value with prices hovering around €16. Off the main tourist track too.

De Windmolen

Map 2, H4. Carmersstraat 135. Daily except Sat 10am–9pm.
Amiable, neighbourhood joint in an old brick house at the east end of Carmersstraat. Dishes up a decent line in inexpensive snacks and light meals – croque monsieur, spaghetti, lasagne and so forth – and possesses a competent beer menu. Has a pleasant outside terrace and the interior is dotted with folksy knick-knacks, especially ceramic windmills – appropriately, given both the name of the place and its proximity to a quartet of old windmills (see p.76), which perch on the grassy bank that marks the course of the medieval city wall.

GHENT

In **Ghent**, where the press of the tourist is much lighter, the city's numerous cafés and restaurants are usually aimed at the domestic market. Consequently, prices tend to be a little lower and standards are more consistently high and on offer is the very best of Flemish and French cuisine with a sprinkling of Italian, Chinese and Arab places for variety. There is a concentration of deluxe restaurants in and around the narrow lanes of the Patershol quarter and another, of less expensive options, on and around the Korenmarkt.

Amadeus

Map 7, E3. Plotersgracht 8
℡ 09/225 13 85.
Mon–Sat 7pm to midnight, Sun
noon–2.30pm & 6pm–midnight.
In the heart of the Patershol,
this busy, well-established
restaurant specializes in spare
ribs. Long tables, oodles of
stained glass, low ceilings and
an eccentric sprinkling of
bygones makes the place
relaxed and convivial;
booking advised. Main
courses at around €18.

Avalon

Map 7, D4. Geldmunt 32.
Mon–Sat noon–2pm.
This spick and span
vegetarian restaurant offers a
wide range of well-prepared
food served in an
environment popular with
locals for its tranquillity. The
key pull are the daily specials,
which cost about €7. Choose
from one of the many
different rooms or the terrace
at the back in the summer.

Bij den wijzen en den zot

Map 7, E3. Hertogstraat 42
℡ 09/223 42 30.
Tues–Sat noon–2pm &
6.30–10pm.
This is one of the best
restaurants in the Patershol,
serving up delicious Flemish
cuisine with more than a dash
of French flair. Soft lighting
and classical music set the
tone. The premises are
charming too – an old brick
house of tiny rooms and
narrow stairs with dining on
two floors. Prices are
moderate, with main courses
averaging about €18; house
specialities include eel,
cooked in several different
ways, and *waterzooi*.

Bistro 't Keteltje

Map 5, E7. Nederkouter 1
℡ 09/233 22 55.
Mon noon–10pm, Tues, Thurs &
Sun 10am–10pm, Sat 10am–
midnight; closed Wed.
Smart and neat little bistro
with bright-white starched
table cloths and a great line in
salads, both warm and cold.
Reasonable prices – a full set
meal will cost you around
€25. Adjacent to the
Ketelvaart canal – though this
is more an industrial eyesore
than an attraction.

153

Het Blauwe Huis
Map 7, B7. Drabstraat 17
℗ 09/233 10 05.
Mon–Fri noon–2pm & daily
3.30–10pm.
The outside of this restaurant
is painted blue – hence its
name. The interior is calm
and subdued, all candles and
varnished woods plus some of
the finest seafood in the city
at affordable prices – main
courses at around €15. A real
treat.

De Blauwe Zalm
Map 7, E2. Vrouwebroersstraat
2 ℗ 09/224 08 52.
Tues–Fri noon–1.45pm plus
Mon–Sat 7–9.30pm.
Brilliant seafood restaurant –
the best in town – serving up
a superb range of seafood
dishes from the more usual
cod, salmon, monkfish and
haddock through to the likes
of seawolf, sea bass, turbot
and John Dory. Fish tanks
keep the crustacea alive and
kicking, and the decor has a
distinctly maritime feel –
though it's all done in
impeccable, ultra cool style.
Main courses from €20 and
conveniently located in the

Patershol. It's a very popular
spot, so reservations are pretty
much essential. Highly
recommended.

Brooderie
Map 7, B6. Jan Breydelstraat 8.
Tues–Sun 8am–6pm.
Pleasant and informal café
with a health-food slant –
and solid wooden tables.
Wholesome breakfasts,
lunches, sandwiches and
salads from around €7.
Central location, near the
Gravensteen castle.

Casa de Las Tapas
Map 7, F3. Corduwaniersstraat
44.
Mon & Wed–Sat 6–11pm, Sun
noon–11pm.
Popular Patershol restaurant-
cum-bar featuring authentic
Spanish tapas eaten either
standing up or sitting down.
All the classic Spanish stuff is
here – spicy chorizo sausage,
Serrano ham, anchovies,
olives and so forth – and if
you're after something more
substantial you can tuck into
a delicious, steaming paella
amongst a limited menu of
larger dishes. For tapas,

GHENT: EATING

reckon on about €6 each.

Greenway Foods

Map 5, E8. Nederkouter 42.
Mon–Sat 11am–9pm.
Tasty, healthy, fresh and fast is
the motto of this "Enviro-
chic" vegetarian cafe serving
salads, pastas, hot baguettes
and burgers. Sparse interior
with high stools – a veggie
fast-food joint with an
environmental conscience.
Inexpensive.

Gwenola

Map 6, F7. Volderstraat 66.
Mon–Sat 11am–6.30pm.
Not much in the way of
atmosphere – the decor is
plain and functional – but this
busy creperie-café serves up
delicious crepes costing
between €2.50 and €5.
Other city centre branches,
with the same opening hours,
are at Bennesteeg 25A (Map
6, F7) and Donkersteeg 16
(Map 7, E8).

De Hel

Map 7, G3. Kraanlei 81
T 09/224 32 40.
Wed–Sun 6–10pm.
This tiny, intimate restaurant

in the Patershol, enhanced by
candle-lit tables, Tiffany glass
and classical music, offers
delicious Franco-Belgian fare
at affordable prices – main
courses average €20. The
building itself, dating from
1669, is adorned by charming
terracotta reliefs of flying deer
and the five senses topped off
by representations of Faith,
Hope and Charity.

'T Klokhuys

Map 7, G3. Corduwaniersstraat
65 T 09/223 42 41.
Daily noon–2pm & 6–11pm.
One of the cheaper options
in the Patershol district, this
smart and brisk little brasserie
serves tasty and affordable
snacks and meals. Offers a
good range of daily specials,
both Flemish and
international dishes.

Koningshuis

Map 6, C5. St Michielsstraat 31
T 09/225 86 33.
Tues–Sat 6pm–midnight, Sun
6–11pm, but closed the last
Tues of the month.
One-time students' favourite
now smartened up into a
cosy restaurant, refurbished in

GHENT: EATING

style with a stained-wood floor and Flemish bygones decorating the walls. Outstanding Flemish cuisine featuring hormone-free meat and the freshest of produce drawn together in an imaginative menu that includes first-rate vegetarian dishes. Main courses average about €15, but the daily specials are often a good deal less expensive.

Malatesta
Map 7, E8. Korenmarkt 35.
Daily except Tues noon–2.30pm & 6–11pm.
Informally fashionable café-restaurant decorated in strong, modern style and offering tasty pizza and pasta dishes at very affordable prices. Handy location, bang in the centre of the city at the corner of Korenmarkt and Hooiaard.

Marco Polo Trattoria
Map 7, I6. Serpentstraat 11
℡ 09/225 04 20.
Tues–Fri noon–2.30pm & 6–10pm, Sat–Sun 6–10pm.
This simple rustic restaurant is part of the Italian "slow

food" movement and serves delicious organic, seasonal food. The menu is small, but all the dishes are freshly prepared – and well worth waiting for. Inexpensive.

'T Marmietje
Map 7, A7. Drabstraat 30
℡ 09/224 30 13.
Tues–Sat noon–2.30pm & 6–10pm. Usually closed Aug for annual holidays.
Traditional, family-run restaurant specializing in Flemish cuisine – a good place to try *Gentse waterzooi van kip* and *Gentse stoverij*. Somewhat eclipsed by the newer and more fashionable restaurants of the Patershol, it's still a good bet and the prices are lower than most of its rivals. Daily specials average around €9. Convenient location too, just off Korenlei.

Othello Wijnrestaurant
Map 5, E7. Ketelvest 8
℡ 09/233 00 09.
Tues–Fri noon–2pm & 7–10pm, Sat 7–10pm. Closed during the town's main annual knees-up, the Gentse Feesten.

Smart little spot serving up a good range of French dishes with main courses costing about €18. The big attraction is, however, the *Othello*'s excellent wine cellar.

Oud Burg
Map 7, G3. Oudburg 2
⓽ 09/233 34 00.
Mon & Thurs–Sun noon–10pm.
Pint-sized Patershol restaurant with Aladdin's cave decor from the beamed ceiling to the painted chairs. French and Flemish dishes, but the big deal here are the mussels, prepared in a variety of styles. Full meals, excluding wine, from around €30.

Pakhuis
Map 7, D11. Schuurkenstraat 4.
Mon–Sat noon–2.30pm & 6.30pm–midnight.
One of Ghent's most fashionable restaurants, attracting a wide-ranging clientele, the Pakhuis is a lively bistro-brasserie offering an extensive menu – Flemish and French and beyond – with main courses averaging around €15. Smashing

premises too – occupies an intelligently remodelled old warehouse with acres of glass and metal down a narrow alley near St Michielsbrug.

Panda
Map 7, H2. Oudburg 38
⓽ 09/225 0786.
Mon–Sat noon–2pm & 6–9pm.
Entrance to this vegetarian restaurant is through the Panda vegetarian supermarket. Delicious, organic food served in a calm setting overlooking the River Leie. Special lunch menus offered for just €8, evening meals at €14. Children under 6 eat for free.

Patisserie Bloch
Map 6, E7. Veldstraat 60.
Mon–Sat 8am–7.30pm.
Something of a local institution, and a favourite with shoppers for donkey's years, this excellent tearoom offers a lip-smacking variety of cakes and confectioneries, washed down by premium coffees and teas. Snacks are available too – though these are no great shakes – and there's a takeaway service.

GHENT: EATING

157

The decor is really rather ordinary, but if you like cakes you won't give a hoot. On the corner with Voldersstraat.

Du Progres

Map 7, E9. Korenmarkt 10. Mon & Thurs–Sun 11.30am–2.30pm & 6–10.30pm; drinks only 8am to midnight. Generations of tourists have plonked themselves down at this long-established café-restaurant, both outside on the pavement terrace and inside amidst the traditional wood-panelled Flemish decor. It's a pleasant spot and although the food isn't exactly memorable, it's certainly good, solid Flemish fare at moderate prices with steak, cooked in several ways, a house speciality. Daily specials for around €5.

St Jorishof

Map 6, H5. Botermarkt 2 Ⓣ 09/224 24 24. Mon–Fri noon–2.30pm & 7–9.30pm, Sat 7–9.30pm, Sun closed. Across the street from the Stadhuis, this polished restaurant has a healthy reputation for the quality of its traditional Flemish cuisine. The neo-baronial fixtures and fittings and the (comparatively) formal atmosphere are not to everyone's tastes, but this is certainly a very good place to try eel. Set menus at around €40, plus à la carte. Booking strongly advised.

Short Order

Map 7, F7. Hoogpoort 11. Mon–Sat 11.30am–9pm. Retro decor with a wall of orange lamps that look like they've been stolen from the nearest road works, this no-frills veggie café serves pasta and Mediterranean dishes, fresh fruit juices and milkshakes, plus sushi on Fridays and Saturdays. You can take out or eat in and pose in the see- and be-seen window. Inexpensive.

Theatercafé de Foyer

Map 6, H6. St Baafsplein 17. Daily except Tues evening 9.30am–midnight. Brisk and efficient café on the first floor of the municipal theatre, an attractively refurbished building dating from the nineteenth century. The café is especially popular at lunch time, when early birds make a beeline for the window seats overlooking the cathedral. A wide-ranging menu features everything, including pastas, seafood and meat. The daily specials (*dagschotels*) are, at €10, a particularly good bet. The theatre is home to the Nederlands Toneel Gent (NTG), the regional repertory company (see p.177).

Togo
Map 7, E2. Vrouwebroersstraat 21.
Daily except Tues 6.30pm–1am. This idiosyncratic café-restaurant, with its pan-African-meets-New Age look, is strong on vegetarian dishes and offers some

African surprises too, like beef wrapped in bananas. In the Patershol; reasonable prices with main courses averaging €15.

Waterzooi
Map 7, D5. St Veerleplein 2 ⓣ 09/225 05 63.
Daily except Sun & Wed noon–1.30pm & 7–9.30pm. Top-notch, split-level restaurant with pastel-painted walls, a wood-beamed ceiling, dappled lighting and stylish furniture. Mixed menu mostly in the French style offering the freshest of ingredients from beef and lamb through to lobster and monkfish, plus a good side-line in Flemish favourites, such as its namesake *waterzooi*. Main courses weigh in at about €20.

Bars, clubs and live music

Few would say **Bruges' bars** are cutting edge, but neither are they staid and dull – far from it if you know where to go. Indeed, drinking in the city can be a real pleasure and one of the potential highlights of any visit. Here as elsewhere in Belgium, the distinction between the city's **cafés** and bars is blurred, with good beer bars often selling excellent food, and cafés frequently boasting an extensive beer list. Nonetheless, the city's specialist bars – from traditional haunts to sleek modern places – are generally more distinctive than the Euro-style pavement cafés which litter the centre and flank the Markt. In **Ghent**, pavement cafés are much less prominent – there are far fewer tourists – and the city centre boasts a superb range of bars, from antique drinking dens with ceilings stained by centuries of smoke through to down-at-heel students' pubs and slick, modern bars with hi-tech furnishings and fittings. Ghent also has a first-rate **club and live music scene**, with several top-ranking, inventive venues, whereas Bruges struggles to muster up any sort of scene at all, though its handful of places are enjoyable enough.

For information on classical music in both Bruges and Ghent, see the Performing Arts chapter (pp.172–178).

Prices for drinks vary enormously, but as a general rule you can expect to pay over the odds on and around the Markt in Bruges and in the Patershol district of Ghent. Generally, if you're paying more than €2.70 for a draught beer, you're paying too much. Spirits are relatively expensive, with a gin and tonic, for example, costing between €3.50 and €4, though the measures are often generous. **Opening hours** are fairly elastic and although we've given them for each of our recommendations, don't be amazed if the bar you're in sails on past the supposed closing time.

Belgium is famous for its beer and in both Bruges and Ghent all the better bars and cafés have a **beer menu**, the pick of which offer a mind-boggling variety of brews, long enough to strain any liver. There are several hundred types of Belgian beer, but for a starter you could sample our list of the "**Top Twenty Belgian beers**" (see pp.291–295).

BRUGES

BARS, CAFÉ-BARS AND CLUBS

De Bolero
Map 3, G12. Garenmarkt 32
ⓣ 050/33 81 11.
Daily except Thurs 9pm–4am.
Currently the only gay and lesbian bar/club in town, but heteros are welcome too. No admission fee and the drinks are very reasonably priced, even the cocktails. Regular dance evenings with a wide range of sounds, from Abba to house. A brief walk south of the Markt via Wollestraat.

Het Brugs Beertje correct order
Map 3, C10. Kemelstraat 5.
Daily except Wed 4pm–1am.
Small and friendly speciality beer bar that claims a stock of three hundred beers, which aficionados reckon is one of the best selections in Belgium. Five minutes' walk southwest of the Markt, off Steenstraat. Opposite *Het Dreupelhuisje* (see opposite).

Cactus Club
Map 3, C7. Sint-Jacobsstraat 36 ⓣ 050/33 20 14, ⓔ info@cactusmusic.be.
Open for concerts/performances only, but note that the *Cactus* is scheduled to be moved to another, as yet unspecified, location in 2003.
Trendiest club in town – groovy and alternative – featuring all sorts of contemporary and world music both live and with well-known DJs. Especially popular at the weekend. Admission usually costs around €10. The *Cactus* organizes the long-established, three-day Cactusfestival held over the second weekend of July (see p.201).

Café Craenenburg
Map 3, D8. Markt 16.
Daily from 10am till late.
The café-restaurants lining the Markt are preoccupied with the tourist trade, the exception being this old-fashioned place, which still attracts a loyal, local clientele. With its leather and wood panelling, wooden benches and stained glass, the Craenenburg has the flavour of old Flanders and although the daytime-only food is routine, it has a good range of beers, including the locally produced, tangy brown ale Brugse Tripel.

Cohiba
Map 3, C11. Zilverstraat 38.
Tues–Sat 11.30am till early in the morning.
Idiosyncratic bar – attached to the smart ersatz-medieval *Cafedraal Restaurant* (see p.146) – whose sprightly, imaginative decor attracts a fashionable, thirty-something crew. Fantastically popular; drinking garden/den too.

Café Du Phare

Map 2, G2. Sasplein 2
ⓣ050/34 35 90.
Daily except Tues from 11am till early in the morning.
Off the beaten track, near the Museum Onze-Lieve-Vrouw ter Potterie (see p.78) in the northeast corner of the city centre, this busy place offers good food, excellent beers and lovely canal views. Every month or so they offer evening blues concerts – come early to get a seat – and there's a pleasant summer terrace too.

Charlie Rockets

Map 3, G7. Hoogstraat 19.
Daily 8am–4am.
American-style bar – or at least an approximation of it – in the same building as the eponymous hostel (see p.135). Five pool tables, youthful clientele.

Het Dreupelhuisje

Map 3, C10. Kemelstraat 9.
Daily except Tues 6pm–2am.
Tiny and eminently agreeable, laid-back bar specializing in jenevers (gins) and advocaats, of which it has

an outstanding range. Opposite the excellent *Het Brugs Beertje* (see opposite).

De Garre

Map 3, E8. De Garre 1.
Daily noon to midnight or 1am.
Down a narrow alley off Breidelstraat between the Markt and the Burg, this cramped but charming tavern (*estaminet*) has a great range of Belgian beers and tasty snacks. Classical music and magazines add to the relaxed air.

De Hobbit

Map 3, C10. Kemelstraat 8.
Closed Mon & Tues.
Kemelstraat is short, but it's home to two great bars, *Het Dreupelhuisje* and *Het Brugs Beertje* (see opposite). If they're full – as they often are – *De Hobbit* is a third (reserve) option, a laid-back, student-style café-bar that's busy till late. They serve inexpensive food, and many people eat here, but the quality and the service are patchy.

Huisbrouwerij De Halve Mann

Map 3, D14. Walplein 26.

BRUGES: BARS, CAFÉ-BARS AND CLUBS

163

Daily 10am–6pm.

The big and breezy bar of the Huisbrouwerij De Halve Mann brewery is a popular tourist spot largely because of the 45-minute brewery tours. These cost €3.72 per person, including a glass of beer (April–Sept frequent tours from 11am to 4pm; Oct–March at 11am & 3pm). The sharp, pale ale that is the house speciality – Straffe Hendrik (Strong Henry) – is one of Flanders' better brews.

Ma Rica rokk
Map 3, A12. 't Zand 7–8.

No fixed times, but open daily from early in the morning till late at night.

Atmospheric spot with sparse functional decor that has long been a local favourite with students and townies alike. Youthful clientele who enjoy some of the best music in town, with house especially popular. Zippy service, a competent beer menu and summer terrace.

Oud Vlissinghe
Map 3, G4. Blekerstraat 2.
Wed–Sun 11am–midnight.

With its wood panelling, antique paintings and long wooden tables, this is one of the oldest and most distinctive bars in Bruges, thought to date from 1515. Relaxed and easy-going atmosphere with the emphasis on quiet conversation – there are certainly no juke boxes here. Garden terrace too. Situated a five-minute walk from Jan van Eyckplein: follow Spinolarei and it's down a turning on the right.

De Republiek
Map 3, C7. Sint-Jacobsstraat 38.

Daily from 11am till 3am or 4am. Arguably one of the most fashionable and certainly one of the most popular café-bars in town with an arty, sometimes alternative crew. Above the café is the excellent art house cinema Lumière (see p.174). Nice snacks also, including vegetarian and pastas.

De Vuurmolen
Map 3, E6. Kraanplein 5.
Daily 10am–7am.

Not far from the Markt, this crowded, youthful bar is a lively spot with a reasonably wide range of beers and some of the best DJs in town playing a good mix of sounds – techno through house and beyond.

De Werf

Map 2, C3. Werfstraat 108
ⓣ 050/33 05 29,
ⓦ www.dewerf.be.
No set opening hours – ring for programme information or consult the website.
Attractive, welcoming place that is excellent for jazz, showcasing both domestic and international talent. Located about fifteen minutes' walk north of the Markt.

Wijnbar Est

Map 3, B9. Noordzandstraat 34.

Daily except Wed from 5pm till late.
The best wine bar in town with an extensive cellar and over twenty different wines available by the glass every day. Especially strong on New World vintages. Also serves inexpensive, tasty lunches. Sedate atmosphere.

De Wittekop

Map 3, C7. Sint Jakobstraat 14.
Tues–Sat from 10am.
The oldest café in town, the decor an appealing mixture of the tasteful and the kitsch. Small and intimate with classy background music – jazz and blues – plus good food, notably a very tasty bouillabaisse and stews. The narrow staircase leads up to an even cosier little room.

GHENT

BARS, CAFÉ-BARS AND CLUBS

Bardot

Map 6, K5. Oude Beestenmarkt

8 ⓣ 0478/26 20 44.
Wed–Sat 8pm–5am.
This new hip venue is one of the top places to be in Ghent. Regular DJs offer funky house, soft-techno and plenty

of the newest sounds. Great place to end the night or dance till dawn.

Bona Dea

Map 5, F8. Lammerstraat 15
℡ 09/234 16 59.
Mon–Sat from 7pm, closed Sun.

Exotic and warm, and a welcome reprieve on a rainy Belgian evening. *Bona Dea* offers an extensive cocktail menu including "Freya" named after the Scandinavian goddess of fertility. Music and dancing at weekends.

Café Central

Map 7, F7. Hoogpoort 32
℡ 09/222 60 56.
Tues–Sun from 7.30pm.

Merengue, salsa, capirinhas and Cuba Libres are top of the bill at this Latin American bar. If you are feeling even more daring you can venture upstairs for a tango class; if that's not to your taste, the cellar plays retro 70s and R&B to strut your funky stuff to.

Damberd Jazzcafe

Map 7, E9. Korenmarkt 19
℡ 09/329 53 37,
ⓦ www.damberd.be.
Daily from 11am.

Jazz café in the centre of Ghent offering a full programme of concerts, but also a great venue to just meet, chat and have a few drinks. The philosophy of the place is to make everyone welcome and provide good sounds. For more about the programme, see their website.

Decadance

Map 5, F12. Overpoortstraat 76
℡ 09 220 55 76.
Sun–Thurs from 8pm.

Student bars in Ghent are not open at the weekend as most of the students go home, but if you're in Ghent during the week and fancy a night out this is the place to be: there's a Friday night party-feeling on a Tuesday and once inside you wouldn't know what time of day or week it is. Reggae, hip-hop, drum 'n' bass and garage-techno vibes.

't Dreupelkot

Map 7, E6. Groentenmarkt 10.
Daily from 11am.
Cosy bar specializing in

jenever, of which it stocks more than 100 brands, all kept at icy temperatures. Down a little alley, next door to the famous *Het Waterhuis* – see p.171.

Dulle Griet

Map 7, I5. Vrijdagmarkt 50.
Mon from 4.30pm,
Tues–Sun from noon.
A long, dark and atmospheric bar with ceiling rugs, all manner of incidental *objets d'art* – and an especially wide range of beers.

De Grote Avond

Map 5, G1. Huidevetterskaai 40.
Wed–Thurs 6pm–1am, Fri–Sat 6pm–2am, Sun 6pm–midnight.
Traditional bar frequented by the artists of Ghent. A good and wide selection of beers and snacks, and – if you are feeling particularly peckish – they claim to make the city's best spaghetti.

Hopduvel

Map 5, B8. Rokerelstraat 10.
Daily from 11am.
Pub with its own brewery, so dozens and dozens of good

beers guaranteed. Traditional Belgian brasserie decor and a great garden terrace for the summer.

Hotsy Totsy

Map 6, B5. Hoogstraat 1
Ⓣ 09/224 20 12,
Ⓦ www.snow.icestorm.com /hotsytotsy.
Tues–Sun from 8pm, closed Mon.
Singers, comedians, artists, poets – all kinds of entertainment at this venue in the centre of Ghent. Music ranges from traditional Dutch *kleinkunst* – literally "small art", the Dutch equivalent of chanson – to international jazz. It's also a regular venue for the Ghent festival.

Magazijn

Map 6, H2. Penitentenstraat 24
Ⓣ 09/234 07 08,
Ⓦ www.magazijn.be.
Mon–Fri noon–2pm & 6pm–2am, Sat–Sun 6pm–4am.
Culture temple for exhibitions, concerts and a venue for the Ghent festival. See the website for what's on. Good food and lots of vegetarian options.

Minor Swing

Map 6, I2. Ottogracht 56
ⓣ 0486/65 66 82.

Wed–Sun from 5pm, closed Mon and Tues.

New live music venue in this cosy café. Advertised as *the* place for jazz lovers, the line-ups have included some real jazz masters. On a balmy summer evening you can sit outside on the terrace and soak up the atmosphere.

Oliver Twist

Map 6, H6. Sint Baafsplein 8.
Daily from 10am.

Almost every Belgian town has an Irish pub, but not many have the English version. This long-established Dickensian effort, in business for over thirty years, offers a good selection of British beers, including, of course, draught bitter. The cuisine is international – some would say mercifully, considering the reputation of English food in Belgium – with a range of pastas and a distinctly spicy chilli con carne.

Opatuur

Map 5, F13. Citadellaan 51

ⓣ 09/221 11 36.

Daily from 6pm.

Another of the city's jazz joints, with gigs often revolving round the bar's piano. Good atmosphere and excellent music.

Pakhuis

Map 7, D11. Schuurkenstraat 4
ⓣ 09/223 55 55,
ⓦ www.pakhuis.be.

Mon–Thurs 11.30am–1am, Fri–Sat 11.30am–2am.

One of the best spots in town, in an intelligently modernized old warehouse. Try out the restaurant (see p.157), or just head on down to the bar. Check their website for forthcoming gigs and events.

Pane & Amore

Map 5, F8. Lammerstraat 10
ⓣ 09/233 13 63.

Mon–Thurs, Sat–Sun from 5pm, closed Fri.

Near to the Vooruit arts centre (see p.178), this place is ideal for a drink after a show. The ground-floor café regularly offers live music and the upstairs café serves excellent pastas. Closed

Friday for private parties.

Pink Flamingos

Map 6, H4. Onderstraat 55
ⓣ 09/233 47 18.
Mon–Wed &Sun noon to
midnight, Thurs–Sat noon–3am.
Weird and wonderful – the
height of kitsch: film stars,
religion, Barbie-dolls, if it's
cheesy it's somewhere in the
decor. Great place for an
aperitif or to sip one of their
large selection of cocktails.
Recommended.

Pole Pole

Map 5, F8. Lammerstraat 8
ⓣ 09/233 21 73.
Daily from 7pm.
Tropical food and a good
cocktail menu imbibed to a
world music – especially
African – soundtrack.
Dancing too.

Rococo

Map 7, F3. Corduwaniersstraat
57.
Daily from 9pm.
Intimate café attracting a
diverse but always cool
clientele, and a perfect place
to be on a cold winter
evening. Home-made cakes

and amazing hospitality
offered by Betty van de
Rococo herself.

Sous-Sol

Map 7, G8. Hoogpoort 41
ⓣ 09/233 71 70.
Tues–Sat from 9pm.
This cellar café-club is part of
the backbone of hip Ghent.
Moody blue interior and
good music. Sit back and
soak up the ambience or go
all out for a real dance night.

Studioskoop

Map 6, M9. Sint Annaplein 63
ⓣ 09/225 08 45,
ⓦ www.studioskoop.be.
Daily from 7pm, Oct–April Sun
from 2pm.
This laid-back, low-key café,
attached to the Studioskoop
cinema, is also a regular
venue for music – see their
website for forthcoming
concerts.

De Tap en de Tepel

Map 6, D3. Gewad 7.
Closed Sun–Tues & most of
Aug.
Charming, candlelit bar with
an open fire and a clutter of
antique furnishings. Wine is

the main deal here, served with a good selection of cheeses. The name translates as "the Tap and Nipple".

De Tempelier

Map 7, H3. Meersenierstraat 9. Mon–Sat from 11am.

Near the Mad Meg cannon, off Vrijdagmarkt. Few tourists venture into this small, dark and intriguing old bar which offers a vast range of beers at lower-than-usual prices. Sometimes eccentric clientele plus occasional live bands.

Trefpunt

Map 6, I3. Bij Sint Jacobs 18 ℡ 09/233 58 48. Daily from 4pm.

The *Trefpunt* (literally "The Meeting Point") has a regular programme of music, chanson and cabaret featuring both established and new talent. Regular venue for the Ghent festival (see p.201).

De Trollekelder

Map 6, I3. Bij St Jacobs 17. Mon, Wed & Thurs 6pm–1.30am & Fri 4pm–2.30am.

Huge selection of beers in an ancient merchant's house. Dark and atmospheric bar – don't be deterred by the trolls stuffed in the window.

Den Turk

Map 6, H5. Botermarkt 3. Daily from 11am; closed Christmas and New Year and during the Ghent festival.

The oldest bar in the city, a tiny rabbit-warren of a place offering a good range of beers and whiskies and a famous plate of cheese with Ghent mustard. Frequent live music, mainly jazz and blues and a great, if slightly highbrow, atmosphere. The beer menu is particularly good on Trappist brews.

Urga

Map 5, E1. Kartuizerlaan 105 ℡ 09/225 29 45. Thurs–Sun from 7.30pm.

Russian food and music in this unique Ghent-Russian experience. Plenty of vodka to wash down the Russian culinary delicacies and guaranteed Russian music too.

't Velootje

Map 7, G2. Kalversteeg 2.
Tues–Sat from 6pm.
A bar to celebrate what the
Flemish love so much – the
bike. And there are plenty of
them to mark this obsession,
hanging from every wall and
ceiling. Good beer and
atmosphere.

Vooruit

Map 5, F8. St
Pietersnieuwstraat 23. Café-bar:
Mon–Thurs 11.30am–2am, Fri &
Sat 11.30am–3am & Sun
4pm–2am.
In a splendid old building,
dating from 1914, the
Vooruit performing arts
centre has good claim to be
the cultural centre of the city
(at least for the under-40s),
offering a wide-ranging
programme of rock and pop
through to dance (see p.178).
The café is a large barn-like
affair that gets jam-packed till
well in the morning.

Het Waterhuis aan de Bierkant

Map 7, E6. Groentenmarkt 9.
Open daily from 11am.
More than 100 types of beer
are available in this engaging,
canal-side bar, just near the
castle. Be sure to try Stropken
(literally "noose"), a delicious
local brew, named after the
time in 1453 when Philip the
Good compelled the
rebellious city burghers to
parade outside the town gate
with ropes around their
necks. Popular with tourists
and locals alike.

Zodiac Cafe

Map 7, G11. Heilige
Geeststraat 3 ⓣ 09/224 32 07.
Wed–Fri from 8pm, Sat–Sun
from 5pm.
Mixed clientele with a shared
passion for cocktails, both
alcoholic and not. Good
starting point for a night out
in Ghent. Occasional DJs.

GHENT: BARS, CAFÉ-BARS AND CLUBS

Performing arts and film

Keen to entertain its many visitors, **Bruges** puts on a varied programme of **performing arts** mostly as part of its annual schedule of festivals and special events (see Chapter 10). Every year the city welcomes a wide range of artists and their companies in classical music, opera, theatre and dance, pressing into service a number of city-centre buildings for their shows. The two principal venues are the municipal theatre, the Stadsschouwburg, and the gleaming new Concert Hall, the Concertgebouw. **Ghent**, on the other hand, tends to focus on resident talent and is particularly strong on theatre, but it also attracts its share of visiting artists.

In terms of **classical music and opera**, Bruges does not have its own full-blown orchestra or opera company, but it does have a renowned chamber orchestra, the (itinerant) Collegium Instrumentale Brugense. Ghent does rather better, possessing its own opera company as well as three first-rate venues. As for **theatre and dance**, Bruges has one professional theatre group, whilst Ghent has half a dozen, but in both cities dance is primarily provided by visiting performers. Inevitably, most of the theatre on offer is in Dutch, but there are occasional plays in English, whereas – good news for English-speakers – the city's **cinemas** normally show films in the original language with Dutch subtitles as required. Both Bruges and Ghent have excellent arthouse cinemas as well as more mainstream establishments.

There are several ways to find out about **forthcoming concerts and performances**. In Bruges, the tourist office, Burg 11 (April–Sept Mon–Fri 9.30am–6.30pm, Sat & Sun 10am–noon & 2–6.30pm; Oct–March Mon–Fri 9.30am–5pm, Sat & Sun 9.30am–1pm & 2–5.30pm, Ⓣ050/44 86 86, Ⓕ44 86 00, Ⓔtoerisme@brugge.be, Ⓦwww.brugge.be), posts information on its notice boards and website and publishes a free bi-monthly, multi-lingual brochure entitled events@brugge. In addition, the Province of West Flanders, covering Bruges and its surroundings, details cultural events on Ⓦwww.tinck.be – or phone Ⓣ070/22 50 05 – whilst the free and very thorough local **listings magazine** *EXit* has reviews and a detailed calendar. It is published monthly and is widely available in bookshops and assorted outlets – including the tourist office – but it is (almost entirely) in Dutch.

For details of forthcoming events in Ghent, simply head for the tourist office (daily: April–Oct 9.30am–6.30pm; Nov–March 9.30am–4.30pm; Ⓣ09/226 52 32) or consult Ⓦwww.gent.be.

BRUGES

CINEMA

- - - - - - - - - - - - - - - - - - - -

Kennedycomplex
Map 3, C10. Zilverstraat 14
Ⓣ050/33 20 70.

Cinema complex, located in the heart of the city, showing mainstream features. It needs refurbishing, but a brand new cinema complex is about to be built near the railway

---

For better or worse, a new mega-cinema complex is under construction beside Bruges railway station; it is scheduled to open in 2003.

---

station, so it may well be left to wither on the cinematic vine. Four screens.

Lumière

Map 3, C7. Sint Jacobstraat 36
ⓣ 050/34 34 65,
ⓦ http://users.skynet.be/lumière.
Blossoming out of a modest art house initiative in 1996, Lumière is Bruges' premier venue for alternative, cult, foreign and art-house movies, with three screens. Every year they organize the Cinema Novo international film festival (see p.198). In the same building as café *De Republiek* (see p.164).

Van Eyck

Map 2, B10. Smedenstraat 12
ⓣ 050/33 20 11.
Small, mainstream cinema showing mainly English- and Dutch-language films. About ten minutes' walk from the Markt. Good acoustics and a bar – the only one on this shopping street.

Het Zwart Huis (aka Ciné Liberty)

Map 3, D6. Kuipersstraat 23
ⓣ 050/33 20 11.
Right in the centre of town, located in a good-looking old building, this cinema offers the better English and American mainstream films, always in the original English-language version.

CLASSICAL MUSIC AND OPERA, THEATRE AND DANCE

De Biekorf

Map 3, D7. Kuipersstraat 3
ⓣ 050/33 00 50.
Features an enterprising programme of theatre and dance in modest premises. Seating for just one hundred.

Concertgebouw

Map 3, A13. 't Zand
ⓣ 050/44 81 11,
ⓦ www.concertgebouw-brugge .be.

To celebrate its year as a cultural capital of Europe in 2002, Bruges has built itself a gleaming new Concert Hall. Its high spec auditoria will host all the performing arts from opera and classical music through to big-name bands.

HET NET

Map 3, C7. Sint-Jakobstraat 36 ℡ 050/33 88 50.
The city's one and only professional theatre group, headed up by the well-known actor Josse De Pauw,

offers a wide-ranging programme from modern drama through to dance.

Stadsschouwburg

Map 3, D6. Vlamingstraat 29 ℡ 050/44 30 60.
Occupying a big and breezy, neo-Renaissance building dating from 1869, the Stadsschouwburg – the municipal theatre – puts on a wide-ranging programme, including theatre, dance, musicals, concerts and opera.

Based in Bruges, the **Collegium Instrumentale Brugense** is a chamber orchestra that was founded in 1970. The performances dip into many historical periods, but Baroque is its speciality. The conductor, Patrick Peire, directs both the orchestra and the choral singers of the associate **Capella Brugensis**. Singers and players perform all over the world, but look out for their concerts in Bruges, and try to catch them.

GHENT

CINEMA

Decascoop

Map 5, G12. Ter Platen 12

℡ 09/265 0600,
ⓦ www.kinepolis.be.
Owned by the Kinepolis group, who certainly believe that big is beautiful. Over

3000 people can watch a film at any one time in twelve auditoria. Mainstream films and Hollywood blockbusters only.

Sphinx

Map 6, C6. Sint-Michielshelling 3 ⓣ09/225 6086, ⓔsphinx.cinema@pi.be, ⓦwww.weekup.be.

A break from the mainstream, the Sphinx focuses on foreign-language and art-house films. The films are never dubbed, but do carry Dutch sub-titles as appropriate. Centrally located just off the Korenmarkt. The Sphinx café is open Mon–Fri 7pm till late, Sat & Sun 2pm till late.

Studioskoop

Map 6, M9. Sint Annaplein 63 ⓣ09/225 0845, ⓦwww.studioskoop.be.

The cosiest of the city's film venues, but with five screens it still competes well with its larger rivals.

CLASSICAL MUSIC AND OPERA

Handelsbeurs

Map 6, F9. Kouter Wwww.handelsbeurs.be.

Opened in September 2002, this is the city's newest concert hall. Two auditoria plus a canalside café/bistro at the back. Music ranges from the traditional to the experimental, from classics to world music. Next door to the Opera House.

De Rode Pomp

Map 6, J4. Nieuwpoort 59 ⓣ09/223 8289, ⓦwww.cevi.be/rp.

This intimate concert hall is the venue for a variety of classical performances and modern opera. Musicians range from international names to new local talent.

Vlaamse Opera

Map 6, E9. Schowburgstraat 3 ⓣ09/225 24 25, ⓦwww.vlaamseopera.be.

Ghent's recently restored opera house has twinned up with the Antwerp opera house to provide top range performances of an international standard. The directors are trying to move away from the exclusive image of opera and are doing well in attracting younger audiences by organizing regular activities and information sessions.

THEATRE AND DANCE

Kopergieterij

Map 6, K1. Blekerijstraat 50
Ⓣ 09/266 11 44,
Ⓦ www.dekopergietery.be.
Arguably the best and certainly the most famous youth theatre in Flanders, this group has gained a national and international reputation under the directorship of Eva Bal. The theatre is part of a "house of art" featuring dance, video and other art forms as performed by young people.

Nieuwpoorttheater

Map 6, J4. Nieuwpoort 31–35
Ⓣ 09/223 0000,
Ⓔ nieuwpoorttheater
@pandora.be.

Contemporary theatre focused on the avant-garde, but polemical rather than abstract. Previous performances have, for example, dealt with conflict and confrontation between theatrical genres and generations. Always inventive, a Flemish trend-setter.

Publiekstheater Groot Huis

Map 6, H6. Sint Baafsplein 17
Ⓣ 09/225 0101,
Ⓦ www.publiekstheater.be or www.ntg.be.
This tastefully refurbished, nineteenth-century theatre house is now home to the Nederlands Toneel Gent (NTG), the regional repertory company. Almost all of their performances are in Flemish, though they do play occasional host to touring English-language theatre companies.

Theater Exces

Map 6, J9. Brabantdam 203
Ⓣ 09/233 0443.
Patrick Vandewalle started this theatre for mime and movement in 1972 and it's still

GHENT: THEATRE AND DANCE

going strong. Offers a wide spectrum of "visual theatre" for both children and adults.

Theater Taptoe

Map 5, I6. Forelstraat 95C Ⓣ 09/223 67 58, Ⓔ theatre.taptoe@ping.be. Theater Taptoe is a very competent puppet theatre, providing regular performances from an imaginative programme. Well worth seeing even if you don't understand Flemish.

Vooruit (Kunstcentrum - Arts Centre)

Map 5, F8. Sint-

Pietersnieuwstraat 23 Ⓣ 09/267 28 28, Ⓕ 267 28 30, Ⓔ info@vooruit.be, Ⓦ www.vooruit.be. Rock, pop, jazz, exhibitions, theatre, dance… this is the cultural centre of Ghent and a place locals are justifiably proud of. Occupies a grand former Festival Hall that was completed in an eclectic version of Art Nouveau in 1914. Once used by the city's socialists for meeting and rallies, it now offers a wide-ranging and well-chosen programme to suit most tastes. There's a café too. Good website with listings.

Shopping

BRUGES

With so much space dedicated to tourism, regular **shopping** plays second fiddle in central **Bruges**. Inevitably, there are scores of souvenir shops, with lace and chocolate being the two most popular items, but nevertheless a number of more interesting establishments still dot the centre, selling everything from locally made lace (a rarity) through to designer clothes and superb handmade chocolates. It is these more distinctive places that we have described in this section along with the city's open-air **markets**, though those in Ghent (see pp.194–195) are much better.

This chapter is divided in two sections – **Shopping in Bruges** (pp.180–188) and **Shopping in Ghent** (pp.188–196). Both of these sections are sub-divided into the following **categories**: art, design and antiques; books and comics; chocolates; department stores; fashion; food and drink; lace; markets and music. In addition, Bruges has a stationery section and Ghent has one on secondhand clothes shops.

The city's main **shopping streets** are located to the west of the Markt with Steenstraat and its continuation

Zuidzandstraat forming the main hub. We have given opening times for all the places listed, but across the city usual **opening hours** are Monday to Saturday 9am to 6pm.

ART, DESIGN AND ANTIQUES

Callebert

Map 3, E9. Wollestraat 25.
Tues–Sat 10am–noon & 2–6pm.
Callebert is strong on contemporary design – the best place in the city – featuring both leading brands – Alessi, Arabia and so forth – as well as less familiar names. Their product range covers the gamut from bags and watches, tableware and clothing to ceramics and wood, glass and metal household implements. In the same premises is an art gallery, which presents the best of contemporary design, primarily in glass and ceramics – along with calligraphy and photography – as well as the B-Shop, featuring the pick of Belgian designers.

Classics

Map 3, E10. Oude Burg 32.

Tues–Sat 10am–noon & 2–6pm.
A mixed bag of an art shop selling everything from icons to tapestries, both antique and modern but in traditional style. Also has Indian applied and fine art – the owner travels to India every year to pick up new tackle. Affordable prices.

Jewellery Quijo

Map 3, E8. Breidelstraat 18.
Mon–Sat 9am–noon & 2–6.30pm.
Made in Bruges, the designer jewellery of Quijo is inventive, creative and pricey. The "Qui-shape", a characteristic style, was, it's claimed, inspired by the city's cobble stones. Regularly exhibits in the front part of the Hallen, on the Markt.

Kasimir's Antique Studio

Map 3, F10. Rozenhoedkaai 3.
Mon–Sat 10.30am–12.30pm & 2–6pm.
Antiques don't come cheap in

Bruges, and Kasimir's is no exception, but the old furniture on sale here is first-rate and there's an interesting assortment of old knick-knacks too. Metres from the rival 't Woonhuisje (see below).

Pollentier

Map 3, C12. Sint-Salvatorskerkhof 8.
Tues–Fri 2–6pm, Sat 10am–noon & 2–6pm.
This antiquarian hideaway specializes in dealing with – and caring for – old and contemporary prints. It also offers a framing service. Seascapes, hunting-scenes and Bruges cityscapes predominate, but there are many other subjects as well.

't Woonhuisje

Map 3, G9. Braambergstraat 4.
Mon–Sat 10.30am–12.30pm & 2–6pm.
Specializing in antique furniture, this smart establishment is very similar to its rival, Kasimir's Antique Studio (see opposite).

BOOKS AND COMICS

Marechal

Map 3, E13. Mariastraat 10.
Mon–Sat 9am–noon & 1.30–6pm.
Browsing is the name of the game in this large bookstore. The Flemish reference section is noticeably weighty, but you can find lots of English books on Bruges too. Also has an interesting antiquarian section.

De Meester (aka De Brugse Boekhandel)

Map 3, F10. Dijver 2.
Mon–Sat 8.30–noon & 1.30–6.30pm.
Good for books about Bruges, both present and past, and sells a wide range of city maps. Also reasonably strong on other topics, notably historical subjects, literature from home and abroad, cookery and gardening.

De Reyghere

Map 3, D8. Markt 12.
Mon–Sat 8.30am–6.15pm.
Founded over one hundred

years ago, De Reyghere is something of a local institution and a meeting place for every book-lover in town. Has a good range of domestic and foreign literature as well as a healthy supply of art and gardening books and travel guides. Also good for international daily newspapers, magazines and periodicals.

De Striep
Map 3, E14. Katelijnestraat 42. Mon 1.30–6pm, Tues–Sat 9am–12.30pm & 1.30–6pm. The only comic strip specialist in town, stocking run-of-the-mill cheapies to collector items in Flemish, French and even English.

Tintin Shop
Map 3, D9. Steenstraat 3. June–Sept Mon–Sat 9.30am–6pm, Sun 11am–6pm; Oct–May same times, but closed Wed. Souvenir-cum-comic shop capitalizing on Hergé's quiffed hero with all sorts of Tintin tackle from T-shirts through to comics.

CHOCOLATES

The Chocolate Line
Map 3, D10. Simon Stevinplein 19. Mon–Sat 9.30am–6.30pm, plus frequent Sundays 10.30am–6.30pm Probably the best chocolate shop in town. Handmade, quality chocolates using natural materials – and therefore more expensive than most of its (plethora of) rivals. Chocolate truffles are a house speciality as are chocolate figurines. Boxes of mixed chocolates are sold in various sizes with a 250grm box, for example, costing €7.75.

Neuhaus
Map 3, D10. Steenstraat 66. Mon–Sat 9am–6pm. Belgium's best – but by no means biggest – chocolate chain sells superb and beautifully presented chocolates. Check out their specialities, most notably the handmade Caprices, which are pralines stuffed with crispy nougat, fresh cream

and soft-centred chocolate, and the delicious Manons, stuffed white chocolates, which come with fresh cream, vanilla and coffee fillings.

Temmerman

Map 3, B11. Zilverpand winkelgalerijen (shopping arcade) 22–23, Zuidzandstraat. Mon–Sat 9am–6pm.

It looks like Roald Dahl's Charlie's Chocolate Factory, and they certainly have a good range of chocolates, but this establishment is much more than a chocolate shop. They sell all kinds of coffees and teas plus old-fashioned sweets. One special thing to try is "Brugse Knapzak", a mix of Bruges specialities guaranteed to undermine the sturdiest of fillings.

DEPARTMENT STORES

INNO

Map 3, D9. Steenstraat 11–15. Mon–Sat 9.15am–6pm.

The best department store in town, spread over four floors

and selling everything you might expect, from high quality clothes and perfumes through to leather goods, underwear, household implements and jewellery. If you don't find what you're looking for here, try HEMA, nearby at Steenstraat 73 (Mon–Sat 9am–6pm; Map 3, D10).

FASHION

L'Angolo

Map 3, C7. Sint-Jacobstraat 28. Mon–Sat 10am–noon & 1.30–7pm.

This mid-range men's shop sells smooth and classy gear from sportswear through to dressy. There's a choice between well-known and less familiar brands.

Knapp Targa

Map 3, B11. Zuidzandstraat 9 and across the street at 16–26. Mon–Sat 9.30am–6.30pm.

Arguably the most enjoyable fashion shop in town, Knapp Targa's chic repertoire of top-quality clothes ranges from the adventurous – or even

BRUGES: DEPARTMENT STORES AND FASHION

challenging – to the classic. They also have a branch to the west of the city centre at Gistelse Steenweg 22–24. Gistelse Steenweg runs west from Canadaplein (Map 2, A11), which itself abuts the Smedenpoort city gate.

Olivier Strelli

Map 3, D7. Eiermarkt 3 (for women): Mon–Sat 10am–6.30pm).
Map 3, C8. Geldmuntstraat 19 (for men : Mon–Sat 10am–12.30pm & 1.30–6.30pm).
One of Belgium's most established designers, Strelli has been creating simple, classic and very modern clothes for years, often with a splash of colour. The rainbow scarves for women are particularly popular. Pricey.

Quicke

Map 3, A12. Zuidzandstraat 21. Mon–Sat 9.30am–6.30pm.
The top shoe shop in Bruges, Quicke showcases the great European seasonal collections, featuring top-rank, exclusive designers. Naturally it's expensive.

Rex Spirou

Map 3, C8. Geldmuntstraat 18. Mon–Sat 9.30am–7pm.
Chic and sharp designer clothes for the young and cool – or at least the self-conscious. Pricey, but with an interesting line in accessories.

FOOD AND DRINK

The Bottle Shop

Map 3, E9. Wollestraat 13. Daily 10am–7pm, 6pm in Jan & Feb.
Just off the Markt – so very popular with tourists – this bright and cheerful establishment stocks several hundred types of beer, oodles of whisky and gin (jenever) as well as all sorts of special glasses to drink them from – the Belgians have specific glasses for many of their beers.

Deldycke

Map 3, E9. Wollestraat 23. Mon–Sat 9.30am–6pm.
There's not much doubt that this is the best delicatessen in town, offering every treat you can think of and then some –

For a top twenty of Belgian beers, see pp.291–295.

from snails and on up the evolutionary tree. Helpful service too.

Javana

Map 3, D9. Steenstraat 6.
Mon–Sat 10am–6.30pm.
Javana has been selling the best coffees and teas in the world from these neat, little premises for over fifty years. Also has the full range of accessories for coffee- and tea-making.

La Pasta

Map 3, D8. Kleine Sint Amandstraat 12.
Tues–Fri 9.30am–1pm & 2–6.30pm, Sat 9.30am–1pm & 2–7pm, Sun 10am–1pm & 3–6pm.
Popular with locals, this cosy shop sells everything Italian, its speciality being ready cooked meals. The same family runs the *Due Venezie* restaurant (see p.147) just along the street. Also stocks a good range of Italian and French wines.

Norma's Asian Market

Map 3, D6. Kuipersstraat 15.
Mon–Sat 10am–noon & 1.30–6pm.
Thai-run grocery store with a good line in Asian and African food and drink (as well as a few knick-knacks). Cheap – but not so cheerful.

LACE

'T Apostelientje

Map 3, I4. Balstraat 11.
Mon–Sat 9.30am–6pm & Sun 9.30am–4pm.
Metres from the Kantcentrum (Lace Centre), this small shop sells a charming variety of handmade lace pieces of both modern and traditional design. If there's nothing here that takes your fancy, then try the (even smaller) shop in the Kantcentrum itself, where they also offer demonstrations of traditional lace-making in the afternoon. For more on the Kantcentrum, see p.72.

BRUGES: LACE

Claeys

Map 3, E14. Katelijnestraat 54. Mon–Sat 10–noon & 2–6pm. Diane Claeys studied lace in various museums in Europe. In 1980, she opened this shop, where she sells authentic, handmade antique-style lace. She also supplies pieces of lace to specialist collections and sometimes organizes lace exhibitions here.

LACE

Renowned for the fineness of its thread and beautiful motifs, **Belgian lace** – or Flanders lace as it was formerly known – is famous the world over. It was once worn in the courts of Brussels, Paris, Madrid and London – Queen Elizabeth I of England is said to have had no less than 3000 lace dresses – and across Europe the ruffs of the royal courtiers were made in Flanders too. Indeed, the Flemings helped their own commercial cause by first using starch to keep the ruffs stiff. Handmade lace reached the peak of its popularity in the early nineteenth century, when thousands of Belgian women and girls worked as home-based lacemakers. The industry was, however, transformed by the arrival of machine-made lace in the 1840s and, by the end of the century, handmade lace had been largely supplanted with the lacemakers obliged to work in factories. This highly mechanized industry collapsed after World War I when lace, a symbol of an old and discredited order, suddenly had no place in the wardrobe of most women.

Bruges' Kantcentrum (Lace Centre; see p.72) has a modest collection of old, handmade lace and there are plans to expand the collection considerably, but in both Bruges and Ghent most **lace shops** – and Bruges has lots – sell lace that is manufactured in the Far East, especially China. The shops listed below (and in Ghent on p.194) sell local, handmade lace, but inevitably prices are higher here than at most of their rivals.

MARKETS

Flea Market
Map 3, E11-G9. Along the Dijver and on the Vismarkt. Mid-March to mid-Nov Sat & Sun.

Not a patch on the flea markets of Ghent (see p.194), but passably entertaining, though the souvenir stalls are starting to rule the roost at the expense of more interesting stalls. Few bargains – there are too many tourists for that – and not much out-of-the-way stuff either.

Food and general goods
Map 3, A12. 'T Zand (Sat 8am–1pm).
Map 3, E8. The Markt (Wed 8am–1pm).

The Saturday market on 't Zand is the city's brightest and best, while Wednesdays on the Markt is OK, but nothing special.

MUSIC

Bilbo
Map 3, B10. Noordzandstraat 82. Mon–Sat 10am–6.30pm.

Not much in the way of service or presentation, but this is the most popular music shop in town, especially with the under-25s. The secret of their success is the bargain-basement prices. Great assortment of secondhand records.

Rombaux
Map 3, F7. Mallebergplaats 13. Mon–Sat 9am–12.30pm & 2–6.30pm.

Here, behind an idiosyncratic facade, are all manner of musical goodies from classical to modern, CD to vinyl. If they can't help you find it, no one else in Bruges can.

STATIONERY

A La Carte
Map 3, F4. Genthof 29. Mon, Tues & Thurs–Sun 10am–12.30pm & 2–6pm.

Showcase for the products of Anne De Loofs' own graphics atelier. Artful cards for almost every occasion plus designer objects in small editions. Reasonable prices.

BRUGES: MARKETS, MUSIC AND STATIONERY

●

Decorte
Map 3, B10. Noordzandstraat 23.
Mon–Sat 9am–noon & 2–6pm.
Stationery nirvana.

Magnificent fountain pens, ball points, coloured pencils, ink pots, wrapping paper, cards and writing paper. Prices for every budget.

GHENT

Larger than Bruges and with a much less dominant tourist industry, the centre of **Ghent** is liberally sprinkled with distinctive shops and stores that primarily cater for the needs of the locals. Ghent is especially strong on fashion, with a string of creative designer shops plus several excellent secondhand clothes shops, and also has a good **flea market**. Other particular strengths are the number of quality bookshops and the range of excellent food shops.

In general terms, the main chain stores are concentrated on Veldstraat, smaller specialist shops on Koestraat, and designer clothes shops on Kalandestraat. Antique shops are grouped together on and around Bij St Jacobs and also along the eastern half of Burgstraat. **Opening times** are given for each establishment listed below, but note that usual opening hours are Monday to Saturday 9am to 6pm.

Shopping in Ghent is divided into the following **categories**: art, design and antiques; books and comics; chocolates; department stores; fashion; food and drink; lace; markets; music; and secondhand clothes shops.

ART, DESIGN AND ANTIQUES

Atmosphere
Map 7, F7. Hoogpoort 3,

ⓦ www.atmosphere-gent.be.
Tues–Sat 10am–noon & 1–6pm.
Specialists in fabric and home decoration, the attractive layout of this shop makes it

definitely worth a visit, if only to browse – or have a look at their website.

Casa

Map 6, E7. Veldstraat 65.
Mon–Sat 9am to 6pm.
This reasonably priced Belgian chain store offers household goods of the latest design. Specializes in tableware, furniture and decorations.

Castle Antiques

Map 7, A5. Burgstraat 18.
Mon & Wed–Sat 2–6.30pm.
Housed in an impressive late-eighteenth-century building, this shop sells select antiques at the top end of the market. Strong on furniture – especially English furniture – with a good supporting line in silverware. One of several antique shops on Burgstraat.

Count's Gallery

Map 7, C5. Rekelingestraat 1.
Tues–Sun 10am–6pm.
Odd little shop, just opposite the castle, selling the weirdest range of souvenirs, miniature models, postcards and so forth. Great for kitsch.

The Fallen Angels

Map 7, B5. Jan Breydelstraat 29–31.
Mon & Wed–Sat 1–6pm.
Mother and daughter run these two adjacent shops, selling all manner of old bric-a-brac from postcards and posters through to teddy bears and toys. Intriguing at best, twee at worst, it can be particularly useful for unusual gifts.

Galerie St John

Map 6, I3. Bij St Jacobs 15.
Mon–Fri 2–6pm, Sat & Sun 10am–noon.
Antique shop selling an alluring range of *objets d'art* from silverware and chandeliers through to oil paintings. Great location too – in an old church overlooking this busy square. One of several antique shops in the vicinity.

Grusenmeyer Interieur

Map 6, D8. Ajuinlei 27,
Ⓦ www.grusenmeyer.be.
Wed–Sat 11am–6pm, Sun 11am–1pm.
Run by a well-known city antiques family - and

something of a local institution – this shop offers a wide-ranging selection of Asian antiques from Chinese furniture to Malayan porcelain and Cambodian bronzes. Visit the website for a preview.

Interphilia

Map 6, H6. St Baafsplein 4. Mon & Wed–Sat 10am–noon & 1–5.30pm.

Specialist stamp shop with a sideline in coins.

Mosiac@home

Map 7, G7. Hoogpoort 39. Wed–Fri 10am–6.30pm, Sat 9am–6.30pm.

From Moroccan tables to Italian art, this is the place for all you ever need in the way of mosaics. Three times a week they offer evening classes in – you guessed it – mosaics.

'T Vlaams Wandtapijt

Map 6, H6. St Baafsplein 6. Mon–Sat 9.30am–6pm.

The great days of Belgian tapestry manufacture are long gone, but the industry survives, albeit in diminished form, and this shop specializes in its products. The large tapestries on sale here are mostly richly decorated, modern renditions of traditional motifs and styles, but – as you might expect – they are expensive, from around €800. Cushion covers, handbags and other smaller knick-knacks, of which there is a good range, are much more affordable.

BOOKS AND COMICS

Atlas and Zanzibar

Map 5, C12. Kortrijksesteenweg 100. Mon–Fri 10am–1pm & 2–7pm, Sat 10am–1pm & 2–6pm.

Specialist travel bookshop offering a comprehensive selection of Belgian hiking maps and many English guidebooks.

Betty Boop

Map 5, F12. Overpoortstraat 110. Daily 11am–6.30pm.

All the best Belgian comics, both traditional and new, plus a selection from America and *Manga* from Japan.

FNAC

Map 6, E7. Veldstraat 88.
Mon–Sat 10am–6.30pm.
Several floors of music, books
and newspapers, including a
good English-language
section. Excellent for maps,
including a comprehensive
range of Belgian hiking maps.
Also sells tickets for most
mainstream cultural events.

De Kaft

Map 5, E9.
Kortrijksepoortstraat 44.
Daily 10am–6pm.
New and used books and
CDs alongside lots of
secondhand vinyl. Also has an
English secondhand fiction
section.

Kiekeboe!

Map 5, E1. Tolhuislaan 126.
Tues–Thurs 2–5.30pm, Fri
2.30–7pm, Sat 2.30–5.30pm.
This place is a favourite haunt
of collectors seeking
particularly rare comics and
music. Also old postcards,
books and newspapers.

CHOCOLATES

Dulce

Map 7, B7. Jan Breydelstraat 1.
Tues–Sat 10am–6pm.
Chains dominate the
chocolate industry in
Belgium, but there are
independent places too – and
this is one of them, the best
in Ghent. The handmade
pralines are delectable.

Neuhaus

Map 6, H6. St Baafsplein 20.
Mon–Sat 9am–6pm.
Belgium's best chocolate
chain – see the description of
their shop in Bruges (p.182)
for further details.

DEPARTMENT
STORES

INNO

Map 6, F6. Veldstraat 86.
Mon–Thurs & Sat 9.30am–6pm,
Fri 9.30am–7pm.
Belgian department store on
the main shopping street,
specializing in clothes for
men, women and kids. Also a
games department and

household goods, plus lots more.

FASHION

Absolute Woman
Map 6, F8. Korte Meer.
Tues–Sat 10.30am–12.30pm & 1.30–6.30pm.
Catering for young women, this shop offers a wide selection of ready-to-wear clothes that are just that little bit different (and more stylish) than the average.

Bethsabis
Map 7, F7. Hoogpoort 5.
Tues–Fri 9.45am–noon & 12.30–6pm, Sat 9.45am–6pm.
Big names at low prices – not the Kwiksave advert, but the slogan for this bargain shoe shop that offers Prada shoes at regular high-street prices.

Cora Kempermann
Map 7, H11. Mageleinstraat 38.
Mon–Thurs10am–6pm, Fri & Sat 10am–7pm.
This Dutch designer is gaining popularity amongst Belgian women for her unique but accessible designs and natural colours and fabrics.

Obius
Map 7, H3. Meerseniersstraat 12.
Mon 1–6.30pm, Tues–Sat 10am–6.30pm.
Shoe and clothes shop stocking all you need in designer gear. Prada, Miu-Miu and Patrick Cox among many others, and the added bonus of incredibly friendly service.

Oona
Map 6, G7. Bennesteeg 12.
Tues 2–6pm, Wed–Sat 11am–1pm & 2–6pm.
The interior may be minimalist, but the clothes are not. This designer shop offers some truly unique creations from Missoni, Barbara Bui and Joseph. Inevitably, the exclusiveness is reflected in the prices.

Sjapoo
Map 6, G1. Sluizeken 29.
Tues–Fri 10am–1pm & 2–6.30pm, Sat 11am–6.30pm.
Beautifully designed and handcrafted hats and accessories from Ria

- -

The former central post office on the Korenmarkt has been
converted into the **Post Plaza shopping centre** (Mon–Thurs
9.30am–6pm, Fri & Sat 9.30am–6.30pm; Map 7, D10), where
the emphasis is on fashion – or at least the mainstream
version of it. There are a lot of shops to look at, but then you
could be in any city in Euroland. The basement is almost
exclusively devoted to club gear.

- -

Dewilde, the owner of this
shop, as well as other selected
designers.

Claudia Sträter

Map 6, G7. Kalandestraat 6.
Mon–Sat 9.30am–6.30pm.
This Dutch designer has
gained an international
reputation in the last few
years and is especially popular
in Belgium. This is one of
her eight shops in the
country and the spacious
light interior is a perfect
setting for her stylish
collections.

Olivier Strelli

Map 6, G7. Kalandestraat 19.
Mon–Sat 9.30am–6.30pm.
Strelli, arguably Belgium's
leading designer, has shops in
both Bruges (see p.184) and
Ghent. Simple, classic clothes
with panache. Expensive.

Stiletto

Map 6, G7. Women:
Voldersstraat 70.
Mon 2–6pm, Tues–Sat
10.30am–12.30pm &
1.30–6.30pm.
Map 6, F7. Men:
Voldersstraat 19.
Mon–Sat 10am–noon
&1.30–6pm.
Wide selection of chic but
practical clothes with a few
nods at the newest and
trendiest names.

FOOD AND DRINK

- -

Coffee Roasters Sao Paulo

Map 6, H8. Koestraat 24.
Mon 12.30–6.30pm, Tues–Sat
8.30am–6.30pm.
Excellent range of coffee,
both pre-packed and, more
importantly, freshly ground as

per your specifications. All sorts of related coffee paraphernalia too.

Himschoot

Map 7, E6. Groetenmarkt 1. Mon–Sat 10am–6pm.
Traditional, family-run bakery right in the centre of town. Has a real old-time feel to the place and its shelves are heaped with all sorts of bread as well as buns, fruit buns (*gebakjes met rozijnen*) and savouries. Don't be surprised if you have to queue. Irresistible.

Kaas Mekka

Map 6, H8. Koestraat 9. Mon–Sat 8am–6pm.
Literally the Cheese Mecca, this small specialist cheese shop offers a remarkable range of traditional and exotic cheese. Try some of the delicious Ghent goats' cheese (*geitenkaas*).

Peeters Delicatessen

Map 6, E7. Hoornstraat 9. Mon–Sat 9am–6.30pm.
Specialist cheese and wine shop with traditional layout. Excellent range. Good lines in jam and marmalade too.

Tierenteyn

Map 7, E6. Groetenmarkt 3. Mon–Sat 10am–6pm.
This traditional shop, one of the city's most delightful, makes its own mustards, wonderful, tongue-tickling stuff that is displayed in shelf upon shelf of ceramic jars. A small jar will set you back about €5.

LACE

Kloskanthuis

Map 7, B7. Jan Breydelstraat 2. Tues–Sat 10am–6pm.
Ghent's one and only specialist lace shop, though the lace is actually part of a wider line in home linen. Well-presented and displayed. Bruges has far more lace shops; see p.186 for further details.

MARKETS

Flea and antique markets

Map 6, I3. Beverhoutplein, Fri, Sat & Sun 7am–1pm.
Map 7, E6. Groetenmarkt.

For more music shops, see the Books and Comics section

March–Nov Mon–Thurs
10am–5pm.
The Beverhoutplein flea
market (*prondelmarkt*), with its
great tangle of bric-a-brac
and junk, makes for enjoyable
browsing – everything from
old pith helmets to fading
sepia photographs. The
Groetenmarkt antique and art
market (*kunstmarkt*) is rather
more polished and staid, but
good fun all the same.

Flower market
Map 7, I5. Vrijdagmarkt.
Sat & Sun 7am–1pm.
Map 6, G9. Kouter.
Daily 7am–1pm.
Of the two markets, the one
on the Vrijdagmarkt is the
better, a first-rate flower
market plus bird market
(which is not for the
squeamish) on Sundays.

Fruit and vegetable
Map 7, E6. Groentenmarkt.
Mon–Fri 7am–1pm, Sat 7am–5pm.
Pile after pile of fresh fruit
and vegetables, including
much local produce.

MUSIC

Fried Chicken Records
Map 5, E8. Nederkouter 47.
Daily 11am–7pm.
Founded by a top Ghent DJ,
this shop is a cave of vinyl,
the house speciality being
drum 'n' bass.

Music Mania
Map 5, E8. Bagattenstraat 197.
Mon–Fri 11am–7pm, Sat
11am–6pm.
Four floors of music covering
pretty much every genre you
could wish for and then
some. The ground floor has
the newest music and the
other floors head back in
time. Happy browsing.

SECONDHAND CLOTHES SHOPS

Aleppo 1
Map 7, H2. Oudburg 72.
Mon–Thurs noon–7pm, Fri–Sat
10.30am–7pm.
Designer secondhand clothes

for men and women, including big names like Ralph Lauren and Armani. You never know when you may need it, but this place specializes in cowboy outfits, with an abundance of leather and denim. First floor dedicated to 60s and 70s retro gear.

Alternatief
Map 6, I2. Baudelostraat 15.
Tues–Sat 2–6.30pm.
Great range of good quality secondhand clothes and paraphernalia. Take a moment to browse the shop at the back too with everything from old cars to the last in kitsch. Second shop at Ottogracht 12A (Map 6, I2).

Boomerang
Map 5, E9.
Kortrijksepoortstraat 142.
Tues–Sat 2–6.30pm.
Retro and secondhand clothes and shoes for men and women.

Festivals and special events

Bruges and Ghent are big on **festivals** and **special events** – everything from religious processions through to film, fairs and contemporary musical binges. These are spread right throughout the year, though, as you might expect, most tourist-orientated events take place in the summer. In both cities, information on upcoming festivals and events is easy to come by.

In **Bruges**, the tourist office, Burg 11 (April–Sept Mon–Fri 9.30am–6.30pm, Sat & Sun 10am–noon & 2–6.30pm; Oct–March Mon–Fri 9.30am–5pm, Sat & Sun 9.30am–1pm & 2–5.30pm; ☎050/44 86 86, ℻44 86 00, ✉toerisme@brugge.be, ⓦwww.brugge.be), posts information on its notice boards and website and publishes a free bi-monthly, multi-lingual brochure entitled events@brugge. In addition, the Province of West Flanders, covering Bruges and its surroundings, details events of every description on ⓦwww.tinck.be – or phone ☎070/22 50 05 – whilst the free and very thorough local **listings magazine** *EXit* has reviews and a detailed calendar. It is published monthly and is widely available in bookshops and assorted outlets –

including the tourist office – but it is (almost entirely) in Dutch.

For details of up-and-coming events in **Ghent**, head for the tourist office, right in the centre of the city (daily: April–Oct 9.30am–6.30pm; Nov–March 9.30am–4.30pm; ⓣ09/226 52 32) or consult ⓦwww.gent.be. One particular feature of Ghent is the city's contribution to the Festival van Vlaanderen (see opposite), which extends from May to November.

CALENDAR

FEBRUARY

Bruges Festival of World Music

Four days in the last week of February. ⓣ050/34 87 47, ⓔrembetika@wol.be. First-rate world music festival with an excellent reputation for sniffing out up-and-coming talent. Held in the Stadsschouwburg, Vlamingstraat 29. Tickets from €16–21.

MARCH

Bruges: Cinema Novo

Ten days in March. ⓣ050/33 54 86, ⓔinfo@cinemanovo.be, ⓦwww.cinemanovo.be.

The prestigious Cinema Novo film festival aims to establish a European foothold for films from Africa, Asia and Latin America. The carrot in this campaign is the annual Karibu Prize, a reward for the distributor that purchases the winning film and releases it onto the market. Films are shown at several cinemas, including the Lumière, Sint-Jacobstraat 36, and Ciné Liberty, Kuipersstraat 23.

Bruges: Europese Biënnale voor grafische kunst (Biennial Graphic Art Exposition)

First half of March.
The Rotary Brugge 't Vrije club turns its attention to

young artists from fifteen European countries in its European Biennial for Graphic Art. The selected works are all for sale. The aim is to raise the profile of the graphic arts amongst the general public and the next exhibition is in 2004. They are held in the Garemijnzaal, at the front of the Hallen, on the Markt.

APRIL

Bruges: Meifoor Brugge
Mid-April to mid-May.
Bruges' main annual funfair with rides, merry-go-rounds and so forth. Held on 't Zand and in the adjoining Koning Albertpark.

Ghent: Gentse Floralien
End of April. ⊤ 09/222 7336.
Held every five years in the Flanders Expo building, Malkouter 1, Sint Denijs Westrem, this is one of the world's biggest flower festivals. The one-and-a-half kilometre "inside garden" which is home to a range of flowers from around the globe, is also the setting for

the main event – the international flower competition. The next festival is scheduled for 2005.

MAY

Flanders: Festival van Vlaanderen
May to November. ⊤ 02/548 9595, Ⓦ www.festival-van-vlaanderen.be.
Begun in 1958, the year of the World Expo in Brussels, the Flanders Festival has provided over four decades of culture in churches, castles and other stylish venues in over sixty Flemish towns. The festival comprises more than 120 classical concerts, attracting international symphony and philharmonic orchestras. In Ghent each year takes on a different theme – see the festival website for details.

Bruges: Heilig Bloedprocessie (Procession of The Holy Blood)
Ascension Day (forty days after Easter).

One of Christendom's holiest relics, the phial of the Holy Blood, believed to contain a few drops of the blood of Christ, is carried through the centre of Bruges once every year on Ascension Day. For safe keeping, the phial is protected by – and held within – an ornate reliquary. Nowadays, the procession is as much a tourist attraction as a religious ceremony, but it remains a prominent event for many Bruggelingen. The procession starts on 't Zand – in front of the new Concertgebouw (Concert Hall) – at 3pm and wends its way round the centre taking in Steenstraat, Simon Stevinplein, Dyver, Wollestraat, the Markt, Geldmunstraat and Noordzandstraat before returning to 't Zand at about 5.30pm.

JUNE

Torhout, West Flanders: House Torhout

Last weekend in June.
Ⓦ www.housetorhout.be.
Three tents showcase top dance music at this three-day festival including special drum 'n' bass and techno tents. Camping possible. Trains run from Bruges to Torhout, where a festival bus will take you on to the site for free. The website only becomes active a couple of months before the event.

Ghent: More Blues Festival

Late June.
Ⓦ www.surf.to/moreblues.
Exactly what it says, a festival almost exclusively focused on the blues. Showcases Belgian and international names – even once attracting The Yardbirds (as in Eric Clapton). Based in Zottegem, a ten-minute drive south of Ghent on the N24.

JULY

Bruges: Axion Beach Rock

Two days over the first or second weekend of July.
Ⓦ www.axionbeachrock.be.
One of Belgium's best rock

festivals, now held on the beach at Ostend, which is readily reached by train from Bruges. The festival formula is simple with lots of dancing in several tents to disco, hip hop and other beats as well as leading live acts on stage. Alanis Morisette, Lou Reed, Deus, Iggy Pop and even Johnny Rotten and the Sex Pistols have all played here. Pray for good weather.

Bruges: Cactusfestival

Three days over the second weekend of July. ⓣ050/33 20 14, ⓦwww.cactusfestival.be. Going strong for over twenty years, the Cactusfestival is something of a classic. Known for its amiable atmosphere, it proudly pushes against the musical mainstream with rock, reggae, rap, roots and R&B all rolling along together. Features both domestic and foreign artists. Recent show-stoppers have included Black Uhuru and Richard Thompson. Held in the park beside the Minnewater.

Ghent: Gentse Feesten

Mid-to late July, but always including July 21. ⓣ09/239 4267, ⓦwww.gentsefeesten .be/.
For ten days every July, Ghent gets stuck into partying in a big way, almost round the clock. Local bands perform free open-air gigs throughout the city and street performers turn up all over the place – fire-eaters, buskers, comedians, actors, puppeteers and so forth. There is also an outdoor market selling everything from Jenever (gin) to handmade crafts.

Werchter: Rock Werchter

Last weekend of July. ⓣ01/660 0406, ⓦwww.rockwerchter.be /index2.htm.
Belgium's most famous open-air rock event, featuring international stars such as Massive Attack, Pulp, Tricky, Beastie Boys and Travis. Werchter is a small town outside Leuven, just to the east of Brussels. Take a train to Leuven and a festival bus will take you to the site.

FESTIVALS AND EVENTS CALENDAR

SFINKS: Boechout, Antwerp

Last weekend of July. ⓣ 03/455 6944, Ⓦ www.sfinks.be or. Belgium's best world music festival held in the suburb of Boechout, about 10km from downtown Antwerp. Sixty concerts showcasing artists from five continents, who perform on six stages. There is a Festa do Brazil, workshops, a kids' festival, exotic bars and restaurants, festival market and camping.

JULY/AUGUST

Bruges: Musica Antiqua

Last week of July and first week of August.

This well-established and well-regarded festival of medieval music offers an extensive programme of live performances at a variety of historic venues – churches, chapels and the like. The evening concerts are built around themes, whilst the lunchtime concerts are more episodic. Tickets go on sale in February at Bruges tourist office (see p.197) and are

snapped up fast.

AUGUST

Bruges: Jazz Brugge

Four days in August. Information from Bruges tourist office (see p.197) or from the Concertgebouw ⓣ 050/44 81 11, Ⓦ www .concertgebouwbrugge.be. A new venture for the city, Jazz Brugge has its first outing in 2003 (Aug 15–18), with concerts held in the spanking new Concertgebouw on 't Zand. The emphasis will be on the contemporary and the avant-garde as played by European musicians, both established names and up-and-coming talent.

Bruges: Klinkers

Two and a half weeks usually from the last weekend of July. Klinkers is Bruges' biggest annual knees-up. City folk really let their hair down, pouring out onto the streets for big-time concerts on the Markt and the Burg, for intimate performances in various bars and cafés or at the Cactus club (see p.162), for film screenings in Astrid Park and for all sorts of other entertainments. It's the city at its best – and most of the events are free.

Ghent: Paterholfeesten

One weekend in mid-August.
ⓣ 09/223 5841.

Three-day knees-up amongst the narrow cobbled lanes of Ghent's lively Patershol district, near the Vrijdagmarkt. Live music and plenty of good spirit (and spirits).

Bruges: Praalstoet van de Gouden Boom (Pageant of the Golden Tree)

Every four years over two days on the last weekend of August. All sorts of mock-medieval heartiness characterize this pageant and thousands congregate in central Bruges to join in the fun. Staged for the first time in 1958, the next one is in 2002. Further details from the tourist office (see p.197).

Hasselt: Pukkelpop

Last weekend in August.
ⓣ 01/140 2267,
ⓦ www.pukkelpop.be or.
Pukkelpop is a summer festival organized by the Humanistic Youth Organisation of Leopoldsburg. The idea behind the festival is to arrange a progressive and contemporary musical happening, clearly focused on alternative youth. However the line-up is not that different to the more "conventional" Werchter. A sample of past performers includes Cypress Hill, De La Soul, Hooverphonic, K's Choice, Levellers, Limp Bizkit, Placebo, St. Germain and Underworld. Hasselt is in eastern Belgium and easily reached by train.

OCTOBER

Ghent Film Festival

Ten days in October.
ⓦ www.filmfestival.be/keuzeEN.asp.
The Flanders International Film Festival in Ghent has

developed into one of Europe's foremost cinematic events. Every year, the Decascoop multiplex, Studioskoop and Sphinx art-house cinemas present a total of around 200 feature films and a hundred shorts from all over the world. Each film is entered into an appropriate competition category. In particular, the festival presents Belgian cinema and the best of world cinema well before it hits the public circuit. There is also a special focus on music in film; the festival has attracted performances from famous film composers including Michael Nyman.

NOVEMBER

Ghent: Zesdaagse an Vlaanderen (The Six days of Flanders – cycling event)

Six days in mid-November.
ⓦwww.kuipke.be.

This annual cycling extravaganza takes place in the velodrome at the Citadelpark in Ghent. It attracts cyclists from all over Europe, who thrash around for dear life in six days of high-speed entertainment.

DECEMBER

Bruges: Kerstmarkt (Christmas Market)

December daily 11am–10pm.
All December Bruges' Christmas Market occupies the Markt with scores of brightly lit stalls selling food, drink, souvenirs and everything Christmasy. The centre of the Markt is turned into an ice-rink (€5) and you can rent skates here too. There's more Christmas jollity at the comparable Christmas Market on the Simon Stevinplein (daily 11am–7pm). Take care with the glühwein.

Directory

Currency In 2002, Belgium abandoned the Belgian franc in favour of the Euro. There are 100 cents in each Euro. At the time of writing, one pound sterling is worth about €1.60, one US dollar €1.10, and one Australian dollar about €0.60.

Disabled travellers Neither Bruges nor Ghent is particularly well equipped to accommodate the traveller with disabilities. Lifts and ramps are comparatively rare, buses, trams and trains are not routinely accessible for wheelchair users, and rough sidewalks are commonplace – and even when an effort has been made, obstacles are frequent. That said, attitudes have changed: most new buildings are required to be fully accessible and the number of premises geared up for the disabled traveller has increased dramatically in the last few years. Consequently, finding an hotel with wheelchair access and other appropriate facilities is not too difficult. For specific advice, contact either the Ghent (see p.198) or Bruges tourist offices (see p.197) in the first instance, but don't be too surprised if they refer you elsewhere.

Electricity The current is 220 volts AC, with standard two-pin plugs. Brits will need an adapter to connect their appliances, North Americans both an adapter and a transformer.

Emergencies Fire & ambulance ☎100; police ☎101.

Health In Belgium, all residents of European Union countries are entitled to free medical treatment and prescribed medicines under the EU Reciprocal Medical Treatment agreement. Most EU countries have a form you have to carry with you to substantiate your right to claim. Brits need a (completed) E111 form, which is available from post offices.

Newspapers and magazines The main Flemish newspapers are the right-leaning *De Standard* and the leftish *De Morgen*, traditionally the favourite of socialists and trade unionists. Most English papers are on sale in both downtown Ghent and Bruges on the day of publication.

Police There are two basic types of police – the Rijkswacht and the Politie. The former, who wear blue uniforms with red stripes on their trousers, patrol the motorways and deal with major crime; the latter, in their dark blue uniforms, cover everything else and many speak English.

Public holidays The main holidays when most shops and banks will be closed are: Jan 1 (New Year's Day); Easter Monday; May 1 (Labour Day); Ascension Day; Whit Monday; July 11 (Flemish Community Day); July 21 (Belgium National Day); Assumption Day (mid-Aug); Nov 1 (All Saints' Day); Nov 11 (Armistice Day); Dec 25 (Christmas Day).

Telephones At public pay phones, local calls cost a minimum of €0.20, but to make an international call you'll need to put in a minimum of €1.20. Many phones accept prepaid cards which can be bought from newsagents, post offices and railway stations for €5 and €10. To make an international call dial ℡ 00, wait for the continuous tone, and then dial the country code followed by the area code – omitting the initial zero – and then the number. For directory enquiries in English, dial ℡ 1405. To ring Bruges and Ghent from abroad dial ℡ 00 32, then the city code without the initial zero, and then the telephone number.

Time One hour ahead of Britain; normally six hours ahead of Eastern Standard Time, nine hours ahead of Pacific Standard Time.

Tipping There's no necessity to tip, but a ten- to fifteen-percent tip is expected by taxi drivers and anticipated by most restaurant waiters.

Toilets Public toilets remain comparatively rare, but many cafés and bars run what amounts to an ablutionary side-line with (mostly middle-aged) women keeping the toilets scrupulously clean and making a minimal charge, though this custom is fizzling out. Where it still applies, you'll spot the plate for the money as you enter.

BRUGES DIRECTORY

Banks and bureaux de change Outside banking hours (usually Mon–Fri 9am–3.30pm) you can change money at the exchange desk in the tourist office (April–Sept Mon–Fri 9.30am–6.30pm, Sat & Sun 10am–6.30pm; October daily 9.30am–5pm; Nov–March Sat & Sun only 9.30am–5.30pm). There are also cash machines dotted right across the city centre.

Bike rental There are half a dozen bike rental places in Bruges, including Belgian Railways at the railway station (T 050/30 23 29; €8.80 per day); Christophe's, Dweersstraat 4 (T 050/33 86 04; €8.70 per day; Map 3, B11); and the Bauhaus

International Youth Hostel, Langestraat 135 (T 050 34 10 93; €8.70 per day; Map 2, H6).

Buses All local bus services are operated by De Lijn. City bus information can be had from the De Lijn kiosk outside the train station (Mon–Fri 7.30am–6pm, Sat 9am–6pm, Sun 10am–5pm). De Lijn's local information line is T 059/56 53 53. The tourist office on the Burg also has bus timetables.

Car rental Europcar, St Pieterskaai 48 (T 050/31 45 44); Luxauto, St Pieterskaai 59 (T 050/31 48 48).

Doctors A list of doctors is available from the tourist office; for weekend doctors (Fri 8pm–Mon 8am) call T 050/81 38 99.

BRUGES DIRECTORY

Football Founded in 1890, Club Bruges is currently Flanders' premier football club and a regular recent winner of the Belgian league and cup. They play on the outskirts of town, a ten-minute drive southwest from the centre along Gistelse Steenweg in the Jan Breydel Stadium; on match days there are special buses to the ground from the train station. Fixture details from the tourist office.

Internet and email access Cafés and coffee shops offering internet access are sprouting up all over central Bruges and computer facilities are now commonplace at the more expensive hotels. One particularly good and convenient spot is *The Coffee Link* (Mon–Fri 10am–9.30pm, Sat & Sun 10am-8.30pm; ⓣ050/34 99 73, ⓔ info@thecoffeelink.com, ⓦ www.thecoffeelink.com; Map 3, C13), in the Oud St-Jan exhibition-cum-shopping centre off Mariastraat. They use American-style keyboards rather than the (slightly different) French ones, which are more common in Belgium. Rates are currently €0.07 per minute, €4 for one hour.

Left luggage Lockers at the train station: large lockers, €3.30 per 24hrs, medium-sized €2.80, small €1.50. Also left luggage office – €2.50 per item.

Pharmacies Two central pharmacies are at 6 St Jakobsstraat (Map 3, C7) and 50 Katelijnestraat (Map 3, E14). Details of late-night pharmacies are available from the tourist office; also, duty rotas are usually displayed in pharmacists' windows.

Post office Markt 5 (Mon–Fri 9am–7pm, Sat 9.30am–12.30pm).

Taxis There's a taxi rank on the Markt (ⓣ050/33 44 44) and outside the train station on Stationsplein (ⓣ050/38 46 60).

Train enquiries Either in person at the train station or call ⓣ050/38 23 82 (daily 7am–9pm). Train information also available at the tourist office.

GHENT DIRECTORY

Banks and bureaux de change
The two most central banks are Fortis, Belfortstraat 41 (Mon–Fri 9am–12.30pm & 1.30–4pm, till 6pm on Thurs; Map 6, H4), and Weghsteen & Driege, St Baafsplein 12 (Mon–Fri 9am–4pm; Map 6, H6). There are also lots of cash machines in the city centre.

Bike rental Bicycles can be rented at St Pieters station (daily 7am–8pm; €8.80 per day, €6.20 per half day) and also at Biker, Sint Michielsstraat 3 (Tues–Sat 9am–12.30pm & 1.30–6pm; ☎ 09/224 29 03; same rates; Map 6, C5).

Buses and trams City and regional transport enquiries at the kiosks on the Korenmarkt (Mon–Fri 7am–7pm & Sat 10.30am–5.30pm) and beside St Pieters station (Mon–Fri 7am–7pm). Information line ☎ 09/210 93 11.

Car rental Avis, Kortrijksesteenweg 676 (☎ 09/222 00 53); Europcar, Brusselsesteenweg 506

(☎ 09/210 46 62); Hertz, Coupure Links 707 (☎ 09/224 04 06); Luxauto, Martelaarslaan 4 (☎ 09/225 30 31).

Gay scene Ghent's gay scene is pretty low-key. Contacts and details from FWH, Kammerstraat 22 (Mon–Fri 9am–4.30pm; ☎ 09/223 69 29).

Internet and email access The handiest place to access the internet and collect emails is the *Coffee Lounge*, across from the tourist office at Botermarkt 6 (daily 10am–10pm; ⓔ coffeelounge@pandora.be; Map 6, H5). Rates are currently €2.50 for one hour, €0.75 for fifteen minutes. Internet and email access are also common-place at the more expensive hotels.

Left luggage Lockers at St Pieters train station: large lockers, €3.30 per 24hrs, medium-sized €2.80, small €1.50. Also left luggage office – €2.50 per item.

Pharmacies Two central pharmacies are at 15 St

Michielsstraat (Map 6, C5) and 123 Nederkouter (Map 5, E8). Duty rotas, detailing late night opening pharmacies, are usually displayed in pharmacists' windows.

Post office The main post office is at Lange Kruisstraat 55 (Mon–Fri 8am–6pm, Sat 9am–12pm; Map 6, H7).

Taxi V-Tax (ⓣ 09/222 22 22).

Train enquiries ⓣ 09/222 44 44 (daily 7am–8pm).

DAY TRIPS

DAY TRIPS

Day trips

A large chunk of Belgium is within easy striking distance of Bruges and Ghent, making the list of possible excursions nearly endless. In this chapter we've picked out seven of the most appealing destinations, all within an hour of either Bruges or Ghent by train or bike. It is possible to make all seven suggested trips from Bruges or Ghent, although travelling time will be slightly longer if your starting point differs from what is proposed below. Bruges and Ghent naturally make excellent day-trips or overnighters from each other too.

From Bruges

The village of **Damme**, just a few kilometres northeast of Bruges, is noted for its easy-going atmosphere, clutch of classy restaurants, and scattering of medieval buildings. Damme marks the start of a delightfully scenic sliver of countryside that is criss-crossed by tree-lined canals and patterned by old causeways – altogether perfect for cycling. Bruges is also close to the seventy kilometre-long Belgian **coast**, where the main event is the **beach**, a sandy fringe that stretches almost without interruption from De Panne in the west to Knokke-Heist in the east. Most of the coast groans under an ugly covering of apartment blocks and bungalow settlements, but **Ostend**, its largest settlement, has the bonus of several good art museums and a thriving restaurant scene – not to mention its own slice of beach. Trams ply the whole of the Belgian coast, making access to all its resorts entirely straightforward, but the prettiest of the lot is **De Haan**, the quintessential family resort. Slightly further afield is **Ieper**, which – as Ypres – is best known for its World War I connections. For almost the entire war, Ieper was on the front line between the Germans and the Allies and a series of sights recall the slaughter, from the monumental Menin Gate through to the many graveyards that dot the surrounding countryside.

Quasimodo offers first-rate guided tours of Ieper and its surroundings beginning in Bruges; see box on p.9.

DAMME

Now a popular day-trippers' destination, the quaint village of **DAMME**, 7km northeast of Bruges, was originally the town's main port and fortified outer harbour and at its height it boasted a population of ten thousand. It stood on the banks of the River Zwin, which gave Bruges direct access to the sea, but the river silted up in the late fifteenth century and Damme slipped into a long decline, its old brick buildings rusting away until the tourists and second-homers arrived to create the pretty and genteel village of today. In its prime, Damme hosted several important events, notably the grand wedding of Charles the Bold and Margaret of York, and it was also the scene of a famous naval engagement on June 24, 1340. In the summer of that year, a French fleet assembled in the estuary of the Zwin to prepare for an invasion of England. To combat the threat the English king, Edward III, sailed across the Channel and attacked at dawn. Although they were outnumbered three to one, Edward's fleet won an extraordinary victory, his bowmen causing chaos by showering the French ships with arrows at what was (for them) a safe distance. A foretaste of the Battle of Crecy, there was so little left of the French force that no one dared tell King Philip of France, until finally the court jester took matters into his own hands: "Oh! The English cowards! They had not the courage to jump into the sea as our noble Frenchmen did." Philip's reply is not recorded.

Nowadays Damme sits beside the canal linking Bruges with tiny Sluis, over the border in Holland, though more importantly, 2km to the northeast of Damme, this waterway also intersects with the modern Leopoldkanaal which cuts down to the coast at the burgeoning container port of Zeebrugge. At right angles to the Sluis canal, Damme's one main street, **Kerkstraat**, is edged by what remains of the medieval town. Funded by a special tax on barrels of herrings, the fifteenth-century **Stadhuis** is easily the best-looking building, its elegant, symmetrical facade balanced by the graceful lines of its exterior stairway. In one of the niches you'll spy Charles the Bold offering a wedding ring to Margaret who stands in the next niche along. Just down the street, **St Janshospitaal** (April–Sept Mon & Fri 2–6pm, Tues–Thurs 11am–noon, Sat & Sun 2–4.30pm; Oct–March Sat & Sun only 2–4.30pm; €1) accommodates a small museum of five rooms and a dainty little chapel. In Room 1 are a couple of curiously crude parchment-and-straw peasants' pictures of St Peter and St Paul and in Rooms 2 and 3 there's some fine old furniture. Room 4, the main room, displays an enjoyable sample of Delftware and pewter, but it's the chimneypiece which grabs the

DAMME

●

attention, a Baroque extravagance with a cast-iron backplate representing the penance of King David for the murder of Bathsheba's husband. Otherwise, the museum holds a mildly diverting assortment of liturgical objects, a potpourri of ceramicware and folksy votive offerings.

From here, it's a couple of minutes' walk further down Kerkstraat to the **Onze Lieve Vrouwekerk** (April–Sept daily 10.30am–noon & 2.30–5.30pm; free), a sturdy brick structure attached to a ruined segment of the original **nave** (open access) that speaks volumes about Damme's decline. The church was built in the thirteenth century, but when the population shrank it was too big and so the inhabitants abandoned part of the nave and the remnants are now stuck between the present church and its clumpy **tower** (same times; €0.50). Climb the tower for the panoramic views over the surrounding polders.

Cycling around Damme

Damme lies at the start of a pretty little parcel of land, a rural backwater criss-crossed by drowsy canals and causeways, each of which is framed by long lines of trees and sprinkled with comely farmhouses. This is perfect **cycling country** and it extends as far as the E34 motorway, about 6km from Damme. There are lots of possible routes and if you want to explore the area in detail you should buy the appropriate Nationaal geografisch instituut map (1:25,000) in Bruges before you set out. One especially delightful itinerary, a 15km round-trip that takes in some of the most charming scenery, begins by leaving Damme to the northeast along the Brugge–Sluis canal. It continues by crossing over the Leopoldkanaal and proceeding on to the hamlet of **Hoeke**. Here, just over the bridge, turn hard left for the narrow causeway – the **Krinkeldijk** – that wanders straight back in the direction of Damme, running to the north of

the Brugge–Sluis canal. Just over 3km long, it drifts across a beguiling landscape and ultimately reaches an intersection where you turn left to regain the Brugge–Sluis waterway.

Cycle hire in Damme is available at Tijl en Nele, round the corner from the Stadhuis at Jacob van Maerlantstraat 2; reservations advised ⓣ050/050/35 71 92; closed Wed; €9 per day.

Practicalities

There are several ways **to get to Damme**, the most rewarding being the seven-kilometre **cycle ride** out along the tree-lined Brugge–Sluis canal, which begins at the Dampoort, on the northeast edge of the city centre. For cycle hire in Bruges see p.207, and in Damme see above.

DAMME

217

You can also get there **by canal boat** from Bruges, with excursions starting behind the Dampoort on the Noorweegse Kaai (Easter–Sept 5 daily; 40min; one-way €4.71, return €6.20). Connecting bus #4 runs to the Noorweegse Kaai from the Markt, except in July and August when you need to catch the Bruges–Damme bus, #799. Finally, you can reach Damme by bus – take **bus #799** from the Markt or the bus station – but note that a day trip is only easy in July and August (6 daily each way; 15min). During the rest of the year, the bus runs less frequently and you'll be consigned to an over-long stay if, indeed, you can make the return journey at all – there's no Sunday service.

Damme's **tourist office**, across from the Stadhuis (mid-April to mid-Oct Mon–Fri 9am–noon & 2–6pm, Sat & Sun 10am–noon & 2–6pm; mid-Oct to mid-April Mon–Fri 9am–noon & 2–5pm, Sat & Sun 2–5pm ☏050/28 86 10), has a good range of local information. There's no strong reason to overnight here, but if you do decide to stay they will also help you find a bed – Damme has a reasonable range of **private rooms**. Alternatively, just wander along Kerkstraat and watch for the signs, though you'll be lucky to find a vacancy in the height of the season. One place to try is *Le Rêve Restaurant*, right by the canal at the top of Kerkstraat at Damse Vaart Zuid 12 (☏050/35 42 17; ❸). There are a handful of rooms here above the restaurant – nothing fancy but perfectly adequate, with en suite costing an extra €10. A good alternative are the slightly smarter rooms above *'t Trompetje Restaurant*, at Kerkstraat 30 (☏050/35 64 30, ℻67 80 91; ❸).

Eating

Damme's real forte is its **restaurants** with a string of first-class places lining up along Kerkstraat. Pick of the bunch is the excellent *Bij Lamme Goedzak*, Kerkstraat 13 (☏050/35

20 03), which serves mouthwatering traditional Flemish dishes, often featuring wild game; main courses run at about €20. Similarly enticing is the French-inspired cuisine of *Le Rêve Restaurant*, by the canal at Damse Vaart Zuid 12 (☎050/35 42 17). If your budget won't stretch that far, head for *'t Uylenspieghel*, Kerkstraat 44, a café-tearoom which serves tasty snacks – croque monsieur through to pancakes – and a good range of beers, including a couple of local village brews.

OSTEND

The 1900 *Baedeker* distinguished **OSTEND**, some 20km west of Bruges, as "One of the most fashionable and cosmopolitan watering places in Europe". The gloss may be long gone, and the town's aristocratic visitors have moved on to more exotic climes, but Ostend remains a likeable, livable seaport with lots of first-rate seafood restaurants, a clutch of enjoyable art museums and – easily the most popular of the lot – a long slice of sandy **beach**.

The old fishing village of Ostend was given a town charter in the thirteenth century, in recognition of its growing importance as a port for trade across the Channel. Flanked by an empty expanse of sand dune, it remained the only important harbour along this stretch of the coast until the construction of Zeebrugge in the nineteenth century. Like so many other towns in the Spanish Netherlands, it was attacked and besieged time and again, winning the admiration of Protestant Europe in resisting the Spaniards during a desperate siege that lasted from 1601 to 1604. Later, convinced of the wholesome qualities of sea air and determined to impress other European rulers with their sophistication, Belgium's first kings, **Leopold I** and II, turned Ostend into a chi-chi resort, demolishing the town walls and dotting the outskirts with prestigious buildings and parks. Heavy

OSTEND

●

OSTEND

NORTH SEA

Casino-Kursaal

James Ensorhuis

MONACO-PLEIN

VAN ISEGHEMLAAN

VLAANDEREN STR.

LOUISA STR.

HOFSTRAAT

LANGE STR.

A. BUYLSTR.

Museum voor Schone Kunsten

ST-SEBASTIAANSSTR.

WAPEN-PLEIN

GROENTE-MARKT

Noordzeeaquarium

KONINGSTRAAT

MARIE JOSE PLEIN

Tram & Bus Stop

JANSSENSLAAN

WITTENONNENSTRAAT

DWARSSTR.

OOST STR.

VISSERS KAAI

Montgomery Dok

LEOPOLD II LAAN

HENDRIK SERRUYSLAAN

KAPEL STR.

KERK STR.

KAAISTRAAT

Leopoldpark

SPILLIAERTSTRAAT

E. BEERNAERTSTRAAT

IEPERSTR.

SINT-PAULUSSTRAAT

Catamaran Terminal

ALFONS PIETERSLAAN

CHRISTINA STRAAT

JOSEF II STR.

BOUDEWIJNSTR.

P. PYPESTR.

Amandine

Museum voor Moderne Kunst

ROMESTRAAT

VINDICTIVELAAN

St. Petrus en Pauluskerk

KAIROSTRAAT

STOCKHOLMSTR.

VUURKRUISEN PLEIN

Mercator

Marina

Train Station

VERENIGDE NATIESLAAN

LEOPOLD III LAAN

Coastal Tram Station

BRANDARISKAAI

GEERWIJNHELLING

N

Voorhaven

G. DE SMET DE NAEYERLAAN

STADHUISKAAI

Maria Hendrikapark

H.M.S. Vindictive Memorial

ACCOMMODATION				RESTAURANTS	
Andromeda	1	Prado	5	Lusitania	C
Du Parc	4	Thermae Palace	3	Mosselbeurs	B
Polaris	6	Youth Hostel	2	Savarin	A

0   200 m

bombing in World War II razed much of the royal resort and today Ostend is largely modern, its seafront crimped by a long line of apartment blocks.

Arrival, information and orientation

There are three trains every hour from Bruges to Ostend and the journey takes a little less than fifteen minutes. Ostend's **train station** is a five-minute walk from the centre of town – and the main square, Wapenplein. It is also next to the docks from where Hoverspeed operates a catamaran service over to Dover (see p.5). In addition, **trams** leave from beside the train station to travel the length of the Belgian coast – east to Knokke-Heist and west to De Panne.

Ostend is the focal point of the coast's public transport system, with fast, frequent and efficient **trams** running behind the beach to Knokke-Heist in the east and De Panne in the west. Winter services in both directions depart every half-hour, in summer every twenty minutes (every 10min in the central section between Nieuwpoort and Blankenberge). Fares are relatively inexpensive – Ostend to either Knokke-Heist or De Panne, for instance, costs €4.20. You can also buy tickets for unlimited tram travel, valid for either one day (€8.20) or three days (€13.90). Tickets from the driver or the tram kiosk by Ostend train station.

Ostend's main **tourist office** is located on Monacoplein, a ten-minute walk from the train station (June–Aug Mon–Sat 9am–7pm, Sun 10am–7pm; Sept–May Mon–Fri 9am–6pm, 10am–6pm & Sun 10am–5pm; ☎059/70 11 99, ⓦwww.oostende.be). They have an excellent range of information about Ostend in particular and the Belgian coast in general. They also operate a hotel room reservation service. Roughly square in shape, the town centre is

OSTEND

221

bounded by the beach to the north, harbours to the east, the marina to the south, and Leopold II-laan to the west; it takes between ten and fifteen minutes to walk from one end to the other.

The Town

Across Visserskaai from the train station is the whopping **St Petrus en Pauluskerk**, which looks old but in fact dates from the early twentieth century. Behind the church, the last remnant of its predecessor is a massive sixteenth-century **brick tower** with a canopied, rather morbid shrine of the Crucifixion at its base. From near here, Kapellestraat, the principal, pedestrianized shopping street, leads to the **Wapenplein**, an attractive piazza with a fancy bandstand. Here also is the **Museum voor Schone Kunsten** (Fine Art Museum; daily except Tues 10am–noon & 2–5pm; €1), which is located on the third floor of the Feest-en Kultuurpaleis (Festival and Culture Hall), a big bruiser of a building that looms over one whole side of the square. The museum has a lively programme of temporary art exhibitions, which supplement a small but enjoyable permanent collection. Highlights of the latter include the harsh surrealism of **Paul Delvaux**'s (1897–1994) *The Ijzer Time* and several piercing canvases by **Leon Spilliaert** (1881–1946), a native of Ostend whose works combine both Expressionist and Symbolist elements. Spilliaert was smitten by the land and seascapes of Ostend, using them in his work time and again – as in *The Gust of Wind*, with its dark, forbidding colours and screaming woman, and the *Fit of Giddiness*.

There's also an excellent sample of the work of **James Ensor**, who was born in Ostend in 1860, son of an English father and Flemish mother. Barely noticed until the 1920s, Ensor spent nearly all his 89 years working in his home town, and is nowadays considered a pioneer of Expressionism. His first paintings were rather sombre portraits and landscapes, but in the early 1880s he switched to brilliantly contrasting colours, most familiar in his *Self-portrait with Flowered Hat*, a deliberate variation on Rubens' famous self-portraits. Less well known is *The Artist's Mother in Death*, a fine, penetrating example of his preoccupation with the grim and macabre.

A couple of minutes' walk north of the Wapenplein, the **James Ensorhuis**, Vlaanderenstraat 27 (June–Sept Wed–Mon 10am–noon & 2–5pm; Oct–May Sat & Sun only 2–5pm; €4), is of some specialist interest as the artist's home for the last thirty years of his life. On the ground floor there's a passable re-creation of the old shop where his aunt and uncle sold shells and souvenirs, while up above the painter's living room and studio have been returned to something like their appearance at the time of his death, though the works on display aren't originals. From here, it's a brief stroll west to the **Casino-Kursaal** (gaming daily from 3pm until early in the morning), an unlovely structure built in 1953 as a successor to the first casino of 1852, and another short stretch to the little lakes, mini-bridges and artificial grottoes of **Leopoldpark**.

Just beyond the south side of the park, at Romestraat 11, is the **Museum voor Moderne Kunst** (PMMK; Modern Art Museum; Tues–Sun 10am–6pm; €3), where a wide selection of modern Belgian paintings, sculptures and ceramics is exhibited in rotation – everything from the Expressionists through to Pop and Conceptual art. Artists represented in the permanent collection and whose works you can expect to see include Delvaux, Spilliaert, Edgard Tygat, Constant Permeke and the versatile Jean Brusselmans (1884–1953), who tried his hand at several different styles. The museum also puts on an imaginative range of temporary exhibitions (when the entry fee is usually increased).

OSTEND

●

The Seafront

To the west of the Casino is Ostend's main attraction, its sandy **beach**, which extends west as far as the eye can see. On summer days thousands drive into the town to soak up the sun, swim and amble along the seafront **promenade**, which runs along the top of the sea wall. Part sea defence and part royal ostentation, the promenade was once the main route from the town centre to the Wellington racecourse 2km to the west. It was – and remains – an intentionally grand walkway designed to pander to Leopold II, whose imperial statue, with fawning Belgians and Congolese at its base, still stands in the middle of a long line of stone columns that now adjoin the **Thermae Palace Hotel**. Built in the 1930s, this is similarly regal, although it spoils the lines of the original walkway.

Heading east from the casino, Albert I Promenade leads along the seashore into the Visserskaai, where the **Noordzeeaquarium** (April–Sept Mon–Fri 10am–noon & 2–6pm, plus Sat & Sun all year 10am–noon & 2–6pm; €2.50), housed in the former shrimp market on the east side of the street, holds a series of displays on North Sea fish, crustacea, flora and fauna. To the south, in the marina, the sailing ship **Mercator** (April–June & Sept daily 10am–1pm & 2–6pm; July & Aug daily 10am–7pm; Oct–March Sat & Sun 11am–1pm & 2–5pm; €2) is the old training vessel of the Belgian merchant navy, converted into a marine museum holding a hotch-potch of items accumulated during her world voyages.

Accommodation

The tourist office (see p.221) will help you find accommodation in one of Ostend's many **hotels** and **guesthouses** at no extra charge. The best option is to head for a beachside hotel, but these are few and far between – most of the seashore is given over to apartment blocks. Alternatively, plump for the area round Leopoldpark on the west side of the centre – it's a pleasant district with a relaxed and easy air. For those on a budget, there's a good HI **hostel** in the centre of town and several bargain basement hotels.

HOTELS

Andromeda

Albert I Promenade 60
ⓣ059/80 66 11, ⓕ80 66 29.
Smart modern high-rise next door to the Casino, and overlooking the town's best beach. Most rooms have balconies and sea views. Four star. ❼

Du Parc

Marie Joséplein 3 ⓣ059/70 16 80, ⓕ80 08 79.
Located in a handsome Art Deco block just south of the Casino, this medium-sized hotel offers comfortable rooms at reasonable prices. The ground-floor café, with its Tiffany glass trimmings, is a favourite with locals. Three star. ❹

Polaris

Groentemarkt 19 ⓣ059/50 16 02, ⓕ51 40 01.

A good-looking *Belle Epoque* exterior hides modest but perfectly adequate rooms right in the centre of town. ❸

Prado

Leopold II-laan 22 ⓣ059/70 53 06, ⓕ80 87 35.
Likeable three-star hotel with neatly furnished modern rooms, just south of the Casino. Ask for a room on the front overlooking Marie Joséplein – and a few floors up from the traffic. Recommended. ❸

HOSTELS

Youth hostel

De Ploate, Langestraat 82
ⓣ059/80 52 97, ⓕ80 92 74,
ⓔdeploate@travel.to.
Spick and span hostel with 100 beds, and some family rooms. The overnight fee of €14.90 per person includes breakfast. Reservations are strongly advised in summer.

OSTEND

Eating and drinking

The sheer variety of places to eat in Ostend is almost daunting. Along Visserskaai (where in summer there's also a long line of seafood stalls) and through the central city streets are innumerable **cafés**, **café-bars** and **restaurants**. Many of them serve some pretty mediocre stuff, but there are lots of good spots too, and everywhere there are plates of fresh North Sea mussels and french fries.

Lusitania

Visserskaai 35 ☎059/70 17 65.
Excellent and long-established restaurant serving great seafood, especially lobster. Main courses from €21 as well as set menus.

Café du Parc

Marie Joséplein 3.
Sociable, old-fashioned café-bar with Art Deco bits and pieces close to the Casino. Part of the Hotel du Parc (see p.225).

Mosselbeurs

Dwarsstraat 10.
One of the liveliest restaurants in town with cheerfully naff nautical fittings and top-notch fishy dishes, especially eels and mussels. Reasonable prices.

Savarin

Albert I Promenade 75
☎059/51 31 71.
Classic Franco-Belgian cuisine with the emphasis on seafood. Expensive, but then it's one of the best restaurants in town. On the seafront a five-minute walk west of the Casino. Reservations advised.

DE HAAN

DE HAAN, some 13km northwest of Bruges, is arguably the prettiest and certainly the most distinctive resort on the coast. Established at the end of the nineteenth century, it was carefully conceived as an exclusive seaside village in a rustic Gothic Revival style, called *style Normand*. The building plots were irregularly dispersed between the tram station and the sea, around a pattern of winding streets reminiscent of – and influenced by – contemporaneous English suburbs such as Liverpool's Sefton Park. The only formality was provided by a central circus set around a casino (demolished in 1929). The casino apart, De Haan has survived pretty much intact, a welcome relief from the surrounding high-rise development, and, flanked by empty sand dunes, it's now a popular family resort, with a good **beach** and pleasant seafront cafés.

Practicalities

To get to De Haan by public transport from Bruges, take the **train** to Ostend and then catch the **tram**, from beside Ostend train station, for the twenty-minute journey east along the coast. Get off at De Haan Aan Zee tram stop. Trams – which carry on beyond De Haan as far as the resort of Knokke-Heist – depart every twenty minutes in summer (Easter–Sept) and every thirty minutes in winter. Alternatively, catch **bus #790** from Bruges bus station (usually 4–6 daily; 40min); buses stop a short distance down and across the street from the De Haan Aan Zee tram stop.

De Haan **tourist office** (April–Oct daily 9am–noon & 2–5/6pm; Nov–March Mon–Fri 10am–noon & 2–5pm; ⊤059/23 44 38, @tourism@dehaan.be) is next to De Haan Aan Zee tram stop, five minutes' walk from the beach along Leopoldlaan. They issue a useful English-language leaflet describing walking and cycling routes in the vicinity of De Haan. **Cycle hire** is available at several outlets, including André at Leopoldlaan 9 (⊤059/23 37 89).

The tourist office also has a small cache of private **rooms** (❷–❹) and in addition there are no fewer than 25 **hotels** in or near the village centre, including a couple of reasonably priced places in Gothic Revival piles a few steps from the tram stop. These are the one-star *Des Brasseurs,* Koninklijk Plein 1 (⊤059/23 52 94, ⓕ23 65 96; ❸), which offers sixteen plain but pleasant rooms, and the rather more enticing and considerably larger three-star *Belle Vue,* at Koninklijk Plein 5 (⊤059/23 34 39, ⓕ23 75 22; 5). However, easily the pick of the hotels is the first-rate *Auberge des Rois,* Zeedijk 1 (⊤059/23 30 18, ⓕ23 60 78, ⓦwww.beachhotel

.be; **❺**), a smart, modern, medium-sized hotel overlooking the beach and adjacent to an undeveloped tract of sand dune; ask for a room with a sea view. Needless to say, it's popular – reservations are advised.

For food, **café-restaurants** line up along the seafront and your best bet is to stroll along until you find somewhere you fancy. Alternatively, *L'Auteuil*, on the central circus at Leopoldlaan 18, serves particularly good mussels, whilst the *Café de Torre*, across from the De Haan Aan Zee tram stop, has a great range of beers, good music and filling snacks.

IEPER – AND WORLD WAR I

At heart, **IEPER**, about 50km southwest of Bruges, is a pleasant, middling sort of place, a typical Flemish small town with a bright and breezy main square that is – in this case – overlooked by the haughty reminders of its medieval heyday as a centre of the cloth trade. Initial appearances are, however, deceptive for all the old buildings of the town centre were built from scratch after World War I, when Ieper – or **Ypres** as it was then known – was literally shelled to smithereens.

Ieper's long and troubled history dates back to the tenth century, when it was founded at the point where the Bruges to Paris trade route crossed the River Ieperlee. Success came quickly and the town became a major player in the cloth trade, its thirteenth-century population of two hundred thousand sharing economic control of the region with rivals Ghent and Bruges. The most precariously sited of the great Flemish cities, **Ypres** was too near the French frontier for comfort, and too strategically important to be ignored by any of the armies whose campaigns criss-crossed the town's environs with depressing frequency. The city governors kept disaster at bay by reinforcing their defences

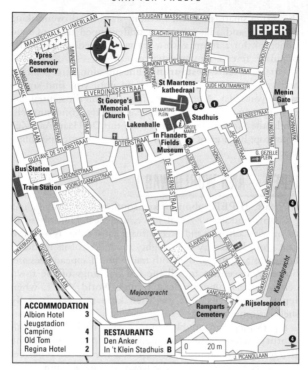

and switching alliances whenever necessary, fighting against
the French at the Battle of the Golden Spurs in 1302, and
with them forty years later at Roosebeke, where the popular Ghentish leader, Philip van Artevelde, was killed. The
first major misjudgement came in 1383 when Ypres sided
with the French against an invading English army and their
Flemish allies. The town was besieged and although the
French eventually saved the day, by the time they arrived

the town was ruined, and most of its weavers promptly migrated. In the event, the process of depopulation proved irreversible, and by the sixteenth century the town had shrunk to a mere five thousand inhabitants.

In World War I, the first German thrust of 1914 left a bulge in the Allied line to the immediate east of Ypres. This bulge – or **Salient** (see box p.235) – preoccupied the generals of both sides and during the next four years a series of futile offensives attempted to use it to break through the enemy's front line. This had disastrous consequences for Ypres, which served as the Allied communications centre. Comfortably within the range of German artillery, Ypres was soon reduced to rubble and its population had to be evacuated. After the war, the returning population determined to rebuild their town, a twenty-year project in which the most prominent medieval buildings – the Lakenhalle (cloth hall) and cathedral – were meticulously reconstructed. The end result must once have seemed strangely antiseptic – old-style edifices with no signs of decay or erosion – but now, after seventy-odd years, the brickwork has mellowed and the centre looks authentically antique. Nonetheless, the main reason to visit is the mementoes of World War I that are scattered around both the town and its environs.

Arrival and information

It takes about an hour to get from Bruges to Ieper by train – change at Kortrijk. Ieper's **train** and **bus stations** stand on the western edge of the town centre, a ten-minute walk from the Grote Markt, straight down Gustave de Stuersstraat. The **tourist office**, in the Lakenhalle on the Grote Markt (April–Sept Mon–Sat 9am–6pm, Sun 10am–6pm; Oct–March Mon–Sat 9am–5pm, Sun 10–5pm; ☏057/22 85 84, ⓦwww.ieper.be), has good town maps, details of suggested car and cycle routes around the Salient and a reasonable range of books on World War I.

Ieper is linked by regular bus with the lovely little town of Veurne (see p.248), some 25km to the north. It is also easy to get to Ieper from Ghent by train; the journey takes a little over an hour (change at Kortrijk).

The Town

A monument to the power and wealth of the medieval guilds, the replica **Lakenhalle**, on the Grote Markt, is a copy of the thirteenth-century original that stood beside the River Ieperlee, which now flows underground. Too long to be pretty and too square to be elegant, it is nonetheless an impressive edifice and one that was built with practical considerations uppermost: no fewer than 58 doors once gave access from the street to the old selling halls, while boats sailed in and out of the jetty on the west wing, under the watchful eyes of the majestic, turreted belfry. The interior of the Lakenhalle holds the ambitious **In Flanders Fields Museum** (April–Sept daily 10am–6pm; Oct–March Tues–Sun 10am–5pm; closed for three weeks after Christmas; €7.50), which focuses on the experiences of those caught up in the war rather than the ebb and flow of the military campaigns. In part this is very successful – the section simulating a gas attack is most effective – but the interactive clutter (touch screens and the like) tends to get in the way and there's not nearly enough about individuals – lots of personal artefacts but precious little about the men and women who owned them. That said, the museum is wide-ranging and thoughtful and the (multilingual) quotations are well-chosen. The photographs are particularly powerful: soldiers grimly digging trenches, the pathetic casualties of a gas attack, flyblown corpses in the mud and panoramas of a blasted landscape.

Back outside, the east end of the Lakenhalle is attached to the **Stadhuis**, whose fancy Renaissance facade rises above an elegant arcaded gallery, and round the back is **St Maartenskathedraal**, built in 1930 as a copy of the thirteenth-century Gothic original. Just to the northwest, near the end of Elverdingsestraat, stands **St George's Memorial Church** (daily 9.30am–4pm, often longer; free), a modest brick building finished in 1929. The interior is crowded with brass plaques honouring the dead of many British regiments and the chairs carry individual and regimental tributes. It's hard not to be moved, for there's nothing vainglorious in this public space, so consumed as it is with private grief.

A few minutes' walk away, just beyond the far side of the Grote Markt, the **Menin Gate** war memorial was built on the site of the old Menenpoort that served as the main route for British soldiers heading for the front. It's a simple, brooding monument, towering over the edge of the town, its walls covered with the names of those fifty thousand British and Commonwealth troops who died in the Ypres Salient but have no grave. The simple inscription above the lists of the dead has none of the arrogance of the victor but rather a sense of great loss. The **Last Post** is sounded beneath the gate every evening at 8pm. Oddly enough, the seventeenth-century brick and earthen **ramparts** on either side of the Menin Gate were well enough constructed to survive World War I intact – the vaults even served as some of the safest bunkers on the front. These massive ramparts and the protective moat still extend right round the east and south of the town centre and there's a pleasant footpath along the top. The stroll takes you past the **Ramparts Cemetery**, a British Commonwealth War Cemetery beside the old Lille Gate (the present Rijselsepoort), and there's another graveyard, the **Ypres Reservoir Cemetery**, on the far side of the town centre – from the cathedral, walk down Elverdingsestraat and turn right along Minneplein.

Accommodation

Albion Hotel

Sint Jacobsstraat 28 Ⓣ057/20 02 20, Ⓦwww.albionhotel.be.

New and appealing three-star hotel with eighteen en-suite rooms decorated in crisp modern style. Excellent breakfasts. A brief stroll from the Grote Markt. ❺

Old Tom Hotel

Grote Markt 8 Ⓣ057/20 15 41, Ⓔoldtom@pandora.be.

Nine plain but pleasant en-suite rooms above a café-bar bang in the centre of town. Much favoured by English visitors. Very reasonably priced. One star. ❸

Regina

Grote Markt 45 Ⓣ057/21 88 88, Ⓕ21 90 20, Ⓦwww.hotelregina.be.

This four-star establishment, housed in a 1920s copy of a grand turn-of-the-century edifice, is the most expensive hotel on the Grote Markt. Frankly, the bland, modern rooms aren't worth the extra – though it's perfectly adequate and often has vacancies when its competitors are full. ❹

Eating and drinking

Den Anker

Grote Markt 29.

Competent, mid-range restaurant that is strong on mussels, cooked in all sorts of ways, and seafood. Main courses from around €15, though the full set menu will set you back much more.

In 't Klein Stadhuis Bar

Adjacent to the Stadhuis on the Grote Markt.

The nearest thing Ieper has to

a hot spot, this lively bar stays open till late.

Old Tom
Grote Markt 8.
Straightforward restaurant offering good-quality Flemish cuisine at affordable prices, and a promising selection of Belgian beers to wash it down.

THE YPRES SALIENT

The **Ypres Salient** occupies a basin-shaped parcel of land about 25km long and never more than 15km deep immediately to the east of Ieper. For the generals of World War I, the area's key feature was the long and low sequence of ridges that sweep south from the hamlet of Langemark to the French border. These gave the occupants a clear view of Ieper and its surroundings, and consequently the British and Germans spent the war trying to capture and keep them. The dips and sloping ridges, which were then so vitally important, are still much in evidence, but today the tranquillity of the landscape makes it difficult to imagine what the war was actually like.

In fact it's surprisingly difficult to find anything which gives any real impression of the scale and nature of the conflict. The most resonant reminders of the blood letting are the 160 or so **British Commonwealth War Cemeteries**, immaculately maintained by the Commonwealth War Graves Commission. Each cemetery has a **Cross of Sacrifice** in white Portland stone, and the larger ones also have a sarcophagus-like **Stone of Remembrance** bearing the legend "Their Name Liveth for Ever More", a quotation selected by Rudyard Kipling from Ecclesiasticus. The graves line up at precisely spaced intervals and, wherever possible, every headstone bears the individual's name, rank, serial number, age, date of death, and the badge of the military unit, or a national emblem, plus an appropriate

THE YPRES SALIENT

The creation of the **Ypres Salient** was entirely accidental. When the German army launched the war in the west by invading Belgium, they were following the principles – if not the details – laid down by a chief of the German General Staff, Alfred von Schlieffen, who had died eight years earlier. The idea was simple: to avoid fighting a war on two fronts, the German army would outflank the French and capture Paris by attacking through Belgium, well before the Russians had assembled on the eastern frontier. It didn't work, with the result that as the initial German offensive ground to a halt, two lines of opposing trenches were dug – and these soon stretched from the North Sea down to Switzerland.

No one knew quite what to do next, but attention focused on the two main bulges – or **salients** – in the line, one at Ieper, the other at Verdun, on the Franco-German frontier just to the south of Luxembourg. To the Allied generals, the bulge at Ieper – the Ypres Salient – was a good place to break through the German lines and roll up their front; to the Germans it represented an ideal opportunity to break the deadlock by attacking key enemy positions from several sides at the same time. Consequently, the salient attracted armies like a giant magnet, but at a time when technological changes had shifted the balance of war in favour of defence: machine guns had become more efficient, barbed wire more effective, and, most important of all, the railways could shift defensive reserves far faster than an advancing army could march. It was a stalemate – and a gory one at that – and neither set of generals proved capable of rethinking their strategy.

Naturally enough, the soldiers of all the armies involved slowly lost confidence in their generals, and by 1917, despite court martials and firing squads, the sheer futility of the endless round of failed offensives made **desertion** commonplace and threatened to bring mass mutiny to the western front. However, although it is undeniably true that few of the military commanders of the day showed much understanding of how to break the deadlock, some of the blame must be apportioned to the politicians. They demanded assault rather than defence, and continued to call for a general "victory" even after it had become obvious that this was beyond reach and that each attack cost thousands of lives. Every government concerned had believed that a clear victor would emerge by Christmas 1914, and none of them was able to adjust to the new situation. There were no moves toward a negotiated settlement, because no one was quite sure what they would settle for – a lack of clarity that contrasted starkly with the jingoistic sentiments stirred up to help sustain the conflict, which demanded victory or at least military success. In this context, how could a general recommend a defensive strategy or a politician propose a compromise? Those who did were dismissed.

This was the background to the four years of war that raged in and around the Ypres Salient. There were four major battles. The first, in October and November of 1914, settled the lines of the bulge as both armies tried to outflank each other; the second was a German attack in the following spring that moved the trenches a couple of miles west. The third, launched by British Empire soldiers in July 1917, was even more pointless, with thousands of men dying for an advance of only a few kilometres. It's frequently called the Battle of Passchendaele, but Lloyd George more accurately referred to it as the "battle of the mud", a disaster that cost 250,000 British lives. The fourth and final battle, in April 1918, was another German attack inspired by General Ludendorff's desire to break the British army. Instead it broke his own and led to the Armistice of November 11.

THE YPRES SALIENT

religious symbol and, at the base, an inscription chosen by relatives. Still, thousands of bodies were buried without ever being properly identified.

To navigate round the scores of sites and to understand the various battles in detail, you'll need *Major & Mrs Holt's Field Guide to the Ypres Salient*, which describes several manageable itineraries and comes complete with a map; it is on sale at Ieper tourist office. Alternatively, the **Peace Route** is a 45-kilometre bike trip round the northern and central portions of the Salient. Again, the Ieper tourist office sells a brochure, though this lacks the background detail provided by the *Holt's* guide. Locally, **guided tours** are provided by **Flanders Battlefield Tours** (☎057/36 04 60), who offer both four- and two-hour excursions. Alternatively, **Quasimodo** operates all-inclusive battlefield tours from Bruges (see box on p.9).

A tour of the Salient

A detailed exploration of the **Salient** would take weeks; below we've outlined an abbreviated itinerary that can be completed comfortably **by car in half a day**. Beginning and ending in Ieper, the route focuses on the Salient's central – and most revealing – section.

Ieper's one-way system initially makes things confusing, but leave the town to the north along the **N369**, the road to Diksmuide. After about 3km, just beyond the flyover, watch for **Essex Farm Cemetery** on the right, where the wounded and dead from the battlefield across the adjacent canal were brought. In the bank behind (and to the left of) the cemetery's Cross of Sacrifice are the remains of several British bunkers, part of a combined forward position and first-aid post where the Canadian John McCrae wrote arguably the war's best-known poem, *In Flanders Fields*:

... We are the Dead. Short days ago
We lived, felt dawn, saw sunsets glow,
Loved and were loved, and now we lie
In Flanders fields...

Retracing your route briefly back along the N369 from
Essex Farm, take the **N38** east by turning right onto the
flyover from its southern side (signed Brugge). The N38
leads straight into – and under a major road – the **N313**
and, after 6.5km, you pass through the village of St Juliaan.
Immediately beyond the village is Vancouver Corner,
where the **Canadian Memorial**, a ten-metre high granite
statue topped by the bust of a Canadian soldier, was raised
in honour of those who endured the first German chlorine
gas attacks in April 1915. On this side of the memorial,
turn right and then first left at the little roadside shrine to
follow the country lane leading 4km east to **Tyne Cot**.
This is the largest British Commonwealth war cemetery in
the world, containing 11,956 graves and the Memorial to
the Missing, a semi-circular wall inscribed with the names
of a further 35,000 men whose bodies were never recovered. The soldiers of a Northumbrian division gave the
place its name, wryly observing, as they tried to fight their
way up the ridge, that the German blockhouses on the
horizon looked like Tyneside cottages. The largest of these
concrete bunkers was, at the suggestion of George V, incorporated within the mound beneath the Cross of Sacrifice –
and you can still see a piece of it where a slab of stone has
been deliberately omitted. The scattered graves behind the
Cross were dug during the final weeks of the war and have
remained in their original positions, adding a further
poignancy to the seemingly endless lines of tombstones
below. Strangely, the Memorial to the Missing at the back
of the cemetery wasn't part of the original design: the
intention was that these names be recorded on the Menin
Gate, but there wasn't enough room.

THE YPRES SALIENT

Tyne Cot cemetery overlooks the shallow valley which gently climbs up to Passendale, known then as **Passchendaele**. This village was the British objective in the Third Battle of Ypres, but torrential rain and intensive shelling turned the valley into a giant quagmire. Men, horses and guns simply sank into the mud and disappeared without trace. The whole affair came to symbolize the futility of the war and the incompetence of its generals: when Field Marshall Haig's Chief of Staff ventured out of his HQ to inspect progress, he allegedly said, "Good God, did we really send men to fight in that?".

Follow the road round the back of Tyne Cot to the right and after about 600m you reach a wider road – the **N303** – which runs along the top of the Passendale ridge. Turn right onto it and shortly afterwards, after 800m, turn right again, down the N332 into **Zonnebeke**. At the far end of the village, fork left onto the **N37**, keep straight over the motorway and you'll soon reach the **N8**, the Ieper–Menen road, which cuts across the back of the Salient – crowded with marching armies at night and peppered by German shrapnel during the day. Go round the island onto the N8 heading east (in the direction of Menen) and after 1.2km turn right up Canadalaan for the 1.3km trip to **Sanctuary Wood Cemetery**, where Gilbert Talbot lies buried. Talbot was the son of the Bishop of Winchester and his death was instrumental in the creation of Toc H, a worldwide Christian fellowship.

Just beyond, the **Sanctuary Wood Museum** (daily 9.30am–7pm or dusk; €4) holds a ragbag of shells, rifles, bayonets, billycans, and incidental artefacts. Outside, things have been left much as they were the day the war ended, with some primitive zigzags of sand-bagged trench, shell craters and a few shattered trees that convey something of the desolateness of it all. The woods and adjacent Hill 62 saw ferocious fighting – and there's a modest Canadian monument on the brow of the hill 300m up the road from the museum. From here, you can see Ieper, 5km away, across the rolling ridges of the countryside. The N8 leads back to the Menin Gate.

From Ghent

Roads, railways, rivers and canals radiate out from Ghent in all directions, slicing across the flatness of the Flemish plain. By and large, this is not Flanders at its prettiest – this is primarily an industrial area – but there are three appealing destinations all within an hour or so by train. The most varied is the big city and port of **Antwerp**, which possesses a flourishing nightlife, medieval churches and first-rate museums as well as an unrivalled collection of the work of its most celebrated son, Peter Paul Rubens. More countrified pleasures are, by contrast, on offer in the picturesque little town of **Veurne**, whilst **Oudenaarde**, a second, small rural town, chimes in with a splendid Stadhuis and a superb selection of the tapestries for which it was once famous.

ANTWERP

Belgium's second city, **ANTWERP** (see also Map 1, I2), fans out from the east bank of the Scheldt about 50km east of Ghent. It's not an especially handsome city – the terrain is too flat and industry too prevalent for that – but it does possess a vibrant and intriguing centre sprinkled with some lovely old churches and distinguished museums, reminders of its auspicious past as the centre of a wide trading empire. In particular, there is the enormous legacy of **Rubens**, whose works adorn Antwerp's galleries and churches. The

ANTWERP

RESTAURANTS, BARS & CAFÉS

Café de Muze	F
Het Elfde Gebod	C
Hippodroom	H
De Matelote	A
Pizzeria Antonio	B
De Stoempot	D
De Vagant	G
De Volle Maan	E

ACCOMMODATION

| Cammerpoorte | 2 |
| Rubens Grote Markt | 1 |

Ⓜ Tram/Metro Stations

0   200m

French laid the foundations of the city's present economic success during the Napoleonic occupation and Antwerp is now one of Europe's premier ports. It has also become the focus of the international diamond industry and, in the last few years, of the more nationalistic amongst the Flemish, who regard the city as their capital in preference to Brussels. It also lays claim to the title of fashion capital of Belgium with many young talents designing here.

Arrival and information

There is a **train** from Ghent to Antwerp every half-hour and the journey takes fifty minutes. These trains stop at Antwerp's two mainline stations, Antwerp Berchem and then **Centraal Station**, which is the one you want for the city centre. Centraal Station is actually on the edge of the city centre, about 2km east of the main square – the Grote Markt (see Map opposite, C2). **Trams** (#2 or #15 to Groenplaats) run from the underground station beside Centraal Station to the centre. A standard single fare **ticket** on any part of the city's transport system costs €1; a ten-strip *Rittenkaart* €7.50; and a 24-hour unlimited travel card, the *dagpas*, €2.90. Tickets are sold at underground stations and, in addition, the Rittenkaarts and the dagpas are sold at selected shops and newsstands all over town. One-way tickets can also be bought direct from the driver, who will give change if required.

Antwerp's **tourist office** is at Grote Markt 15 (Mon–Sat 9am–6pm, Sun 9am–5pm; ℡03/232 01 03, Ⓔtoerisme @antwerpen.be, Ⓦwww.visitantwerpen.be). They have a comprehensive range of information on the city and its sights, including maps and a number of specialist leaflets – principally those detailing where to see the works of Rubens and his contemporary, Jacob Jordaens. They will also make **hotel reservations** on your behalf at no charge:

ANTWERP

●

the modest deposit you pay is subtracted from your final hotel bill.

The City

The centre of Antwerp is the spacious **Grote Markt** (Map p.242, C2), at the heart of which stands the **Brabo fountain**, a haphazard pile of rocks surmounted by a bronze of Silvius Brabo, the city's first hero, depicted flinging the hand of the giant Antigonus – who terrorized passing ships – into the Scheldt. The north side of Grote Markt is lined with daintily restored sixteenth-century **guildhouses**, though they are overshadowed by the **Stadhuis** (tours Mon, Tues, Wed & Fri 11am, 2pm & 3pm, Sat 2pm & 3pm; €1), completed in 1566, and one of the most important buildings of the Northern Renaissance. Among rooms you can visit are the Leys Room, named after Baron Hendrik Leys, who painted the frescoes in the 1860s, and the Wedding Room, which has a chimneypiece decorated with two caryatids carved by Cornelius Floris, architect of the building.

Southeast of Grote Markt, the **Onze Lieve Vrouwe Cathedral** (Map p.242, D3; Mon–Fri 10am–5pm, Sat 10am–3pm, Sun 1–4pm; €2.50) is one of the finest Gothic churches in Belgium, mostly the work of Jan and Pieter Appelmans in the middle of the fifteenth century. Inside, the seven-aisled nave is breathtaking, if only because of its sense of space, an impression that's reinforced by the bright, light stonework revealed by a recent refurbishment. Four early paintings by **Rubens** are displayed here, the most beautiful of which is the *Descent from the Cross*, a triptych painted after the artist's return from Italy that displays an uncharacteristically restrained realism, derived from Caravaggio.

It takes about five minutes to walk southwest from the

ANTWERP

cathedral to the **Plantin-Moretus Museum**, on Vrijdagmarkt (Map p.242, B4; Tues–Sun 10am–5pm; €4), which occupies the grand old mansion of Rubens' father-in-law, the printer Christopher Plantin. One of Antwerp's most interesting museums, it provides a marvellous insight into how Plantin and his family conducted their business.

From here it's a brief stroll to the riverfront **Nationaal Scheepvaartmuseum** (Map p.242, B2; National Maritime Museum; Tues–Sun 10am–5pm; €4), which is located at the end of Suikerrui and inhabits the Steen, the remaining gatehouse of what was once an impressive medieval fortress. Inside, the cramped rooms feature exhibits on inland navigation, shipbuilding and waterfront life, while the open-air section has a long line of tugs and barges under a rickety corrugated roof. Crossing Jordaenskaai, it's a short walk east to the impressively gabled **Vleeshuis** (Map p.242, C2; Tues–Sun 10am–5pm; €2.50), built for the guild of butchers in 1503 and now used to display a substantial but incoherent collection of applied arts – everything from antique musical instruments to medieval woodcarvings.

Just north of here, along Vleeshouwersstraat, **St Pauluskerk** (Map p.242, D1; May–Sept daily 2–5pm; free) is a dignified late Gothic church built for the Dominicans in the early sixteenth century. Inside, the airy and elegant nave is decorated by a series of paintings depicting the "Fifteen Mysteries of the Rosary", including Rubens' exquisite *Scourging at the Pillar* of 1617.

East to the Rubenshuis and St Jacobskerk

It's a ten-minute walk east from the cathedral to the **Rubenshuis** at Wapper 9 (Map p.242, G4; Tues–Sun 10am–5pm; €5), the former home and studio of the artist, now restored as a (very popular) museum. Unfortunately, there are only one or two of his less distinguished paintings here, but the restoration of the rooms is convincing.

ANTWERP

Rubens died in 1640 and was buried in **St Jacobskerk**, just to the north at Lange Nieuwstraat 73 (Map p.242, G3; April–Oct Mon–Sat 2–5pm; €1.80). Rubens and his immediate family are buried in the chapel behind the high altar. Here, in one of his last works, *Our Lady Surrounded by Saints*, he painted himself as St George, his two wives as Martha and Mary, and his father as St Jerome.

South of the centre

About ten minutes' walk southeast of Groenplaats, the **Mayer van den Bergh Museum**, at Lange Gasthuisstraat 19 (Map p.242, E5; Tues–Sun 10am–5pm; €4), contains delightful examples of the applied arts, from tapestries to ceramics, silverware, illuminated manuscripts and furniture, in a crowded reconstruction of a sixteenth-century town house. There are also some excellent paintings, including works by Quentin Matsys and Jan Mostaert, but the museum's most celebrated work is **Piefer Bruegel the Elder**'s *Dulle Griet* or "Mad Meg", a misogynistic allegory in which a woman, loaded down with possessions, stalks the gates of Hell.

Further south still (tram #8 from Groenplaats), the **Museum voor Schone Kunsten** (Map p.242, A9; Fine Art Museum; Tues–Sun 10am–5pm; €4) has one of the country's better fine-art collections. Its early Flemish section features paintings by Jan van Eyck, Memling, Rogier van der Weyden and Quentin Matsys. Rubens has two large rooms to himself, in which one very large canvas stands out: the *Adoration of the Magi*, a beautifully human work apparently completed in a fortnight. The museum also displays a comprehensive collection of modern Belgian art with Paul Delvaux and James Ensor being particularly well represented.

ANTWERP

Accommodation

Cammerpoorte

Map p.242, C5. Nationalestraat
38 ⓣ03/231 97 36; ⓕ226 29 68.
Budget, two-star hotel with
forty, plain modern rooms,
but it is – and this is something
of a rarity in Antwerp – close
to the Grote Markt. ❹

Rubens Grote Markt

Map p.242, D2. Oude Beurs 29
ⓣ03/226 95 82, ⓕ225 19 40,
ⓔhotel.rubens@glo.be.
One of the best hotels in
town, the *Rubens* is a lovely
little place with tastefully
furnished, modern rooms in
an old building just a couple
of minutes' walk north of the
Grote Markt. ❺

Scoutel
Jeugdverblifcentrum

Stoomstraat 3 ⓣ03/226 46 06,
ⓕ232 63 92, ⓦwww.vvksm.be.
Spick and span hostel-cum-
hotel offering frugal but
perfectly adequate doubles
and triples with breakfast. It's
situated about 5min walk
from Centraal Station.
There's no curfew (guests
have their own keys), but be
sure to check in before 6pm
when reception closes.
Reservations are advised.
€27 for a single room,
€43.50 for a double with
discounts for the under-26s.

Eating

Hippodroom

Map p.242, A8. Léopold de
Waelplaats 10 ⓣ03/248 52 52.
Smooth and polished
restaurant offering a wide
range of Flemish dishes from
around €18 per main course.

De Matelote

Map p.242, B3. Haarstraat 9
ⓣ03/231 3207.
Modish, pastel-painted fish
restaurant off Grote Pieter
Potstraat, near the Grote
Markt. Serves delicious – if
expensive – food.

ANTWERP

●

Pizzeria Antonio

Map p.242, C3. Grote Markt 6.
Tasty and swiftly served pasta
and pizza.

De Stoemppot

Map p.242, B3. Vlasmarkt 12

Ⓣ03/231 36 86.
Stoemp is a traditional Flemish
dish consisting of puréed
meat and vegetables – and
this is the best place to eat it.
Closed Wed.

Drinking

Café de Muze

Map p.242, D3. Melkmarkt 15.
With its bare brick walls and
retro film posters, this laid-
back and central little place is
a busy spot. Occasional live
music – mainly jazz and
blues.

Het Elfde Gebod

Map p.242, D3. Torfbrug 10.
On one of the tiny squares
fronting the north side of the
cathedral, this bar is
something of a tourist trap,
but it's still worth visiting for
the kitsch religious statues
which cram the interior; the
food is mediocre.

De Vagant

Map p.242, C4. Reyndersstraat
21.
Specialist gin bar serving an
extravagant range of Belgian
and Dutch jenevers in spruce,
modern surroundings.

De Volle Maan

Map p.242, C3. Oude
Koornmarkt 7.
Lively, likeable and offbeat
bar close to the Grote Markt.

VEURNE

VEURNE is a charming market town, rural Flanders at its
prettiest, situated near the coast some 75km west of Ghent.
It was originally part of a chain of fortresses built to defend
the region from the raids of the Vikings, but without much
success. The town failed to flourish and two centuries later

it was small, poor and insignificant. All that changed when Robert II of Flanders returned from the Crusades in 1099 with a piece of the True Cross. His ship was caught in a gale, and in desperation he vowed to offer the relic to the first church he saw if he survived. The church was St Walburga at Veurne, and the annual procession that commemorated the gift made the town an important centre of medieval pilgrimage for some three hundred years. Today, Veurne's main attraction is its amiable, easy-going atmosphere and trim appearance, especially in the Grote Markt, one of the best-preserved town squares in Belgium.

Arrival and information

There's a direct train from Ghent to Veurne; it leaves every hour and takes an hour. Veurne **train station** is a ten-minute stroll from the town centre – turn right out of the station building, first left along Statiestraat and go over the canal straight down Ooststraat. The **tourist office**, at Grote Markt 29 (April–Sept daily 10am–noon & 1.30–5.30pm; Oct–March Mon–Sat 10am–noon & 2–4pm; ☎058/33 05 31, ⓦwww.veurne.be), issues a useful and free town brochure, which includes an events' calendar and accommodation listings.

Veurne is actually nearer to Bruges than Ghent – it's only about 40km away – but there's no direct train; you have to change at Lichtervelde and the journey takes a little over an hour. Veurne is also linked by bus with Ieper (see p.229), some 25km to the south. Veurne bus station is next to its train station; for bus timetable details, call the bus company, De Lijn, on ☎059/56 53 53.

VEURNE

●

The Town

All the main sights are on or around the **Grote Markt**, beginning in the northwest corner with the **Stadhuis** (Town Hall), an engaging mix of Gothic and Renaissance styles built between 1596 and 1612. Inside, a **museum** (April–Sept guided tours 4 times daily, Oct–March Mon–Sat twice daily; €2) displays items of unexceptional interest, the pick of which is a set of leather wall coverings made in Cordoba. The Stadhuis connects with the more austere classicism of the **Gerechtshof** (Law Courts), whose symmetrical pillars and long, rectangular windows now hold the tourist office, but once sheltered the Inquisition as it set about the Flemish peasantry with gusto. The attached tiered and balconied **Belfort** (belfry; no public access) was completed in 1628, its Gothic lines culminating in a dainty Baroque tower, from where **carillon concerts** (Wed 10.30–11.30am, plus July & Aug Sun 8–9pm) ring out over the town. The belfry is, however, dwarfed by the adjacent **St Walburga** (June–Sept daily 10am–noon & 3–6pm; free), the objective of the medieval pilgrims, an enormous buttressed and gargoyled affair with weather-beaten brick walls dating from the thirteenth century. It's actually the second church to be built on the spot; the original version – which in turn replaced a pagan temple dedicated to Wotan – was razed by the Vikings. The hangar-like interior has one virtue, the lavishly carved Flemish Renaissance choir stalls.

Moving on to the northeast corner of the Grote Markt, the **Spaans Paviljoen** (Spanish Pavilion), at the end of Ooststraat, was built as the town hall in the middle of the fifteenth century, but takes its name from its later adaptation as the officers' quarters of the Habsburg garrison. It's a self-confident building, the initial square brick tower, with its castellated parapet, extended by a facade of long, slender windows and flowing stone tracery in the true Gothic manner

VEURNE

THE PENITENTS' PROCESSION

In 1650 a young soldier named Mannaert was on garrison duty in Veurne when he was persuaded by his best friend to commit a mortal sin. After receiving the consecrated wafer during Communion, he took it out of his mouth, wrapped it in a cloth, and returned to his lodgings where he charred it over a fire, under the delusion that by reducing it to powder he would make himself invulnerable to injury. The news got out, and he was later arrested, tried and executed, his friend suffering the same fate a few weeks later. Fearful of the consequences of this sacrilege in their town, the people of Veurne resolved that something must be done and decided on a procession to commemorate the Passion of Christ. This survives as the **Penitents' Procession** (*Boetprocessie*), held on the last Sunday in July – an odd and distinctly macabre reminder of a superstitious past. Trailing through the streets, the leading figures dress in the brown cowls of the Capuchins and carry wooden crosses that weigh anything up to 50kg.

– an obvious contrast to the Flemish shutters and gables of the old **Vleeshuis** (Meat Hall) standing directly opposite. Crossing over to the southeast side of the square, the **Hoge Wacht**, which originally served as the quarters of the town watch, displays a fetching amalgam of styles, its brick gable cheered up by a small arcaded gallery. The east side of this building edges the Appelmarkt, home to the clumping medieval mass of **St Niklaaskerk**, whose detached **tower** (mid-June to mid-Sept 10–11.45am & 2–5.15pm; €1.50) gives spectacular views over the surrounding countryside.

Accommodation and eating

There's no strong reason to overnight in Veurne, but the tourist office does have a small cachet of private **rooms**

(**②**–**③**) and there is one very recommendable **hotel**. This is the three-star *Croonhof* (**☎**058/31 31 28, **Ⓕ**31 56 81, **Ⓔ**croonhof@online.be; **⑤**), a smart, well-cared-for little place in an attractively converted old house with spotless rooms just off the Grote Markt at Noordstraat 9. Call ahead in summer to be certain of a bed.

The Grote Markt is lined with **cafés** and **bars**. One of the more popular places is *'t Centrum,* Grote Markt 33 (closed Mon Sept–June), which offers reasonably priced snacks and meals from a straightforward Flemish menu. Another option is the comparable *Flandria,* at Grote Markt 30 (closed Thurs). Moving upmarket, the *Croonhof* (closed Sun eve & Mon plus last 2 weeks in Sept) has an excellent restaurant, featuring Flemish regional dishes.

OUDENAARDE

The attractive and gently old-fashioned town of **OUDE-NAARDE**, literally "old landing place", hugs the banks of the River Scheldt as it twists its way north toward Ghent, 30km away. The town has a long and chequered history. Granted a charter in 1193, it concentrated on cloth manu-facture until the early fifteenth century, when its weavers cleverly switched to tapestry-making, an industry that made its burghers rich and the town famous with the best tapes-tries becoming the prized possessions of the kings of France and Spain. So far so good, but Oudenaarde became a key military objective during the religious and dynastic wars of the sixteenth to the eighteenth centuries and time and again it was attacked and besieged, making sustained expan-sion impossible. Nevertheless, it was the demise of the tapestry industry in the 1780s that pauperized the town, rendering it an insignificant backwater in one of the poorest parts of Flanders. In the last few years, however, things have improved considerably due to its skilful use of regional

OUDENAARDE

0   100 m

Bus Station

Train Station

STATIONSPLEIN

BREDESTRAAT

PAUWEL VANDERSCHELDESTR

DIJKSTRAAT

BLEKERSTRAAT

FORTSTRAAT

LIZERSTRAAT

GROENSTRAAT

J. LACOPSSTRAAT

STATIONSSTRAAT

BEVERSTRAAT

Coupere

GEVAERTSDREEF

GEN. PERSSINGSTR

DE VOSTR

DIJKSTRAAT

PRINS LEOPOLDSTR

A. BROUWERSSTR

Park
Liedts

PARKSTRAAT

GASPER H. STR

TACAMBARO-
PLEIN

MEINAERT

HOOGSTRAAT

WIJNGAARDSTR

ACHTER DEWACHT

WOEKER

SIMON DE PAPPESTRAAT

CAPUC. LIN
STEEG

NEDERSTRAAT

KATTESTRAAT

BEKSTRAAT

GENTIEL
ANTHEUNISPLEIN

LAPPERSFORT

JEZUIETENPLEIN

Lakenhalle

Stadhuis

A

1

B

C

EINESTRAAT

KONINGSTR

REFUGESTR

GRACHT

E

MARKT

D

BROODSTRAAT

KREKEL PUT TUSSENBRUGGERN

MAARLBORGHLAAN

BOURGONDISTRAAT

F

VOORBURG

BURGSCHELDE

Huis de
Lalaing

St Walburgakerk

IST WAL-BURGASTR

LEVIEN
STR

BURG

ACHTER
BURG

KASTEELSTR

BERGSTRAAT

MATTHIJS CASTELENSTRAAT

SMALLENDAM

DE HAM

ZAKSE

Begijnhof

2

MANGARETHA VAN PARMASTRAAT

LOUISE MARIEKAAI

Schelde

SPEI

BAARSTR

O.L.V.
Van
Pamelekerk

ACCOMMODATION

| De Rantere | 2 |
| La Pomme d'Or | 1 |

**RESTAURANTS,
CAFÉS & BARS**

Cesar	B
De Carillon	F
De Cridts	E
Fox	C
Harmonie	A
N'oni's	D

OUDENAARDE

development funds, and today's town – with its clutch of fascinating old buildings – makes an interesting and pleasant day out.

Arrival and information

There is a train from Ghent to Oudenaarde every half-hour and the journey takes just thirty minutes. Oudenaarde's **train station** is a modern affair – the old neo-Gothic station next door stands forlorn and abandoned – and from here it's a fifteen-minute walk to the town centre. The **tourist office**, in the Stadhuis on the Markt (April–Oct Mon–Fri 9am–6pm, Sat & Sun 10am–6pm; Nov–March Mon–Fri 8.30am–noon & 1.30–4.30pm, Sat 2–5pm; ⓣ055/31 72 51, ⓦwww.oudenaarde.be), issues a free town brochure and has an accommodation list, though there are no private rooms and only three central hotels.

The Town

Heading into Oudenaarde along Stationsstraat, the middle of the **Tacambaroplein** is taken up by a romantic war memorial commemorating those who were daft or unscrupulous enough to volunteer to go to Mexico and fight for Maximilian, son-in-law of the Belgian king, Leopold I. Unwanted and unloved, Maximilian was imposed on the Mexicans by a French army provided by Napoleon III, who wanted to create his own American empire. It was all too fanciful and the occupation rapidly turned into a fiasco. Maximilian paid for the adventure with his life in 1867, and few of his soldiers made the return trip.

The Markt: the Stadhuis and Lakenhalle
Further south, the wide open space of the **Markt** is edged by the **Stadhuis**, one of the finest examples of Flamboyant

OUDENAARDE

Gothic in the country. An exquisite creation of around 1525, its elegantly symmetrical facade spreads out on either side of the extravagant tiers, balconies and parapets of a slender central tower, topped by the gilded figure of a knight, *Hanske de Krijger* ("Little John the Warrior"). Underneath the knight, the cupola is in the shape of a crown, a theme reinforced by the two groups of cherubs on the dormer windows below, who lovingly clutch at the royal insignia. To the rear of the Stadhuis sulks the dour and gloomy exterior of the adjoining Romanesque **Lakenhalle**, or cloth hall, which dates from the thirteenth century.

Inside the Stadhuis (April–Oct tours: Mon–Thurs at 11am & 3pm, Fri 11am, Sat & Sun 2pm & 4pm; €4) a magnificent oak **doorway** forms the entrance to the old *Schepenzaal* (Aldermen's Hall). Of the paintings displayed here, the most distinguished are those by Adriaen Brouwer, a native of Oudenaarde, whose representations of the five senses are typical of his ogre-like, caricaturist's style. Beyond, in the Lakenhalle, is a superb collection of **tapestries**, the first being the eighteenth-century *Nymphs in a Landscape*, a leafy romantic scene in which four nymphs pick and arrange flowers. The adjacent *Return from Market*, which also dates from the eighteenth century, features trees in shades of blue and green, edged by sky and bare earth – a composition reminiscent of Dutch landscape paintings. In the sixteenth century, classical tapestries were all the rage and there are several superb examples here, beginning with *Hercules and the Stymphalian Birds*, a scene set among what appear to be cabbage leaves. Equally impressive is *Scipio and Hannibal*, in which the border is decorated with medallions depicting the Seven Wonders of the World – though the Hanging Gardens of Babylon appear twice to create the symmetry.

OUDENAARDE

> Over the last few years, the days and times of the guided tours of the Stadhuis have been changed frequently. To avoid disappointment, call Oudenaarde tourist office ahead of time.

South of the Markt

Immediately southwest of the Markt, **St Walburgakerk** (Thurs 10–11am and usually July–Sept Tues & Sat 2.30–4.30pm) is a hulking mass of masonry, which was badly in need of the restoration work that is now well underway. Inside, there are several locally manufactured tapestries and a monument to the four Catholic priests who were thrown into the Scheldt in 1572 from the windows of the town castle (since demolished). Across the road, opposite the church, a group of old mansions follows the bend in what was once the line of the town wall. These are also being repaired and refurbished – not before time – and, close by, narrow Voorburg and then Kasteelstraat lead down to the river past a trim seventeenth-century **portal**, the entrance to the former *Begijnhof*. Finally, if you're keen to discover more about tapestries, head for the municipal repair workshops sited in a grand old mansion, the **Huis de Lalaing** (Mon–Fri 9am–noon & 1.30–4.30pm; free), on the far side of the river at Bourgondiestraat 9. The workshops don't make a big thing out of showing visitors around, but everyone seems quite friendly and you can poke around looking at the various restorative processes.

Accommodation, eating and drinking

Oudenaarde has two recommendable **hotels**, the better of which is the enjoyable *De Rantere*, Jan zonder Vreeslaan 8 (☎055/31 89 88, ℱ33 01 11, ⊛www.derantere.be; ➏), a spruce and comfortable modern hotel overlooking the

OUDENAARDE

Scheldt on the south side of the Markt. The other option is *La Pomme d'Or*, Markt 62 (℡055/31 19 00, ℱ30 08 44, ⓦwww.lapommedor.be; ❺), which occupies a big old house on the main square and offers plain, but perfectly adequate, high-ceilinged rooms.

The Markt is lined with **cafés** and bars, one good option being *De Cridts*, at no. 58, an old-fashioned café-restaurant serving standard-issue Flemish dishes at very reasonable prices. Close by, at no. 63, the *Harmonie Restaurant* (Mon–Thurs 10am–9pm, Fri 6–9pm & Sun 10am–9pm) is a tad more formal, but there's a wider choice, with snacks from €7 and tasty main courses for around €18.

As for **drinking**, the local Roman brewery rules the municipal roost, its most distinctive products being Tripel Ename, a strong blond beer, and Roman Dobbelen Bruinen, a snappy, filtered stout. These are usually available at the best bars in town: try *N'oni's*, a fashionable, pastel-decorated bar off the east side of the Grote Markt at Einestraat 3, and the *Fox*, a similarly lively and youthful spot directly opposite. A third option is *De Carillon*, a quieter place in the old brick-gabled building in the shadow of St Walburgakerk.

CONTEXTS

A brief history of Bruges and Ghent

Early settlement to the ninth century

Little is known of the prehistoric settlers of Flanders, though it is probable that **Neolithic peoples** extracted salt from the sea near Bruges and that their kinsmen eked out a precarious existence amongst the marshes of today's Ghent. More certainly archeologists believe the **Celts** had established an Iron Age culture across much of Flanders by about the fifth century BC, though these tribes only begin to emerge from the prehistorical soup after Julius Caesar's conquest of Gaul (broadly France and southern Belgium) in 57 to 50 BC. The **Romans** did not consider Flanders worthy of colonization, but instead used its warlike inhabitants as a source of recruitment for their legions and curiosity for imperial travellers. Early reports were hardly flattering: in 50 AD, Pliny commented that they were a "wretched race". The Roman occupation of Gaul continued for five hundred years, until the legions were pulled back to protect the heartland of the crumbling empire. As the western empire collapsed in chaos and confusion, the Germanic **Franks** filled the power vacuum, though in Flanders they were jostled by their northern neighbours, the Saxons and the Frisians. The Franks were probably the first to settle Ghent, on account of its strategically important location at the confluence of the rivers Scheldt and Leie, though the Celts may well have been here before them. Whatever the truth, there was definitely a significant settlement here when the French missionary **St Amand** arrived in about 625 AD. Eager to turn the locals Christian, St Amand founded both St Pietersabdij (see p.120) and St Baafsabdij (see p.108), but despite – or perhaps because of – these successes, his putative parishioners ended up chucking him into the Scheldt.

At the end of the eighth century, most of Flanders had been incorporated into Charlemagne's empire and it was in Ghent, in 811, that the emperor assembled a massive fleet for an expedition against the **Vikings**, whose raids were becoming increasingly troublesome. In the event, Charlemagne's campaign was inconclusive and the Vikings, emboldened by the collapse of central authority after the emperor's death in 814, returned with depressing regularity, sacking Ghent in 851 and again in 879. Flanders proved an easy target for the raiders, but slowly local barons rectified matters, no one more so than the first count of Flanders, **Baldwin Iron Arm**, who founded Bruges as a coastal stronghold against the Vikings in 865. By the tenth century, with the Vikings no longer a menace, Flanders had developed into a fully fledged feudal society governed, however roughly, by its own count. The complication – and this was to dog medieval Flanders – was that the count held most of his possessions as a vassal of the King of (what was then a very small) France. This didn't matter much in the tenth century, when the French king was remote and weak, but in the long term it had complicated ramifications for the Flemings.

The tenth century to 1384

In the tenth century, Flanders developed its own **wool industry**. Sheep flourished on the coastal salt-flats and inland on the Flemish plain, though the wool produced was of poorer quality than English wool, which supplanted the local product in the first years of the twelfth century. This soon led to the development of an **international cloth trade** in which high-quality English wool was imported and turned into clothing, which was then exported all over the known world. The leading Flemish cloth town was Bruges, with Ghent and Ypres not far behind. It proved to be an immensely profitable business and it made Flanders – or at least its merchants – immensely rich. Bruges, in particular, became a key member of – and showcase for – the Hanseatic League, a mainly German association of towns which acted as a trading group, protecting its interests by an exclusive system of trading tariffs. Through the city's harbours and docks, Flemish cloth and Hansa goods were exchanged for hogs from Denmark, spices from Venice, hides from Ireland, wax from Russia, gold and silver from Poland and furs from Bulgaria. The business of these foreign traders was protected by no fewer than 21 consulates, and Bruges developed a wide range of support services, including banking, money-changing, maritime insurance and an elementary shipping code, known as the Roles de Damme.

Despite (or because of) this lucrative state of affairs, Bruges, Ghent and Ypres were plagued by **war**. The cities' weavers and merchants were dependent on the goodwill of the kings of England for the proper functioning of the wool trade, but their feudal overlords, the counts of Flanders, were vassals of the rival king of France. Although some of the dukes and counts were strong enough to defy their king, most felt obliged to obey his orders and thus take his side against the English when the two countries were at war. This conflict of interests was compounded by rivalry between the Flemish guilds, class tensions between the cities's landowners, merchants and guildsmen and the designs the French monarchy had on the independence of Flanders itself. Time and again, the French sought to assert control over the towns of West Flanders, but more often than not they encountered armed rebellion. In Bruges, the most famous insurrection was precipitated by Philip the Fair, the King of France, at the beginning of the fourteenth century. Philip and his wife, Joanna of Navarre, had held a grand reception in Bruges, but it had only served to feed their envy. In the face of the city's splendour, Joanna moaned "I thought that I alone was Queen; but here in this place I have six hundred rivals." The opportunity to flex royal muscles came shortly afterwards when the town's guildsmen flatly refused to pay a new round of taxes. Enraged, Philip dispatched an army to restore order and garrison the town, but at dawn on Friday, May 18, 1302, a rebellious force of Flemings crept into the city and massacred Philip's sleepy army – an occasion later known as the **Bruges Matins**. Anyone who couldn't correctly pronounce the Flemish shibboleth *schild en vriend* ("shield and friend") was put to the sword. In July of the same year, Philip the Fair suffered another disastrous reverse at the **Battle of the Golden Spurs**, when the army he had sent to Flanders to avenge the Bruges Matins was slaughtered outside Kortrijk. The two armies, Philip's heavily armoured cavalry and the lightly armed Flemish weavers, had met on marshy ground, which the Flemish had disguised with brushwood. Despising their lowly-born adversaries, the French knights made no reconnaissance and fell into the trap, milling around in the mud like cumbersome dinosaurs. They were massacred, victims of their own arrogance, and the battle was a military landmark, the first time an amateur civilian army had defeated professional mail-clad knights.

Burgundian rule and the arrival of the Habsburgs

Throughout the fourteenth century, Bruges and Ghent pretty much held their own against the many attempts to curb their independence – in part because of the interminable warfare between France and England. The **dukes of Burgundy** were, however, a much more powerful kettle of ducal fish and, after they inherited Flanders in 1384, they hacked away at the cloth towns' rights and privileges to great effect. In 1419, **Philip the Good** succeeded to the ducal throne and established a strong central administration in Bruges. The city was firmly under his thumb, but it did prosper and the Burgundian court patronized the early and seminal Nederlandish painters like Jan van Eyck and Hans Memling. Philip died in 1467 to be succeeded by his son, **Charles the Bold**. An inveterate warmonger, Charles was killed besieging Nancy ten years later and Flanders was inherited by his daughter, **Mary of Burgundy**, who was married to **Maximilian**, a **Habsburg** prince and future Holy Roman Emperor. Mary died in a riding accident in 1482 – her tomb stands beside that of her father in the Onze Lieve Vrouwekerk in Bruges (see p.51) – and her territories went to her husband. Thus Flanders, as well as the rest of present-day Belgium and Holland, was incorporated into the Habsburg Empire. A sharp operator, Maximilian continued where the Burgundians had left off, whittling away at the power of the Flemish cities and despite the odd miscalculation – the burghers of Bruges temporarily imprisoned him in 1488 (see p.23) – he was largely successful.

When Maximilian became Holy Roman Emperor in 1494, he transferred control of the Low Countries to his son, Philip the Handsome, and then – after Philip's early death – to his grandson **Charles V**, who also became king of Spain and Holy Roman Emperor in 1516 and 1519 respectively. Charles ruled his vast kingdom with skill and energy, but, born in Ghent, he was (just like Maximilian) very suspicious of the turbulent Flemish burghers. Consequently, he favoured **Antwerp** at their expense and this city now became the greatest port in the Habsburg empire, part of a general movement of trade and prosperity away from Flanders to the cities further north. In addition, the Flemish cloth industry had, by the 1480s, begun its long decline, mainly because of England's new-found cloth-manufacturing success. Bruges was especially badly hit and, as a sign of its decline, failed to dredge the silted-up River Zwin, the city's trading lifeline to the North Sea. By the 1510s, the stretch of water between Sluis and Damme was only navigable by smaller ships, and by the 1530s the town's sea trade had collapsed completely. Bruges simply withered away, its houses deserted, its canals empty and its money spirited north with the merchants. Ghent did much better, in part because many of its merchants switched to exporting surplus grain from France, and was sufficiently confident – or foolhardy – to refuse to pay a tax imposed by Charles in 1537. Furious, the emperor seized the city, beheaded the leaders of the opposition, annulled the town's ancient privileges and built a new fortress there entirely at the city's expense.

By sheer might, Charles had bent Ghent to his will, but regardless of this display of force, a spiritual trend was emerging that would soon not only question the rights of the emperor but also rock the power of the Catholic Church itself.

The Reformation and the revolt against Spain

The **Reformation** was a religious revolt that stood sixteenth-century Europe on its head. The first stirrings were in the welter of debate that spread across much of western Europe under the auspices of theologians like **Erasmus**, who wished to cleanse the Catholic church of its corruptions and extravagant ceremony; only later did some of these same thinkers – principally **Martin Luther** – decide to support a breakaway church. The seeds of this **Protestantism** fell on fertile ground among the merchants of Ghent and Bruges, whose wealth and independence had never been easy to accommodate within a rigid caste society. Similarly, their employees, the guildsmen and their apprentices, who had a long history of opposing arbitrary authority, were easily convinced of the need for reform. In 1555, **Charles V abdicated**, transferring his German lands to his brother Ferdinand, and his Italian, Spanish and Low Countries territories to his son, the fanatically Catholic **Philip II**. In the short term, the scene was set for a bitter confrontation between Catholics and Protestants, while the dynastic ramifications of the division of the Habsburg empire were to complicate European affairs for centuries.

After his father's abdication, Philip II decided to teach his heretical subjects a lesson. He garrisoned Bruges, Ghent and the other towns of the Low Countries with Spanish mercenaries, imported the Inquisition and passed a series of anti-Protestant edicts. However, other pressures on the Habsburg Empire forced him into a tactical withdrawal and he transferred control to his sister, **Margaret of Parma**, in 1559. Based in Brussels, the equally resolute Margaret implemented the policies of her brother with gusto. Initially, the repression worked, but in 1566 the Protestant workers struck back. A Protestant sermon in the tiny Flemish textile town of Steenvoorde incited the congregation to purge the local church of its papist idolatry. The crowd smashed up the church's reliquaries and shrines, broke the stained glass windows and terrorized the priests, thereby launching the **Iconoclastic Fury**. The rioting

THE REFORMATION AND THE REVOLT AGAINST SPAIN

spread like wild fire and within ten days churches had been ransacked from one end of the country to the other, including Bruges and Ghent, where the *Adoration of the Mystic Lamb* altarpiece (see p.82) had the first of its many lucky escapes.

Protestantism had infiltrated the nobility, but the ferocity of the Fury shocked the upper classes into renewed support for Spain. Philip was keen to capitalize on the increase in support and, in 1567, he dispatched the **Duke of Albe**, with an army of 10,000 men, to the Low Countries to suppress his religious opponents absolutely. Margaret was not at all pleased by Philip's decision and, when Albe arrived in Brussels, she resigned in a huff, initiating a long period of what was, in effect, military rule. One of Albe's first acts was to set up the Commission of Civil Unrest, which was soon nicknamed the "**Council of Blood**" after its habit of executing those it examined. No fewer than 12,000 citizens went to the block.

Once again, the repression backfired. The region's greatest landowner, Prince William of Orange-Nassau, known as **William the Silent** (1533–84), raised the Low Countries against the Habsburgs and swept all before him, making a triumphant entrance into Brussels. Momentarily, it seemed possible for the whole of the Low Countries to unite behind William and all signed the **Union of Brussels**, which demanded the departure of foreign troops as a condition for accepting a diluted Habsburg sovereignty. This was followed, in 1576, by the **Pacification of Ghent**, an agreement that guaranteed freedom of religious belief, a necessary precondition for any union between the predominantly Catholic south (Belgium) and the mainly Protestant north (the Netherlands). But Philip was not inclined to compromise, especially when he realized that William's Calvinist sympathies were giving many of the prince's newly-found Catholic allies the jitters. In 1578, Philip gathered together another army which he dispatched to the Low Countries under the command of Alessandro Farnese, the **Duke of Parma**. Parma was successful, recapturing most of modern Belgium, including Bruges and Ghent in 1584 and finally Antwerp the year after. He was, however, unable to advance any further north and the Low Countries were divided into two – the **Spanish Netherlands** and the **United Provinces** – beginning a separation that would lead, after many changes, to the creation of Belgium and the Netherlands.

The Spanish Netherlands

Parma was surprisingly generous in victory, but Philip II was not inclined to tolerate his newly recovered Protestant subjects. As a result, and as Spanish control grew ever more proscriptive, thousands of Flemish weavers, apprentices and skilled workers – the bedrock of Calvinism – fled north to escape the new Catholic regime, thereby fuelling an economic boom in Holland. Ghent alone haemorrhaged 20,000 workers. It took a while for this migration to take effect, and for several years the **Spanish Netherlands** had all the trappings – if not the substance – of success, though a complete economic catastrophe was warded off by the fostering of new enterprises to meet the luxury tastes of the Habsburg elite. Silk weaving, diamond processing and lace-making were particular beneficiaries and a new canal was cut linking Ghent and Bruges to the sea at Ostend. This commercial restructuring underpinned a brief flourishing of artistic life centred on **Rubens** and his circle of friends, including Anthony van Dyck and Jacob Jordaens, in Antwerp during the first decades of the seventeenth century.

Meanwhile, months before his death in 1598, Philip II had granted control of the Spanish Netherlands to his daughter and her husband, appointing them the **Archdukes Isabella** and **Albert**. Failing to learn from experience, the ducal couple continued to prosecute the war against the Protestant north, but with so little success that they were obliged to make peace – the **Twelve Year Truce** – in 1609. When the truce ended, the new Spanish king Philip IV stubbornly resumed the campaign against the Protestants, this time as part of a general and even more devastating conflict, the **Thirty Years War** (1618–48), a largely religious-based conflict between Catholic and Protestant countries that involved most of western Europe. Finally, the Habsburgs were compelled to accept the humiliating terms of the **Peace of Westphalia**, a general treaty whose terms formally recognized the independence of the United Provinces and closed the Scheldt estuary, thereby crippling Antwerp. By these means, the commercial preeminence of Amsterdam was assured and its Golden Age began.

The Thirty Years War had devastated the Spanish Netherlands, but the peace was perhaps as bad. Politically dependent on a decaying Spain, economically in steep decline and deprived of most of its more independent-minded citizens, the country turned in on itself, sustained by the fanatical Catholicism of the **Counter-Reformation**. Literature disappeared, the sciences vegetated and religious orders multiplied to an extraordinary degree. In painting, artists – principally Rubens – were used to confirm the ecclesiastical orthodoxies, their canvases full of muscular saints and angels, reflecting a religious faith of mystery and hierarchy; others, such as David Teniers, retreated into minutely observed realism. Flanders was especially hard hit, sinking into poverty and decay, a static and traditional society where nearly every aspect of life was controlled by decree, and only three percent of the population could read or write. As Voltaire quipped:

In this sad place wherein I stay,
Ignorance, torpidity,
And boredom hold their lasting sway,
With unconcerned stupidity;
A land where old obedience sits,
Well filled with faith, devoid of wits.

The Peace of Westphalia had also freed the king of France from fear of Germany, and the political and military history of the Spanish Netherlands after 1648 was dominated by the efforts of **Louis XIV** to add the country to his territories. Fearful of an over-powerful France, the United Provinces and England, among others, determinedly resisted French designs and, to preserve the balance of power, fought a long series of campaigns beginning in the 1660s. The **War of the Spanish Succession** – the final conflict of the series – was sparked by the death in 1700 of Charles II, the last of the Spanish Habsburgs, who had willed his territories to the grandson of Louis XIV. An anti-French coalition refused to accept the settlement and there ensued a haphazard series of campaigns that dragged on for eleven years. Eventually, with the **Treaty of Utrecht** of 1713, the French abandoned their attempt to conquer the Spanish Netherlands, which now passed under the control of the Austrian Habsburgs in the figure of Emperor Charles VI.

The Austrian Netherlands

The transfer of the country from Spanish to **Austrian control** made little appreciable difference: a remote imperial authority continued to operate through an appointed governor in Brussels and the country as a whole remained poor and backward. This sorry state of affairs began to change in the middle of the eighteenth century when the Austrian oligarchy came under the influence of the **Enlightenment**, a belief in reason and progress – as against authority and tradition – that had first been proselytized by French philosophers. In 1753, the arrival of a progressive governor, the **Count of Cobenzl**, signified a transformation of Habsburg policy. Cobenzl initiated an ambitious programme of public works and both Ghent and Bruges benefited. New canals were dug, old canals deepened, new industries were encouraged – especially in Ghent – and public health was at least discussed, the main result being regulations forbidding burial inside churches and the creation of new cemeteries outside the city walls. This was, however, all a little too late: Ghent had a population of just 50,000 and Bruges 30,000 at a time when Amsterdam had swollen to 200,000 and Paris 550,000.

In 1780, the **Emperor Joseph II** came to the throne, determined to "root out silly old prejudices", as he put it – but his reforms were opposed by both left and right. The liberal-minded **Vonckists** demanded a radical, republican constitution, while their enemies, the conservative **Statists**, insisted on the Catholic status quo. There was pandemonium and, in 1789, the Habsburgs dispatched an army to restore order. Against all expectations, the two political groups combined and defeated the Austrians near Antwerp in what became known as the **Brabant Revolution**. In January 1790, the rebels announced the formation of the United States of Belgium, but the country remained in turmoil and when Emperor Joseph died in 1790, his successor, **Léopold**, quickly withdrew the reforming acts and sent in his troops to restore imperial authority.

French occupation and the Kingdom of the Netherlands

The new and repressive Habsburg regime was short-lived. French Republican armies brushed the imperial forces aside in 1794, and the Austrian Netherlands were annexed the following year, an annexation that was to last until 1814. The **French** imposed radical reforms: the Catholic church was stripped of much of its worldly wealth, local government was entirely reorganized, feudal privileges were abolished, and so were the guilds. Despite their Republican claims to the contrary, the French were, however, very much an army of occupation. Particularly in the early years, looting and destruction were commonplace: in Bruges, the French razed St Donatian's Cathedral (see p.33) and in Ghent they swiped the *Adoration of the Mystic Lamb* altarpiece and carted it off to Paris. Most unpopular of all, the French introduced conscription, prompting the Flemish peasantry to a series of insurrections, each of which was crushed with great severity. The only bonus – at least as far as Ghent was concerned – was the arrival of Lieven Bauwens (see p.106) with a Spinning Jenny he had stolen from England. Bauwens used the technology he had acquired to establish the city's first mechanized cotton mill, thereby kick-starting an industry that was to revive Ghent's economy. Bauwens success did not, of course, make the French any more popular and French authority in Ghent and Bruges had largely evaporated long before **Napoleon**'s final defeat just outside Brussels at the battle of Waterloo in 1815.

At the **Congress of Vienna**, called to settle Europe at the end of the Napoleonic Wars, the main concern of the great powers was to bolster the Low Countries against France. With scant regard to the feelings of those affected, they therefore decided to establish the **Kingdom of the Netherlands**, which incorporated both the old United Provinces and the Austrian Netherlands, and on the throne they placed Frederick William of Orange, appointed **King William I**. From the very beginning, the union proved problematic – there were even two capital cities, Brussels and The Hague – and William simply wasn't wily enough to hold things together. Nonetheless, the union struggled on until August 25, 1830, when the singing of a duet, *Amour sacré de la Patrie*, in the Brussels opera house hit a nationalist nerve. The audience poured out onto the streets to raise the flag of Brabant in defiance of King William, thereby initiating a countrywide **revolution**. William sent in his troops, but Great Britain and France quickly intervened to stop hostilities. In January of the following year, at the **Conference of London**, the great powers recognized Belgium's independence, with the caveat that the country be classified a "neutral" state – that is one outside any other's sphere of influence. To bolster this new nation, they dug out the uncle of Queen Victoria, Prince Léopold of Saxe-Coburg, to present with the crown. Despite these national tribulations, Ghent did reasonably well from the joint kingdom: the cotton mills flourished and the Dutch established the city's university and built a bigger and better canal from the city to the sea.

Independent Belgium

Léopold I (1830–65) was careful to maintain his country's neutrality and encouraged an industrial boom that saw coal mines developed, iron-making factories established and the rapid expansion of the railway system. His successor, **Léopold II** (1865–1909), further boosted industry and supervised the emergence of Belgium as a major industrial power. In particular, Ghent's textile industry flourished, spearheading a more general expansion that involved everything from paper-making and sugar-processing to steel manufacture. Indeed, its entrepreneurial mayor, Emile Braun, even managed to get the Great Exhibition, showing the best in design and goods, staged here in 1913. Things were much more low-key in Bruges, but machine-made lace proved a profitable concern and the opening of a brand new seaport and harbour at nearby Zeebrugge in 1907 helped boost local trade. Determined to cut an international figure, Léopold II also decided to build up a colonial empire. The unfortunate recipients of his ambition were the Africans of the Congo River basin, who were effectively given to him by a conference of European powers in 1885. Ruling the Congo as a personal fiefdom, Léopold established an extraordinarily cruel colonial regime – so cruel in fact that even the other colonial powers were appalled and the Belgian state was obliged to end the embarrassment by taking over the region, as the **Belgian Congo**, in 1908.

Domestically, the first fly in the royal ointment came in the 1860s and 1870s with the initial stirrings of (a more virulent form of) **Flemish nationalism**. These nascent nationalists felt little enthusiasm for the unitary status of Belgium, divided as it was between a French-speaking majority in the south of the country – the Walloons – and the minority Dutch-speakers of the north. The Catholic party ensured that, under the Equality Law of 1898, Dutch was ratified as an official language, equal in status to French – the forerunner of many long and difficult debates. In Ghent, the language debate focused on the university, where the nationalists won a significant victory with the adoption of Dutch as an official language of tuition – alongside French. Bruges was following a rather different course, with the city remaining very small-town conservative and its most influential citizen, the priest **Guido Gezelle** (1830–99; see p.74), conflating the survival of the medieval town with the continuity of the Catholic faith – and the maintenance of Flemish "purity". This mind-set tallied neatly with the historicism of Bruges's sizeable English émigré community, a prosperous and powerful bunch of Victorians who were eager to preserve the city's medieval appearance, even "improving" it as and where necessary. Between them, Gezelle and the émigrés laid the basis of the city's tourist industry (however accidentally), but it was **Georges Rodenbach**'s novel of 1892, *Bruges-la-Morte* (see p.304), that alerted the whole of western Europe to the town's aged, quiet charms.

1900 to 1945

At the beginning of the twentieth century, Belgium was an industrial powerhouse with a booming economy and a rapidly increasing workforce – 934,000 in 1896, 1,176,000 in 1910. It was also determined to keep on good terms with all the great powers, but could not prevent getting caught up in **World War I**. Indifferent to Belgium's proclaimed neutrality, the Germans had decided as early as 1908 that the best way to attack France was via Belgium, and this is precisely what they did in 1914. They captured almost all of the country, the exception being a narrow strip of territory around De Panne. Undaunted, **King Albert I** (1909–34) and the Belgian army bravely manned the northern part of the Allied line, and it made the king a national hero. The trenches ran through western Flanders and all the towns and villages lying close to them – principally Ieper (Ypres) – were simply obliterated by artillery fire. Belgium also witnessed some of the worst of the slaughter in and around a bulge in the line, which became known as the **Ypres Salient** (see p.235). The destruction was, however, confined to a narrow strip of Flanders, and Ghent and Bruges were almost untouched, though the local population did suffer during the occupation from lack of food, and hundreds of men were forced to work in German factories.

The Germans returned in May 1940, launching a blitzkrieg that overwhelmed both Belgium and the Netherlands. This time there was no heroic resistance by the Belgian king, now **Léopold III** (1934–51), who ignored the advice of his government and surrendered unconditionally and in great haste. It is true that the Belgian army had been badly mauled and that a German victory was inevitable, but the manner of the surrender infuriated many Belgians, as did the king's refusal to form a government in exile. At first the occupation was relatively benign and most of the population waited apprehensively to see what would happen. The main exception – setting aside the king, who at best played an ambivalent role – was the right-wing edge of the Flemish Nationalist movement, which co-operated with the Germans and (unsuccessfully) sought to negotiate the creation of a separate Flemish state. Popular opinion hardened against the Germans in 1942 as the occupation became more oppressive. The Germans stepped up the requisitioning of Belgian equipment, expanded its forced labour schemes, obliging thousands of Belgians to work in Germany, and cracked down hard on any sign of opposition. By the end of the year, a **Resistance** movement was mounting acts of sabotage against the occupying forces and this, in turn, prompted more summary executions – of both Resistance fighters and hostages. The summer of 1942 also witnessed the first round-ups of the country's **Jews**. In 1940, there were approximately 50,000 Jews in Belgium, mostly newly arrived refugees from Hitler's Germany. Much to their credit, many Belgians did their best to frustrate Nazi efforts to transport the Jews out of the country – mostly to Auschwitz. Some members of the Belgian police did not co-operate, Belgian railway workers tried to leave carriages unlocked and/or sideline trains, and many other Belgians hid Jews in their homes for the war's duration. The result was that the Germans had, by 1944, killed about half the country's Jewish population, much lower than in other parts of occupied Europe. The Allied armies landed in France in

1900 TO 1945

June 1944 and the **liberation** of Belgium began in September with the Americans in the south and the British and Canadian divisions sweeping across Flanders in the north.

Modern times

After the war, the Belgians set about the task of economic **reconstruction**, helped by aid from the United States, but hindered by a divisive controversy over the wartime activities of King Léopold. Many felt his surrender to the Germans was cowardly and his subsequent willingness to work with them treacherous; others pointed to his efforts to increase the country's food rations and his negotiations to secure the release of Belgian prisoners. Inevitably, the complex shadings of collaboration and forced co-operation were hard to disentangle, and the debate continued until 1950 when a referendum narrowly recommended his return from exile. Léopold's return was, however, marked by rioting in Brussels and across Wallonia, where the king's opponents were concentrated, and Léopold abdicated in favour of his son, **Baudouin** (1951–93).

The development of the postwar Belgian economy follows the pattern of most of western Europe: reconstruction in the 1950s, boom in the 1960s, recession in the 1970s, and retrenchment in the 1980s and 1990s. In the meantime, Brussels, which had been one of the lesser European capitals, was turned into a major player when it became the home of the EU and NATO – the latter was ejected from France on the orders of de Gaulle in 1967. But, above all, the postwar period has been dominated by the increasing **tension between the Walloon and Flemish communities**, a state of affairs that has been entangled with the relative economic decline of Wallonia, formerly the home of most of the country's heavy industry, as compared with burgeoning Flanders. Every national institution is now dogged by the prerequisites of bilingualism – speeches in parliament have to be delivered in both languages – and in Brussels, the country's one and only **bilingual region**, every instance of the written word, from road signs to the yellow pages, has to be bilingual as well.

Bogged down by these linguistic preoccupations – the current Prime Minister (Guy Verhofstadt) and his cabinet squeeze in four hours of language classes every week – the federal government often appears extraordinarily cumbersome. In addition, much of the political class is at least partly reliant on the linguistic divide for their jobs and, institutionally speaking, has little reason to see the antagonisms resolved. For the most part, things just rumble on, but in 1996 the Belgian police, also dogged by language and regional divides, proved itself at best hopelessly inefficient and at worst complicit in the gruesome activities of the child murderer and pornographer **Marc Dutroux**. Over 350,000 people – from both sides of the language divide – took to the streets, demanding the police and justice system be overhauled. This rare outburst of public protest peaked again two years later when, amazingly enough, Dutroux escaped his police guards, stole a car and headed out of the city, and, although he was subsequently recaptured, most Belgians were simply appalled.

The Dutroux affair dented the national psyche – and few Belgians believe that the reforms imposed on the police have made much difference – but into this psychological breach rode the **royal family**, one of the few institutions to bind the country together. In 1999, the heir to the throne, Prince Philippe, broke with tradition and married a Belgian, Mathilde d'Udekem d'Acoz – and, to top that, one of non-royal descent and with family on both sides of the linguistic divide. The marriage may well have healed a few wounds, but its effects should not be over-estimated.

MODERN TIMES

Over 400,000 people snapped up the free travel tickets offered by the Belgian railways to celebrate the event, but only around twenty percent were used to come to Brussels, and out of them one can only speculate as to how many loyal subjects chose to wave the flag on a cold December day rather than head for the nearest bar.

An Introduction to Belgian Art

What follows is a brief introduction to a subject that has rightly filled volumes: it is designed to serve only as a quick reference. Inevitably, it covers **artists** that lived and worked in both the Netherlands and Belgium as these two countries have both been, for most of their history, bound together as the so-called Low Countries. For more in-depth and academic studies, see the recommendations in the "Books" listings on p.298.

In both Bruges and Ghent, paintings and sculptures are displayed in all the important churches and a clutch of lesser museums, but there are three principal collections. These are the Groeninge in Bruges (see p.35), which is world-famous for its Early Flemish Masters, the Museum voor Schone Kunsten in Ghent (see p.115), with a good all-round collection, and Ghent's contemporary art gallery, S.M.A.K. (see p.119).

The Early Flemish Masters

Throughout the medieval period, Flanders was one of the most artistically productive parts of Europe with all of the cloth towns, but especially Bruges and Ghent, trying to outdo its rivals with the quality of their religious art. Today, the works of these early Flemish painters, known as the **Flemish Primitives**, are highly prized and an excellent sample is displayed in both Ghent and Bruges as well as in Brussels. **Jan van Eyck** (1385–1441) is generally regarded as the first of the Flemish Primitives, and has even been credited with the invention of oil painting itself – though it seems more likely that he simply perfected a new technique by thinning his paint with (the newly discovered) turpentine, thus making it more flexible. His fame partially stems from the fact that he was one of the first artists to sign his work – an indication of how highly his talent was regarded by his contemporaries. Van Eyck's most celebrated work is the *Adoration of the Mystic Lamb*, a stunningly beautiful altarpiece displayed in St Baafskathedraal in Ghent (see p.82). The painting was revolutionary in its realism, for the first time using elements of native landscape in depicting Biblical themes, and was underpinned by a complex symbolism which has generated analysis and discussion ever since. Van Eyck's style and technique were to influence several generations of Low Countries artists.

Firmly in the Eyckian tradition was **Rogier van der Weyden** (1400–64), one-time official painter to the city of Brussels. Weyden's paintings do, however, show a greater degree of emotional and religious intensity than those of van Eyck, whilst his serene portraits of the bigwigs of his day were much admired across a large swathe of western Europe. Van der Weyden influenced many painters, but one of the most talented was **Dieric Bouts** (1415–75). Born in Haarlem but active in Leuven, Bouts is recognizable by his stiff, rather elongated figures and horrific subject matter, all set against carefully drawn landscapes. **Hugo van der Goes** (d.1482) was the next Ghent master after van Eyck, most famous for the Portinari Altarpiece in Florence's Uffizi. After a short painting career, he died insane, and his late works have strong hints of his impending madness in their subversive use of space and implicit acceptance of the viewer's presence. Few doubt that **Hans Memling** (1440–94) was a pupil of van der Weyden. Active in Bruges throughout his life, he is best remembered for the pastoral charm of his landscapes and the quality of his portraiture, much of which survives on the rescued side panels of triptychs. The Memling collection in Bruges (see p.57) has a wonderful sample of his work.

Both **Gerard David** (1460–1523) and **Jan Provoost** (1465–1529) moved to Bruges at the back end of the fifteenth century. Mostly they painted religious scenes, but their secular works are much more memorable, especially David's *Judgement of Cambyses* (see p.39), exhibited in the Groeninge. David's best-known apprentice was **Adriaen Isenbrant** (d 1551), whose speciality was small, precisely executed panels – his *Madonna of the Seven Sorrows* in Bruges' Onze Lieve Vrouwekerk (see p.55) is quite superb. Isenbrant was the last of the great painters to work in that city before it was superseded by Antwerp – which itself became the focus of a more Italianate school of art in the sixteenth century.

Hieronymus Bosch (1450–1516) lived for most of his life in Holland, though his style is linked to that of his Flemish contemporaries (see p.40). His frequently reprinted religious allegories are filled with macabre visions of tortured people and grotesque beasts, and appear at first faintly unhinged, though it's now thought that these are visual representations of contemporary sayings, idioms and parables. While their interpretation is far from resolved, Bosch's paintings draw strongly on subconscious fears and arche-types, giving them a lasting, haunting fascination.

The sixteenth century

At the end of the fifteenth century, the Flemish cloth towns – including Bruges and Ghent – were in decline and the leading artists of the day were drawn instead to the boom-ing port of Antwerp. The artists who worked here soon began to integrate the finely observed detail that character-ized the Flemish tradition with the style of the Italian painters of the Renaissance. **Quentin Matsys** (1464–1530) introduced florid classical architectural details and intricate landscapes to his works, influenced perhaps by the work of Leonardo da Vinci. As well as religious works, he painted portraits and genre scenes, all of which have recognizably Italian facets, and paved the way for the Dutch genre painters of later years. **Jan Gossart** (1478–1532) made the pilgrimage to Italy, and his dynamic works are packed with detail, especially finely drawn classical architectural back-drops. He was the first Low Countries artist to introduce the subjects of classical mythology into his works, part of a steady trend through the period towards secular subject matter.

The latter part of the sixteenth century was dominated by the work of **Pieter Bruegel the Elder** (c.1525–69), whose gruesome allegories and innovative interpretations of religious subjects are firmly placed in Low Countries set-tings. Pieter also painted finely observed peasant scenes, though he himself was well-connected in court circles in Antwerp and, later, Brussels. **Pieter Aertsen** (1508–75) also worked in the peasant genre, adding aspects of still life: his paintings often show a detailed kitchen scene in the foreground, with a religious episode going on behind. Bruegel's two sons, **Pieter Bruegel the Younger**

(1564–1638) and **Jan Bruegel** (1568–1625), were lesser painters: the former produced fairly insipid copies of his father's work, while Jan developed a style of his own – delicately rendered flower paintings and genre pieces that earned him the nickname "Velvet". Towards the latter half of the sixteenth century highly stylized Italianate portraits became the dominant fashion, with **Frans Pourbus the Younger** (1569–1622) the leading practitioner. Frans hobnobbed across Europe, working for the likes of the Habsburgs and the Medicis, his itinerant life in contrast to that of his grandfather, the Bruges-based **Pieter Pourbus** (1523–1584), the founder of this artistic dynasty.

The seventeenth century – Rubens and his followers

Belgian painting of the early seventeenth century is dominated by **Pieter Paul Rubens** (1577–1640), who was easily the most important exponent of the Baroque in northern Europe. Born in Siegen, Westphalia, he was raised in Antwerp, where he entered the painters' Guild in 1598. He became court painter to the Duke of Mantua in 1600, and until 1608 travelled extensively in Italy, absorbing the art of the High Renaissance and classical architecture. By the time of his return to Antwerp in 1608 he had acquired an enormous artistic vocabulary: the paintings of Caravaggio in particular were to influence his work strongly. His first major success was *The Raising of the Cross*, painted in 1610 and displayed today in Antwerp cathedral. A large, dynamic work, it caused a sensation at the time, establishing Rubens' reputation and leading to a string of commissions that enabled him to set up his own studio. *The Descent from the Cross*, his next major work (also in the cathedral), consolidated this success: equally Baroque, it is nevertheless quieter and more restrained.

The division of labour in Rubens' studio, and the talent of the artists working there (who included Antony van Dyck and Jacob Jordaens) ensured a high output of excellent work. The degree to which Rubens personally worked on a canvas would vary – and would determine its price. From the early 1620s onwards he turned his hand to a plethora of themes and subjects – religious works, portraits, tapestry designs, landscapes, mythological scenes, ceiling paintings – each of which was handled with supreme vitality and virtuosity. From his Flemish antecedents he inherited an acute sense of light, and used it not to dramatize his subjects (a technique favoured by Caravaggio and other Italian artists), but in association with colour and form. The drama in his works comes from the vigorous animation of his characters. His large-scale allegorical works, especially, are packed with heaving, writhing figures that appear to tumble out from the canvas.

Rubens' influence on the artists of the period was enormous. The huge output of his studio meant that his works were universally seen, and widely disseminated by the engravers he employed to copy his work. Chief among his followers was the portraitist **Anthony van Dyck** (1599–1641), who worked in Rubens' studio from 1618, often taking on the depiction of religious figures in his master's works that required particular sensitivity and pathos. Like Rubens, he was born in Antwerp and travelled widely in Italy, though his initial work was influenced less by the Italian artists than by Rubens himself. Eventually van Dyck developed his own distinct style and technique, establishing himself as court painter to Charles I in England, and creating portraits of a nervous elegance that would influence the genre there for the next hundred and fifty years. Most of his great portraiture remains in England, but his best religious works – such as the *Lamentation* in Antwerp's Museum voor Schone Kunsten – can be found in Belgium. **Jacob**

Jordaens (1593–1678) was also an Antwerp native who studied under Rubens. Although he was commissioned to complete several works left unfinished by Rubens at the time of his death, his robustly naturalistic works have an earthy – and sensuous – realism that's quite distinct in style and technique.

As well as the Baroque creations of Rubens and his acolytes, another style emerged in the seventeenth century, that of **genre painting**. Often misunderstood, the term was initially applied to everything from animal paintings and still lifes through to historical works and landscapes, but later came to be applied only to scenes of everyday life. In the southern Netherlands the most skilful practitioner was Oudenaarde's **Adriaen Brouwer** (1605–38), whose peasant figures rivalled those of the painters Jan Steen and Adriaen van Ostade to the north. Brouwer's output was unsurprisingly small given his short life, but his riotous tavern scenes and tableaux of everyday life are deftly done, and were well received in their day, collected by, among others, Rubens and Rembrandt. Brouwer studied in Haarlem for a while under Frans Hals (and may have picked up much of his painterly technique from him), before returning to his native Flanders to influence **David Teniers the Younger** (1610–1690), who worked in Antwerp, and later in Brussels. Teniers' early paintings are Brouwer-like peasant scenes, although his later work is more delicate and diverse, including *kortegaardje* – guardroom scenes that show soldiers carousing. This was all grist to the artistic mill, but meanwhile Bruges and Ghent had hit the skids with only **Jacob van Oost the Elder** (1603–1671), Bruges's most prominent artist during the Baroque period, showing any talent, though frankly his canvases are somewhat clichéd and uninspired.

The eighteenth century

By the end of the seventeenth century, French influences had overwhelmed Belgium's native artistic tradition with painters like **Jan Joseph Horemans I** and **Balthasar van den Bossche** modifying the Flemish genre painting of the previous century to suit Parisian tastes. Towards the end of the century Neoclassicism came into vogue, a French-led movement whose leading light was **Jacques Louis David** (1748–1825), the creator of the iconic *Death of Marat*. **Laurent Delvaux** (1696–1778) was also an important figure during this period, a Flemish sculptor who produced a large number of works for Belgian churches, including the pulpit of Ghent's cathedral.

The nineteenth century

French artistic fashions ruled the Belgian roost well into the nineteenth century, and amongst them Neoclassicism remained the most popular. Of the followers of Jacques Louis David, **François Joseph Navez** (1787–1869) was the most important to work in Belgium, furthering the influence of the movement via his position as director of the Brussels academy. With Belgian independence (from the Netherlands) in 1830 came, as might be expected, a new interest in nationalism, and artists such as **Louis Galliat** (1810–1887) and **Henri Dobbelaere** (1829–1885) spearheaded a romantic interpretation of historical events, idealizing Belgium's recent and medieval history.

    Antoine Wiertz (1806–1865) was celebrated for his grandiose amalgamation of romantic and Neoclassical themes in his sculptures and paintings, whilst **Henri de Braekeleer** (1840–1888) was highly regarded for his Dutch-inspired interiors and landscapes. Indeed, landscape painting underwent a resurgence of popularity in France in the mid-nineteenth century, and once again Belgian artists flocked to reflect that country's tastes. More positively, **Emile Claus** (1849–1924) adapted French Impressionist ideas to create an individual style known as Luminism, and **Théo Rysselberghe** (1862–1926) followed suit. The talented **Fernand Khnopff** (1858–1921) developed his own style too, in his case inspired by the English Pre-Raphaelites.

One artist who stands out during this period is **Constantin Meunier** (1831–1905), a painter and sculptor whose naturalistic work depicting brawny workers and mining scenes was the perfect mirror of a fast-industrializing Belgium. But the most original Belgian artist of the late nineteenth century was **James Ensor** (1860–1949). Ensor, who lived in Ostend for most of his life, painted macabre, disturbing works, whose haunted style can be traced back to Bosch and Bruegel and which was itself a precursor of Expressionism. He was active in a group known as **Les XX** (Les Vingt; see p.44), which organized exhibitions of new styles of art from abroad, and greatly influenced contemporary Belgian painters.

The twentieth century

Each of the major modern art movements had its followers in Belgium, and each was diluted or altered according to local taste. **Expressionism** was manifest in a local group of artists established in a village near Ghent, with the most eye-catching paintings produced by **Constant Permeke** (1886–1952), whose bold, deeply coloured canvases can be found in many Belgian galleries. There was also **Jean Delville** (1867–1953), not as talented as Permeke perhaps, but an artist who certainly set about his religious preoccupations with gigantic gusto. **Surrealism** also caught on in a big way, perhaps because of the Belgian penchant for the bizarre and grotesque. **René Magritte** (1898–1967), one of the leading lights of the movement, was born and trained in Belgium and returned there after being involved in the movement's birth in 1927. His Surrealism is gentle compared to the work of Dalí or de Chirico: ordinary images are used in a dreamlike way, often playing on the distinction between a word and its meaning. His most famous motif was the man in the bowler hat, whose face was always hidden from view. **Paul Delvaux** (1897–1994) adopted his own rather salacious interpretation of the movement – a sort of "What-the-butler-saw" Surrealism.

Most of the interwar artists were influenced by van Doesburg and de Stijl in Holland, though none figured highly in the movement. The abstract geometrical works of **Victor Severanckx** (1897–1965) owed much to de Stijl, and he in turn inspired the postwar group known as **La Jeune Peinture**, which gathered together some of the most notable artists working in Belgium, the antecedents of the Abstract Expressionists of the 1950s. A similar collective function was served by **CoBrA**, founded in 1948 and taking its name from the first letters of Copenhagen, Brussels and Amsterdam. While none of the Belgian participants in CoBrA achieved the fame of one of its Dutch members, Karel Appel, the name of **Pierre Alechinsky** (1927–) is certainly well known in his hometown, Brussels. Probably the most famous recent Belgian artist is **Marcel Broodthaers** (1924–1976). He initially worked in the Surrealist manner, but soon branched out, quickly graduating from cut-paper geometric shapes into both the plastic arts and, most famously, sharp and brightly coloured paintings of everyday artefacts, especially casseroles brimming with mussels.

A top twenty of Belgian beers

Belgium's beer-making history goes back centuries and whatever bar of the world you come from you'll know that this is serious beer country. Official estimates suggest that there are more than **700 beers** to choose from with the rarest and most precious given all the reverence of fine wine. The professional beer drinker will already know the brews listed below, but for the tippling amateur we have produced this **top twenty** to get you started. Most bars in Bruges and Ghent have a **beer menu** and although it's unlikely that any one establishment will have all those listed, all of them will (or should) have at least a couple.

DON'T DRINK THE WATER!

In the eleventh century, a Benedictine monk dipped his crucifix into a Belgian brewer's kettle to encourage the populace to drink beer instead of plague-contaminated water: the plague stopped. The monk was later beatified as **St Arnold** and he became – logically enough – the patron saint of brewers.

Chapter 7 recommends good places to
drink in both Ghent and Bruges.

Brugse Straffe Hendrik
(Blond 6.5%, Bruin 8.5%)

Straffe Hendrik, a smart little
brewery located in the centre of
Bruges (see p.164), produces
zippy, refreshing ales. Their
Blond is a light and tangy pale
ale, whereas the Bruin is a classic brown ale with a full body.

Bush Beer (7.5% and 12%)

A Wallonian (southern Belgium)
speciality. It's claimed that the
original version is – at 12% –
the strongest beer in Belgium,
but it's actually more like a barley wine and has a lovely golden
colour and an earthy aroma.
The 7.5% Bush is a tasty pale
ale with a zip of coriander.

Chimay (red top 7%,
blue top 9%)

Made by the Trappist monks of
Forges-les-Chimay, in southern
Belgium, Chimay beers are
widely regarded as being
amongst the best in the world.
Of the several brews they produce, these two are the most

readily available, fruity and
strong, deep in body, and
somewhat spicy with a hint of
nutmeg and thyme.

La Chouffe (8%)

Produced in the Ardennes, this
distinctive beer is instantly
recognizable by the red hooded
gnome (or *chouffe*) which
adorns its label. It's a refreshing
pale ale with a hint of coriander
and it leaves a peachy aftertaste.

Corsendonk Pater
Noster (5.6%)

The creation of Jef
Keersmaekers, this bottled beer
is easily the pick of the many
Corsendonk brews. It is known
for its Burgundy-brown colour
and smoky bouquet.

De Koninck (5%)

Antwerp's leading brewery, De
Koninck, is something of a
Flemish institution – for some a
way of life. Its standard beer, De
Koninck, is a smooth, yellowish

pale ale that is better on draft than in the bottle. Very drinkable and with a sharp aftertaste.

Delirium Tremens (9%)

Great name for this spicy amber ale that is the leading product of Ghent's Huyghe brewery.

Gouden Carolus (8%)

Named after – and allegedly the favourite tipple of – the Habsburg emperor Charles V, Gouden Carolus is a full-bodied dark brown ale with a sour and slightly fruity aftertaste. Brewed in the Flemish town of Mechelen.

Gueuze (Cantillon Gueuze Lambic 5%)

A type of beer rather than an individual brew, Gueuze is made by blending old and new lambic (see p.294) to fuel re-fermentation with the end result being bottled. This process makes Gueuze a little sweeter and fuller bodied than lambic. Traditional Gueuze – like the two brands mentioned – can, however, be hard to track down and you may have to settle for the sweeter, more commercial brands,

notably Belle Vue Gueuze (5.2%), Timmermans Gueuze (5.5%) and the exemplary Lindemans Gueuze (5.2%).

Hoegaarden (5%)

The role model of all Belgian wheat beers, Hoegaarden – named after a small town east of Leuven – is light and extremely refreshing, despite its cloudy appearance. It is brewed from equal parts of wheat and malted barley and is the ideal drink for a hot summer's day. The history of wheat beers is curious: in the late 1950s, they were unloved and unsung and facing extinction, but within twenty years they had been taken up by a new generation of drinkers and are now extremely popular. Hoegaarden is as good a wheat beer as any.

Kriek (Cantillon Kriek Lambic 5%, Belle Vue Kriek 5.2%, Mort Subite Kriek 4.3%)

A type of beer rather than a particular brew, Kriek is made from a base beer to which is added cherries or, in the case of the more commercial brands, cherry juice and perhaps even sugar. It is decanted from a bottle with a cork – as in sparkling wine. The better examples – including the three mentioned above – are not too sweet and taste simply wonderful. Other fruit beers are available too, but Kriek is perhaps the happiest.

Kwak (8%)

This Flemish beer, the main product of the family-run Bosteels brewery, is not all that special – it's an amber ale sweetened by a little sugar – but it's served in dramatic style with its distinctive hourglass placed in a wooden stand.

Lambic beers (Cantillon Lambik 5%, Lindemans Lambik 4%)

Representing one of the world's oldest styles of beer manufacture, lambic beers are tart because they are brewed with at least thirty percent raw wheat as well as the more usual malted barley. The key feature is, however, the use of wild yeast in their production, a process of spontaneous fermentation in which the yeasts of the atmosphere gravitate down into open wooden casks over a period of

between two and three years. This balance of wild yeasts is specific to the Brussels area. Draught lambic is extremely rare, but the bottled varieties are more commonplace, even though most are modified in production. Cantillon Lambik is entirely authentic, an excellent drink with a lemony zip. Lindemans Lambik is similar and a tad more available.

Leffe (Leffe Brune 6.5%, Leffe Blond 6.6%)

Brewed in Leuven, just to the east of Brussels, Leffe is strong and malty and comes in two main varieties. Leffe Blond is bright, fragrant, and has a slight orangey flavour, whereas Leffe Brune is dark, aromatic, and full of body. Very popular, but a little gassy for some tastes.

Orval (6.2%)

One of the world's most distinctive malt beers, Orval is made in the Ardennes at the Abbaye d'Orval, which was founded in the twelfth century by Benedictine monks from Calabria. The beer is a lovely amber colour, refreshingly bitter, and makes a great aperitif.

Rochefort (Rochefort 6 7.5%, Rochefort 8 9.2%, Rochefort 10 11.3%)

Produced at a Trappist monastery in the Ardennes, Rochefort beers are typically dark and sweet and come in three main versions. These are Rochefort 6, Rochefort 8 and the extremely popular Rochefort 10, which has a deep reddish-brown colour and a delicious fruity palate.

Rodenbach (Rodenbach 5% and Rodenbach Grand Cru 6.5%)

Located in the Flemish town of Roeselare, the Rodenbach brewery produces a reddish brown ale in several different formats with the best brews aged in oak containers. Their widely available Rodenbach (5%) is a tangy brown ale with a hint of sourness. The much fuller – and sourer – Rodenbach Grand Cru is far more difficult to get hold of, but is particularly delicious.

Verboden Vrucht (Forbidden Fruit 9%)

Forbidden Fruit is worth buying just for the label, which depicts a fig-leaf clad Adam offering a strategically covered Eve a glass of beer in the garden of Eden. The actual drink is dark, strong and has a spicy aroma, and something of a cult following in Flanders. Produced by Hoegaarden.

Westmalle (Westmalle Dubbel 7%, Tripel 9%)

The Trappist monks of Westmalle, just north of Antwerp, claim their beers not only cure loss of appetite and insomnia, but reduce stress by half. Whatever the truth, the prescription certainly tastes good. Their most famous beer, the Westmalle Tripel, is deliciously creamy and aromatic, while the popular Westmalle Dubbel is dark and supremely malty.

Westvleteren (Special 6° 6.2%, Extra 8° 8%)

Made at the abbey of St Sixtus in West Flanders, Westvleteren beers come in several varieties. These two are the most common, dark and full-bodied, sour with an almost chocolate-like taste.

Books

M ost of the following books should be readily available in the UK, US and Canada. We have given **publishers** for each title in the form UK/US publisher; o/p means out of print.

History

Neal Ascherson *The King Incorporated* (Granta in UK & US). Belgium's own King Léopold II was responsible for one of the cruellest of colonial regimes, a savage system of repression and exploitation that devastated the Belgian Congo. Ascherson details it all.

J. C. H. Blom (ed) *History of the Low Countries* (Berghahn Books in US & UK). Belgian history books are thin on the round, so this heavyweight volume fills a few gaps, though it's hardly sun-lounge reading. A

series of historians weigh in with their specialities, from Roman times onwards. Taken as a whole, its forte is in picking out those cultural, political and economic themes that give the region its distinctive character.

Martin Conway *Collaboration in Belgium* (Yale UP in UK & US). Detailed analysis of wartime collaboration and the development of Fascism in Belgium in the 1930s and 1940s. Authoritative and well-written, but something of a special-interest text.

Niall Ferguson *The Pity of War* (Penguin in UK, Basic Books in

US). A controversial account of World War I, which challenges many of the beliefs concerning the start and continuation of the war. An immensely readable and well-researched history.

Galbert of Bruges *The Murder of Charles the Good* (University of Toronto). A rather specialist book, this is a contemporary chronicle of the tempestuous events that rattled early twelfth-century Bruges. A detailed yarn giving all sorts of insights into medieval Flanders.

Pieter Geyl *The Revolt of The Netherlands* 1555–1609 (o/p in UK/Littlefield Adams in US). Geyl presents a concise account of the Netherlands during its formative years, chronicling the uprising against the Spanish and the formation of the United Provinces. The definitive book on the period.

Martin Gilbert *First World War* (Harper Collins in UK, Henry Holt in US). Highly regarded account of the war focused on the battles and experiences of the British army. Very thorough – at 640 pages.

Adam Hochschild *King Leopold's Ghost* (Macmillan in UK, Houghton Mifflin in US). Harrowing account of King Leopold's savage colonial regime in the Congo. A detailed assessment – perhaps a little too long – explains and explores its gruesome workings. Particularly good on Roger Casement, the one-time British consul to the Congo, who publicised the cruelty and helped bring it to an end. After his return to Europe, Casement became a fervent Irish nationalist, who sought German assistance for the cause during World War I. The Germans landed him in Ireland by U-boat in 1916, but he was quickly captured and subsequently executed by the British just before the Easter Rising. Hochschild's last chapter – "The Great Forgetting" – is a stern criticism of the Belgians for their failure to acknowledge their savage colonial history.

E. H. Kossmann *The Low Countries 1780–1940* (OUP in UK & US). Gritty, technically detailed but ultimately rather turgid narrative of the Low

HISTORY

Countries from the Austrian era to World War II. Concentrates on the arena of party politics and is therefore a tad specific. Only available in hardback, it also costs a bomb.

A. de Meeüs *History of the Belgians* (o/p). Entertaining if rather confused attempt at an exhaustive history of the Belgians, from "prehistoric dawns" to modern times. Good on incidental detail.

Geoffrey Parker *The Dutch Revolt* (Penguin in the UK & US o/p). Compelling account of the struggle between the Netherlands and Spain. Probably the best work on this topic. Also *The Army of Flanders and the Spanish Road 1567–1659* (Cambridge UP in UK & US). The title may sound academic, but this book gives a fascinating insight into the Habsburg army which occupied what is now Belgium for well over a hundred years – how it functioned, was fed and moved from Spain to the Low Countries along the so-called Spanish Road.

A.J.P. Taylor *The First World War: An Illustrated History* (Penguin in UK, Perigee in US). First published in 1963, this superbly written and pertinently illustrated history offers a penetrating analysis of how the war started and why it went on for so long. Many of Taylor's deductions were controversial at the time, but such was the power of his arguments that much of what he said is now mainstream history. Recommended.

Art and architecture

Ulrike Becks-Malorny *Ensor* (Taschen in UK & US). Eminently readable and extensively illustrated account of James Ensor's life and art. Very competitively priced too.

Kristin Lohse Belkin *Rubens* (Phaidon Press in UK & US). Too long for its own good, this book details Rubens' spectacularly successful career as both artist and diplomat. Belkin is particularly thorough in her discussions of technique and the workings of his workshop. Extensive reference is made to Rubens' letters. Excellent illustrations.

Robin Blake *Anthony van Dyck* (Ivan R Dee in UK & US). Whether or not van Dyck justifies 448 pages is a moot point, but he did have an interesting life and certainly thumped out a fair few paintings. This volume explores every artistic nook and cranny.

Max J. Friedlander *From Van Eyck to Bruegel* (o/p). Scholarly and thoughtful account of the early Flemish masters, though stylistically and factually (in the light of modern research) beginning to show its age.

R. H. Fuchs *Dutch Painting* (Thames & Hudson in UK & US). If the sample of Dutch paintings at either the Groeninge in Bruges or the Museum voor Schone Kunsten in Ghent whets your appetite, then the first book you should turn to is this thoughtful and well-researched title which tracks the subject from the fifteenth century onwards.

R. H. Fuchs et al *Flemish and Dutch Painting (from Van Gogh, Ensor, Magritte and Mondrian to Contemporary)* (Rizzoli in US). Excellent, lucid account giving an overview of the development of Flemish and Dutch painting.

Suzi Gablik *Magritte* (Thames & Hudson in UK & US). Suzi Gablik lived in Magritte's house for six months in the 1960s and this personal contact informs the text, which is lucid and thoughtful. Most of the illustrations are, however, black and white.

Walter S. Gibson *Bosch* (Thames & Hudson in UK & US). Everything you wanted to know about Bosch, his paintings and his late fifteenth-century milieu. Superbly illustrated. Also, try the beautifully illustrated *Bruegel* (Thames & Hudson), which takes a detailed look at the artist with nine well-argued chapters investigating the components of Pieter Bruegel the Elder's art.

Paul Haesaerts *James Ensor* (Thames & Hudson o/p). It may weigh a ton, but this excellent volume is an outstanding exploration of the work of this often neglected, Ostend-born painter. The illustrations and photos are well-chosen.

ART AND ARCHITECTURE

A. M. Hammacher *René Magritte* (Thames & Hudson in UK, Harry N Abrams in US). Thames & Hudson produce some of the finest art books in the world and this is an excellent example, beautifully illustrated and featuring a detailed examination of Magritte's life, times and artistic output. One of the competitively priced "Masters of Art" series.

Craig Harbison *Jan van Eyck: The Play of Realism* (Reaktion Books in UK & US). Not much is known about van Eyck, but Harbison has done his best to root out every detail. The text is accompanied by illustrations of all of his major paintings.

Bruce McCall *Sit!: The Dog Portraits of Thierry Poncelet* (Workman in UK). This weird and wonderful book features the work of the Belgian Thierry Poncelet, who raids flea markets and antique shops for ancestral portraits, then restores them and paints dogs' heads over the original faces.

Dirk de Vos *Rogier van der Weyden* (Harry N Abrams in UK & US). One of the most talented and influential of the Flemish Primitives, Weyden was the official city painter to Brussels in the middle of the fifteenth century. This 400-page volume details everything known about him and carries illustrations of all his works – but then no more than you would expect from such an expensive tome.

Peter Weiermair *Eros & Death: Belgian Symbolism* (Oehrli in UK, Art Books in US). Great title and an original book exploring the nature of Belgian symbolism with reference to drawings, prints, paintings and sculptures. Artists featured include James Ensor and Felician Rops.

Christopher White *Peter Paul Rubens: Man and Artist* (o/p). A beautifully illustrated introduction to both Rubens' work and social milieu.

Guides and commentaries

Paul van Buitenen *Blowing the Whistle* (Politico's Publishing in UK). All your worst fears about the EU confirmed. Buitenen was an assistant auditor in the EU's Financial Control Directorate in Brussels and this book, published in 1998, exposed the fraud and corruption. Needless to say, the EU was far from grateful for his revelations and forced him to resign, but even so the scandal stories became so widespread that the entire Commission was obliged to resign en bloc. Since then, there have been earnest declarations that things would be much better. Don't hold your breath.

Michael Jackson *The Great Beers of Belgium* (Prion in UK/Running Press in US). Belgium produces probably the

TINTIN BOOKS

Plenty of books exist on everyone's favourite Belgian, but here are the top recommendations in English. For more on where to buy Tintin comics and memorabilia, see Shopping, p.182.

Michael Farr *Tintin: The Complete Companion* (John Murray). A Tintinologists' treat, this immaculately illustrated book – written by the world's leading Tintinologist – explores every aspect of Hergé's remarkably popular creation. Particularly strong on the real-life stories that inspired Hergé, but you do have to be seriously interested in Tintin to really enjoy this book.

Hergé *The Calculus Affair* (Mammoth in UK, Little Brown in US); *The Making of Tintin: Cigars of the Pharaoh & the Blue Lotus* (Methuen in UK, Little Brown in US). Tintin oomio strips come in and out of print at a rapid rate and there is a wide selection of audio cassettes too. The two anthologies listed here are a good place to start.

Benoit Peeters *Tintin and the World of Hergé: An Illustrated History* (Methuen/Joy St Books). Examines the life and career of Hergé, particularly the development of Tintin, and the influences on his work. No less than 300 illustrations.

GUIDES AND COMMENTARIES

best beers in the world. Michael Jackson is probably one of the best beer writers in the world. The result is cheeky, palatable and sinewy with just a hint of fruitiness.

Harry Pearson *A Tall Man in a Low Land* (Abacus in UK, Trafalgar in US). The product of an extended visit to the lesser known parts of Belgium, this racy book is in the style of (but not as perceptive as) Bill Bryson. Pearson has oodles of comments to make on Belgium and the Belgians – on everything from DIY to architecture – and although he sometimes tries too hard, this is a very enjoyable read.

Ed Marianne Thys *Belgian Cinema* (Ludion in UK & US). This authoritative and weighty volume has reviews of every Belgian film ever made. Published in 1999.

San van de Veire *Belgian Fashion Design* (Ludion in UK). The staggering success of Flemish fashion designers is chronicled in this well-illustrated book. Particularly interesting on the factors underpinning the burgeoning of Belgian fashion in the early 1980s.

Tim Webb *Good Beer Guide to Belgium, Holland & Luxembourg* (CAMRA Books in UK, Storey in US). Detailed and enthusiastic guide to the best bars, beers and breweries. A good read, and extremely well informed to boot. Undoubtedly, the best book on its subject on the market.

Literature

Mark Bles *A Child at War* (Warner in UK, Mercury House in US). This powerful book describes the tribulations of Hortense Daman, a Belgian girl who joined the Resistance at the tender age of fifteen. Betrayed to the Gestapo, Daman was sent to Ravensbruck concentration camp, where she was used in medical experiments, but remarkably survived. This is her story, though the book would have benefited from some editorial pruning.

Hugo Claus *The Sorrow of Belgium* (o/p in UK; Penguin in US). Born in Bruges in 1929,

Claus is generally regarded as Belgium's foremost Flemish-language novelist, and this is considered his best novel. It charts the growing maturity of a young boy living in Flanders under the Nazi occupation. Claus' style is somewhat dense to say the least, but the book gets to grips with the guilt, bigotry and mistrust of the period, and caused a minor uproar when it was first published in the early 1980s. His *Swordfish* (Dufour) is a story of an isolated village rife with ethnic and religious tensions. The effects of this prove too much for a boy in his spiral down to madness. Also *Desire* (Penguin in UK) is a strange and disconcerting tale of two drinking buddies, who, on an impulse, abandon small-town Belgium for Las Vegas, where both of them start to unravel.

Michael Frayn *Headlong* (Faber & Faber in UK, Picador in US). Subtle, gripping yarn in which the protagonist, Martin Clay, an English art historian, stumbles across – or thinks he does – a "lost" Flemish medieval painting of immense value. But he does-n't own it and the lies – and moral slide – begin.

Robert Graves *Goodbye To All That* (Penguin in UK, Anchor in US). Written in 1929, this is the classic story of life in the trenches. Bleak and painful memories of First World War army service written by Graves, a wounded survivor.

Alan Hollinghurst *The Folding Star* (Vintage in UK & US). British writer Hollinghurst's evocation of a thinly disguised Bruges, in a compelling novel of gay sex, mystery and obsession.

Amelie Nothomb *Loving Sabotage* (New Directions in UK & US). English translations of modern Belgian writers (from both French and Dutch) are a rarity, but Nothomb, one of Belgium's most popular writers, has made the linguistic leap. This particular novel deals with a daughter of a diplomat stationed in Peking in the 1970s, a rites-of-passage story with a Maoist backdrop. Also by Nothomb is *The Stranger Next Door* (Henry Holt in UK & US), concerning weird and disconcerting happenings in the

LITERATURE

Belgian countryside, and perhaps her most successful translated work. *Fear and Trembling* (St Martins, US only) is a sharply observed tale of the shoddy treatment meted out to a young Western businesswoman in a big corporation in Tokyo.

Jean Ray *Malpertuis* (Atlas in UK). This spine-chilling Gothic novel, set in Belgium, was written in 1943. The suffocating Catholicism of the Inquisition provides a perfect backcloth.

Georges Rodenbach *Bruges la Morte* (Atlas in UK & US). First published in 1892, this slim and subtly evocative novel is all about love and obsession – or rather a highly stylized, decadent view of it. It's credited with starting the craze for visiting Bruges, the "dead city" where the action unfolds.

Luc Sante *The Factory of Facts* (Granta in UK, Vintage in US). Born in Belgium but raised in the US, Sante returned to his native land for an extended visit in 1989 – at the age of 35. His book is primarily a personal reflection, but he also uses this as a base for a thoughtful exploration of Belgium and the Belgians – from their art to their food and beyond. Highly recommended.

Siegfried Sassoon *The Memoirs of an Infantry Officer* (Faber & Faber in UK & US). Sassoon's moving and painfully honest account of his experiences in the trenches of the First World War. A classic and infinitely readable. Also try Siegfried Sassoon's *Diaries 1915–1918* (Faber & Faber o/p).

Emile Zola *Germinal* (Penguin in UK, Viking in US). First published in 1885, *Germinal* exposed the harsh conditions of the coal mines of northeast France. It was also a rallying call to action with the protagonist, Etienne Lantier, organizing a strike. A vivid, powerful work, Zola had a detailed knowledge of the mines – how they were run and worked – and makes passing reference to the coal fields of southern Belgium, where conditions and working practices were identical. This novel inspired a whole generation of Belgian radicals.

LITERATURE

Language

Throughout the northern part of Belgium, in the provinces of Antwerp, Limburg and Flemish Brabant as well as West and East Flanders, which cover, respectively, Bruges and Ghent, the principal language is **Dutch**, which is spoken in a variety of distinctive dialects commonly (if inaccurately) lumped together as **Flemish**. Most Flemish-speakers, particularly in the tourist industry, speak English to varying degrees of excellence. Indeed, Flemish-speakers have a seemingly natural talent for languages, and your attempts at speaking theirs may be met with bewilderment – though this can have as much to do with your pronunciation (Dutch is very difficult to get right) as surprise you're making the effort.

Flemish, or Dutch, is a Germanic language – the word "Dutch" itself is a corruption of Deutsch, a tag inaccurately given by English sailors in the seventeenth century. Though Dutch-speakers are at pains to stress the differences between the two languages, if you know any German you'll spot many similarities. As noted above, English is very widely spoken across Flanders, but the notes that follow may still prove handy. We have also provided two lists of **Flemish words and terms**, one for general use, the other to help decipher restaurant and café menus, though multilingual

menus are commonplace. For further reference, consult the
Rough Guide Dutch dictionary and phrase book.

Pronunciation

Dutch is pronounced much the same as English. However,
there are a few Dutch sounds that don't exist in English,
which can be difficult to pronounce without practice.

Consonants
v is like the English f in **f**ar
w like the v in **v**at
j like the initial sound of **y**ellow
ch and g are considerably harder than in English, enunciat-
ed much further back in the throat.
ng is as in bri**ng**
nj as in o**ni**on
Otherwise double consonants keep their separate sounds –
kn, for example, is never like the English "knight".

Vowels and diphthongs
Doubling the letter lengthens the vowel sound:
a is like the English **a**pple
aa like c**a**rt
e like l**e**t
ee like l**a**te
o as in p**o**p
oo in p**o**pe
u is like the French **tu** if preceded but not followed by a
consonant (eg nu); it's like w**oo**d if followed by a consonant
(eg bus).
uu the French **tu**
au and ou like h**ow**
ei and ij as in f**i**ne, though this varies and sometimes it can
sound more like l**a**ne.

oe as in s**oo**n

eu is like the diphthong in the French l**eur**

ui is the hardest Dutch diphthong of all, pronounced like h**ow** but much further forward in the mouth, with lips pursed (as if to say "oo").

FLEMISH WORDS AND PHRASES

Basics and greetings

yes	*ja*
no	*nee*
please	*alstublieft*
(no) thank you	*[nee] dank u or bedankt*
hello	*hallo or dag*
good morning	*goedemorgen*
good afternoon	*goedemiddag*
good evening	*goedenavond*
goodbye	*tot ziens*
see you later	*tot straks*
do you speak English?	*spreekt u Engels?*
I don't understand	*ik begrijp het niet*
women/men	*vrouwen/mannen*
children	*kinderen*
when?	*wanneer?*
I want	*ik wil*
I don't want	*ik wil niet... (+verb)*
	ik wil geen... (+noun)
how much is...?	*wat kost...?*

Finding the way

how do I get to...?	*hoe kom ik in...?*
where is...?	*waar is...?*
how far is it to...?	*hoe ver is het naar...?*
far/near	*ver/dichtbij*
left/right	*links/rechts*
straight ahead	*recht uit gaan*
platform	*spoor*
through traffic only	*doorgand verkeer*

Money

post office	*postkantoor*
stamp(s)	*postzegel(s)*
money exchange	*wisselkantoor*
cashier	*kassa*
ticket office	*loket*

Useful words

good/bad	*goed/slecht*
big/small	*groot/klein*
open/shut	*open/gesloten*
push/pull	*duwen/trekken*
new/old	*nieuw/oud*
cheap/expensive	*goedkoop/duur*
hot/cold	*heet/koud*
with/without	*met/zonder*
here/there	*hier/daar*
men's/women's toilets	*heren/dames*

Days and times

Sunday	*Zondag*	tomorrow	*morgen*
Monday	*Maandag*	tomorrow	*morgenocht*
Tuesday	*Dinsdag*	morning	*-end*
Wednesday	*Woensdag*	minute	*minuut*
Thursday	*Donderdag*	hour	*uur*
Friday	*Vrijdag*	day	*dag*
Saturday	*Zaterdag*	week	*week*
yesterday	*gisteren*	month	*maand*
today	*vandaag*	year	*jaar*

continues overleaf

FLEMISH WORDS AND PHRASES

Numbers

When saying a number, the Dutch generally transpose
the last two digits: eg, *vijf en twintig* is 25.

0	*nul*	13	*dertien*	70	*zeventig*
1	*een*	14	*veertien*	80	*tachtig*
2	*twee*	15	*vijftien*	90	*negentig*
3	*drie*	16	*zestien*	100	*honderd*
4	*vier*	17	*zeventien*	101	*honderd een*
5	*vijf*	18	*achttien*	200	*twee*
6	*zes*	19	*negentien*		*honderd*
7	*zeven*	20	*twintig*	201	*twee*
8	*acht*	21	*een en twintig*		*honderd*
9	*negen*	30	*dertig*		*een*
10	*tien*	40	*veertig*	500	*vijf honderd*
11	*elf*	50	*vijftig*	1000	*duizend*
12	*twaalf*	60	*zestig*		

FLEMISH FOOD AND DRINK TERMS

Basics

Boter	Butter
Brood	Bread
Broodje	Sandwich/roll
Dranken	Drinks
Eieren	Eggs
Gerst	Semolina: the type of grain used in Algerian couscous, popular in vegetarian restaurants
Groenten	Vegetables
Honing	Honey
Hoofdgerechten	Entrées
Kaas	Cheese
Koud	Cold
Nagerechten	Desserts
Peper	Pepper
Pindakaas	Peanut butter
Sla/salade	Salad
Smeerkaas	Cheese spread
Stokbrood	French bread
Suiker	Sugar
Vis	Fish
Vlees	Meat
Voorgerechten	Appetizers, hors d'oeuvres
Vruchten	Fruit
Warm	Hot
Zout	Salt

continues overleaf

FLEMISH FOOD AND DRINK TERMS

Appetizers and snacks

Erwtensoep/snert	Thick pea soup with bacon or sausage
Huzarensalade	Egg salad
Koffietafel	A light midday meal of cold meats, cheese, bread and perhaps soup
Patats/Frites	French fries
Soep	Soup
Uitsmijter	Ham or cheese with eggs on bread

Meat and poultry

Biefstuk (hollandse)	Steak
Eend	Duck
Fricandeau	Roast pork
Fricandel	A frankfurter-like sausage
Gehakt	Ground meat
Ham	Ham
Hutsepot	Beef stew with vegetables
Kalfsvlees	Veal
Kalkoen	Turkey
Karbonade	Chop
Kip	Chicken
Kroket	Spiced meat in bread crumbs
Lamsvlees	Lamb
Lever	Liver
Rookvlees	Smoked beef
Spek	Bacon
Worst	Sausages

Fish

Forel	Trout	*Mosselen*	Mussels
Garnalen	Shrimp	*Paling*	Eel
Haring	Herring	*Schelvis*	Shellfish
Haringsalade	Herring salad	*Schol*	Flounder
Kabeljauw	Cod	*Tong*	Sole
Makreel	Mackerel	*Zalm*	Salmon

Vegetables

Aardappelen	Potatoes	*Komkommer*	Cucumber
Bloemkool	Cauliflower	*Prei*	Leek
Boerenkool	A kind of cabbage	*Rijst*	Rice
		Sla	Salad, lettuce
Bonen	Beans	*Uien*	Onions
Champignons	Mushrooms	*Wortelen*	Carrots
Erwten	Peas	*Zuurkool*	Sauerkraut
Knoflook	Garlic		

Desserts

Appelgebak	Apple tart or cake
Drop	Dutch liquorice, available in zoet (sweet) or zout (salted) varieties
Gebak	Pastry
Ijs	Ice cream
Koekjes	Cookies
Oliebollen	Doughnuts
Pannekoeken	Pancakes
Poffertjes	Small pancakes, fritters
(Slag) room	(Whipped) cream

continues overleaf

FLEMISH FOOD AND DRINK TERMS

Speculaas	Spice- and honey-flavoured biscuit
Stroopwafels	Waffles
Vla	Custard

Fruit and nuts

Aardbei	Strawberry
Amandel	Almond
Appel	Apple
Appelmoes	Apple purée
Citroen	Lemon
Druif	Grape
Framboos	Raspberry
Hazelnoot	Hazelnut
Kers	Cherry
Kokosnoot	Coconut
Peer	Pear
Perzik	Peach
Pinda	Peanut
Pruim	Plum/prune

Drinks

Anijsmelk	Aniseed-flavoured warm milk
Appelsap	Apple juice
Bessenjenever	Blackcurrant gin
Chocomel	Chocolate milk
Citroenjenever	Lemon gin
Droog	Dry
Frisdranken	Sodas
Jenever	Dutch gin

Karnemelk	Buttermilk
Koffie	Coffee
Koffie verkeerd	Coffee with warm milk
Kopstoot	Beer with a Jenever chaser
Melk	Milk
Met ijs	With ice
Met slagroom	With whipped cream
Pils	Dutch beer
Proost!	Cheers!
Sinaasappelsap	Orange juice
Thee	Tea
Tomatensap	Tomato juice
Vieux	Dutch brandy
Vruchtensap	Fruit juice
Wijn	Wine
(wit/rood/rose)	(white/red/rosé)
Zoet	Sweet

Terms

Doorbakken	Well done
Gebakken	Fried/baked
Gebraden	Roasted
Gegrild	Grilled
Gekookt	Boiled
Geraspt	Grated
Gerookt	Smoked
Gestoofd	Stewed
Half doorbakken	Medium
Hollandse saus	Hollandaise (butter and egg sauce)

FLEMISH FOOD AND DRINK TERMS

●

315

Glossaries

Flemish terms

Abdij Abbey or group of monastic buildings.

Begijnhof Convent occupied by béguines (*begijns*), members of a sisterhood living as nuns but without vows and with the right of return to the secular world.

Beiaard Carillon – a set of tuned church bells, either operated by an automatic mechanism or played by a keyboard.

Belfort Belfry.

Beurs Stock exchange.

Botermarkt Butter market.

Brug Bridge.

Burgher Member of the upper or mercantile classes of a town, usually with civic powers.

Fietspad Bicycle path, and **fiets** — bicycle.

Gasthuis Hospital.

Gemeente Municipal: eg Gemeentehuis – town hall.

Gerechtshof Law Courts.

Gilde Guild.

Groentenmarkt Vegetable market.

Grote Markt Central town square and the heart of most Belgian communities.

Hal Hall.

Hof Court(yard).

Huis House.

Ingang Entrance.

Jeugdherberg Youth hostel.

Kaai Quai.

Kapel Chapel.

Kasteel Castle.

Kerk Church; eg Grote Kerk – the principal church of the town; Onze Lieve Vrouwekerk – church dedicated to the Virgin Mary.

Koninklijk Royal.

Korenmarkt Corn market.

Kunst Art.

Kursaal Casino.

Lakenhalle Cloth hall. The building in medieval weaving towns where cloth would be weighed, graded and sold.

Luchthaven Airport.

Markt Marketplace.

Molen Windmill.

Ommegang Procession.

Paleis Palace.

Plein A square or open space.

Polder Low-lying land that has been – at one time or another – reclaimed from the sea or a river.

Poort Gate.

Rijk State.

Schepenzaal Alderman's Hall.

Schone kunsten Fine arts.

Schouwburg Theatre.

Sierkunst Decorative arts.

Spoor Track (as in railway) – trains arrive and depart on track (as distinct from platform) numbers.

Stadhuis Town hall.

Station (Railway or bus) station.

Stedelijk Civic, municipal.

Steen Fortress.

Stitching Institute or foundation.

Toren Tower.

Tuin Garden.

Uitgang Exit.

Volkskunde Folklore.

FLEMISH TERMS

Art and architectural terms

Ambulatory Covered passage around the outer edge of the choir of a church.

Apse Semicircular protrusion at (usually) the east end of a church.

Art Deco Geometrical style of art and architecture especially popular in the 1930s.

Art Nouveau Style of art, architecture and design based on highly stylized vegetal forms. Particularly popular in the early part of the twentieth century.

Baroque The art and architecture of the Counter-Reformation, dating from around 1600. Distinguished by its extreme ornateness, exuberance and by the complex but harmonious spatial arrangement of interiors.

Basilica Roman Catholic church with honorific privileges.

Carillon A set of tuned church bells, either operated by an automatic mechanism or played by a keyboard.

Caryatid A sculptured female figure used as a column.

Classical Architectural style incorporating Greek and Roman elements – pillars, domes, colonnades, etc – at its height in the seventeenth century and revived, as Neoclassical, in the nineteenth century.

Clerestory Upper storey of a church, incorporating the windows.

Diptych Carved or painted work on two panels. Often used as an altarpiece.

Flamboyant Florid form of Gothic (see opposite).

Fresco Wall painting – durable through application to wet plaster.

Gable The triangular upper portion of a wall – decorative or supporting a roof.

Gobelins A rich French tapestry, named after the most famous of all tapestry manufacturers, based in Paris, whose most renowned period was in the reign of Louis XIV. Also loosely applied to all tapestries of similar style.

Gothic Architectural style of the thirteenth to sixteenth centuries, characterized by pointed arches, rib vaulting, flying buttresses and a general emphasis on verticality.

Misericord Ledge on choir stall on which the occupant can be supported while standing; often carved with secular subjects (bottoms were not thought worthy of religious ones).

Nave Main body of a church.

Neoclassical Architectural style derived from Greek and Roman elements – pillars, domes, colonnades, etc – popular across the Low Countries – including Belgium – during French rule in the early nineteenth century.

Renaissance Movement in art and architecture developed in fifteenth-century Italy.

Rococo Highly florid, light and graceful eighteenth-century style of architecture, painting and interior design, forming the last phase of Baroque.

Retable Altarpiece.

Romanesque Early medieval architecture distinguished by squat forms, rounded arches and naive sculpture.

Stucco Marble-based plaster used to embellish ceilings and other parts.

Transept Arms of a cross-shaped church, placed at ninety degrees to nave and chancel.

Triptych Carved or painted work on three panels. Often used as an altarpiece.

Tympanum Sculpted, usually recessed, panel above a door.

Vault An arched ceiling or roof.

ART AND ARCHITECTURAL TERMS

Index

Visit us online
roughguides.com

Information on over 25,000 destinations around the world

- **Read** Rough Guides' trusted travel info
- **Share** journals, photos and travel advice with other readers
- Get exclusive Rough Guide **discounts** and travel **deals**
- Earn membership points every time you contribute to the
  Rough Guide **community** and get **free** books, flights and trips
- Browse thousands of CD reviews and artists in our **music** area

around the world

Alaska ★ Algarve ★ Amsterdam ★ Andalucía ★ Antigua & Barbuda ★
Argentina ★ Auckland Restaurants ★ Australia ★ Austria ★ Bahamas ★
Bali & Lombok ★ Bangkok ★ Barbados ★ Barcelona ★ Beijing ★ Belgium &
Luxembourg ★ Belize ★ Berlin ★ Big Island of Hawaii ★ Bolivia ★ Boston
★ Brazil ★ Britain ★ Brittany & Normandy ★ Bruges & Ghent ★ Brussels ★
Budapest ★ Bulgaria ★ California ★ Cambodia ★ Canada ★ Cape Town ★
The Caribbean ★ Central America ★ Chile ★ China ★ Copenhagen ★
Corsica ★ Costa Brava ★ Costa Rica ★ Crete ★ Croatia ★ Cuba ★ Cyprus ★
Czech & Slovak Republics ★ Devon & Cornwall ★ Dodecanese & East
Aegean ★ Dominican Republic ★ The Dordogne & the Lot ★ Dublin ★
Ecuador ★ Edinburgh ★ Egypt ★ England ★ Europe ★ First-time Asia ★
First-time Europe ★ Florence ★ Florida ★ France ★ French Hotels &
Restaurants ★ Gay & Lesbian Australia ★ Germany ★ Goa ★ Greece ★
Greek Islands ★ Guatemala ★ Hawaii ★ Holland ★ Hong Kong & Macau ★
Honolulu ★ Hungary ★ Ibiza & Formentera ★ Iceland ★ India ★ Indonesia
★ Ionian Islands ★ Ireland ★ Israel & the Palestinian Territories ★ Italy ★
Jamaica ★ Japan ★ Jerusalem ★ Jordan ★ Kenya ★ The Lake District ★
Languedoc & Roussillon ★ Laos ★ Las Vegas ★ Lisbon ★ London ★

in twenty years

London Mini Guide ★ London Restaurants ★ Los Angeles ★ Madeira ★ Madrid ★ Malaysia, Singapore & Brunei ★ Mallorca ★ Malta & Gozo ★ Maui ★ Maya World ★ Melbourne ★ Menorca ★ Mexico ★ Miami & the Florida Keys ★ Montréal ★ Morocco ★ Moscow ★ Nepal ★ New England ★ New Orleans ★ New York City ★ New York Mini Guide ★ New York Restaurants ★ New Zealand ★ Norway ★ Pacific Northwest ★ Paris ★ Paris Mini Guide ★ Peru ★ Poland ★ Portugal ★ Prague ★ Provence & the Côte d'Azur ★ Pyrenees ★ The Rocky Mountains ★ Romania ★ Rome ★ San Francisco ★ San Francisco Restaurants ★ Sardinia ★ Scandinavia ★ Scotland ★ Scottish Highlands & Islands ★ Seattle ★ Sicily ★ Singapore ★ South Africa, Lesotho & Swaziland ★ South India ★ Southeast Asia ★ Southwest USA ★ Spain ★ St Lucia ★ St Petersburg ★ Sweden ★ Switzerland ★ Sydney ★ Syria ★ Tanzania ★ Tenerife and La Gomera ★ Thailand ★ Thailand's Beaches & Islands ★ Tokyo ★ Toronto ★ Travel Health ★ Trinidad & Tobago ★ Tunisia ★ Turkey ★ Tuscany & Umbria ★ USA ★ Vancouver ★ Venice & the Veneto ★ Vienna ★ Vietnam ★ Wales ★ Washington DC ★ West Africa ★ Women Travel ★ Yosemite ★ Zanzibar ★ Zimbabwe

also look out for our maps, phrasebooks, music guides and reference books

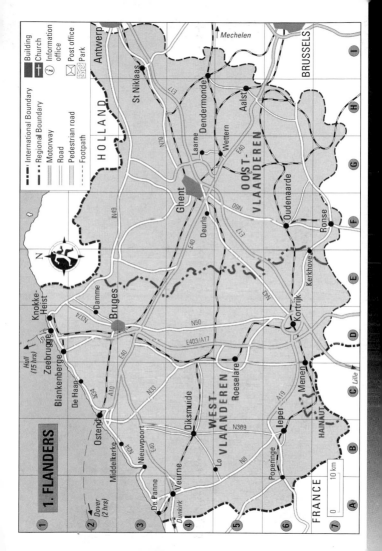

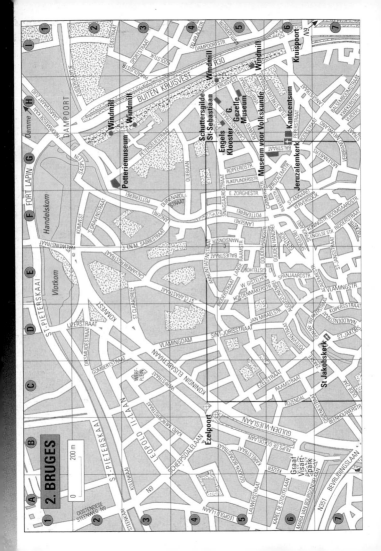

2. BRUGES

0   200 m

A B C D E F G H

1 2 3 4 5 6 7

OOSTENDSE STEENWEG N9

Damme → DAMPOORT

Handelskom

Vlotkom

FORT LAPIN

ST-PIETERSKAAI

N9

LEOPOLD II-LAAN

KONINGIN ELISABETHLAAN

VLAMINGDAM

VLAMINGSTR

Ezelpoort

GULDEN-VLIESLAAN

Graaf Visart-park

BEVRIJDINGSLAAN

N357

BUITEN KRUISVEST

Windmill

Windmill

R30

Windmill

Windmill

DAMPOORT STR

Kruispoort

N9

Potteriemuseum

Schuttersgilde St-Sebastiaan

Engels Klooster

G. Gezelle Museum

Museum voor Volkskunde

Kantcentrum

Jeruzalemkerk

St Jakobskerk

SINT-JORISSTRAAT

EZELSTRAAT

ST ANNA

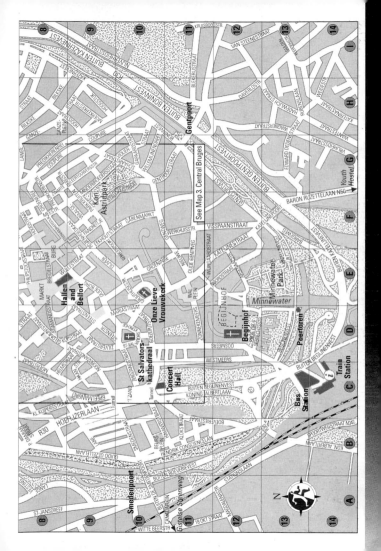

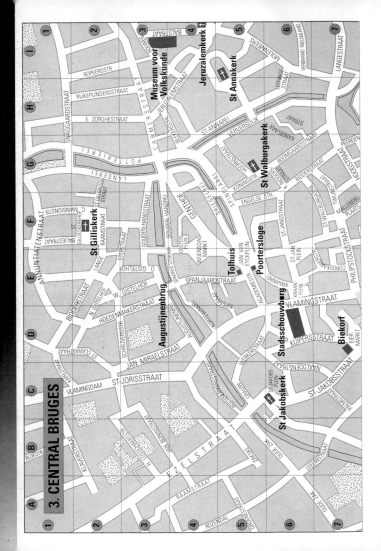

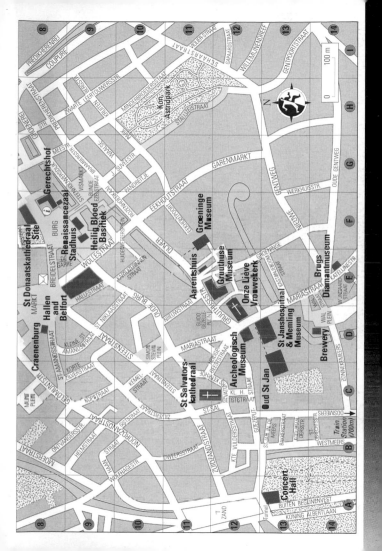

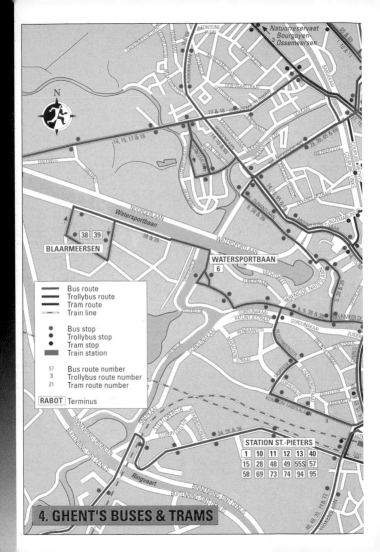

4. GHENT'S BUSES & TRAMS

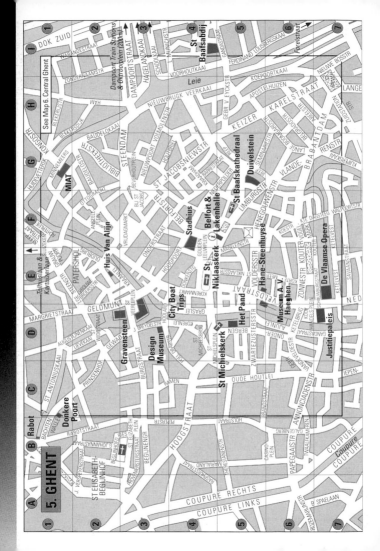

5. GHENT

DOK ZUID

See Map 6. Central Ghent

Dampoort Train Stations & Oktroolplein (200m)

St Baafsabdij

Leie

MIAT

Stadhius

St Baafskathedraal

Duivelstein

Befort & Lakenhalle

St Niklaaskerk

Huis Van Alijn

Hane-Steenhuys

Design Museum

City Boat Trips

Gravensteen

Het Pand

Museum A. V. Haeghen

De Vlaamse Opera

St Michielskerk

Justitiepaleis

Rabot

Donkere Poort

ST ELISABETH-BEGIJNHOF

COUPURE RECHTS

COUPURE LINKS

Coupure

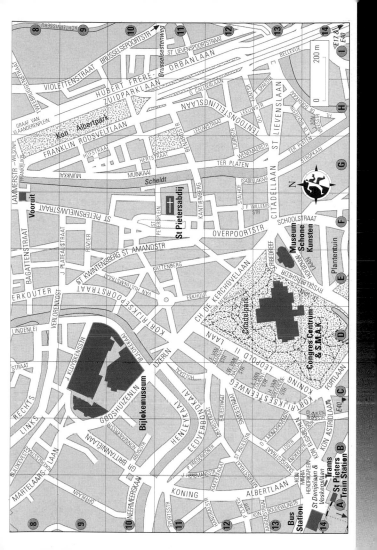

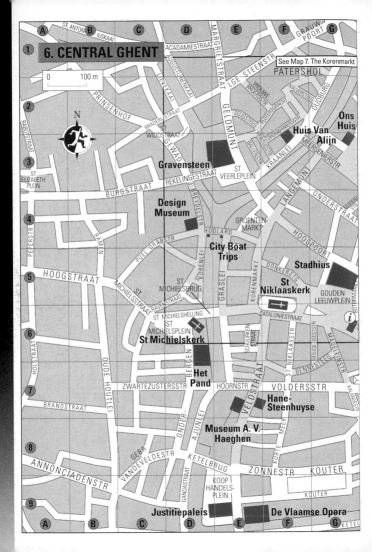

6. CENTRAL GHENT

0   100 m

See Map 7. The Korenmarkt

A **B** **C** **D** **E** **F** **G**

ST ANTONIUSKAAI
ACADAMIESTRAAT
PATERSHOL
GRAUW POORT

MARGRIETSTRAAT
LGE STEENSTR
KALVERSTEEG
OUDBURG

PRINSENHOF
BRADERIESTRAAT
ST WIDOSTRAAT
MEVE KAAI
AUGUSTIJNENKAAI
GELDMUNT
VROUWE BROERSTR
ZEUGSTEEG
KETELGRACHT
SCHOONVANBRISERSTR
BALTENSTR
MEERSENIERSTR

Huis Van Alijn

Ons Huis

RABOTSTRAAT

Gravensteen

ST VEERLEPLEIN

ST ELIZABETH PLEIN

REKELINGESTRAAT
BURGSTRAAT

GREYSTR
KRAANLEI
LANGEMUNT
ONDERSTRAAT

Design Museum

HOOLARD
GROENTEN-MARKT
HOOGPOORT

PEPERSTR
RAMEN

POEL
DRABSTR

KORENLEI

City Boat Trips

GRASLEI
KORENMARKT
DONKERSTG
Stadhius

HOOGSTRAAT
ST MICHIELSSTRAAT
ST RAVENSTRAAT
ST MICHIELSBRUG

St Niklaaskerk

GOUDEN LEEUWPLEIN
BOTERMKT

ST MICHIELSHELLING
ST MICHIELSPLEIN
CATALONIESTRAAT
SCHUURKEN STRAAT

St Michielskerk

ST NIKLAASSTR
HEILIGE GEESTSTR
BENNESTEEG
MAGELEINSTR
KALANDBERG

HOLSTRAAT
OUDE HOUTLEI
BERGEN

Het Pand

ZWARTEZUSTERSSTR
HOORNSTR
Hane-Steenhuyse

VELDSTRAAT
VOLDERSSTR

BRANDSTRAAT

GEBR VANDEVELDESTR
ONDER
A JUNLEI
KETELBRUG
Museum A. V. Haeghen

KORTE MEER
ZONNESTR
KOUTER

ANNONCIADENSTR

GANDASTRAAT
KOOP HANDELS-PLEIN

Justitiepaleis

De Vlaamse Opera

KOUTER
KETEL

1 **2** **3** **4** **5** **6** **7** **8** **9**

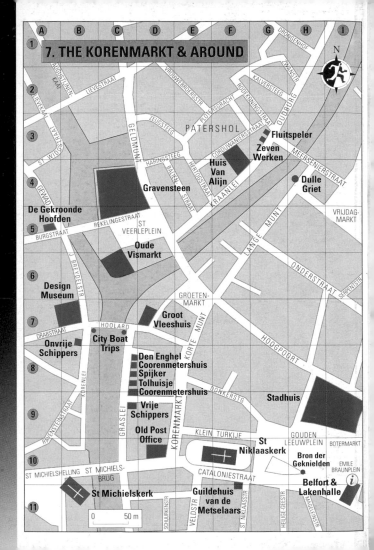